DIALOGUE BETWEEN GIOVANNI
AND A LETTER

medieval & renaissance texts & studies

VOLUME 59

The Renaissance Society of America

Renaissance Texts Series

VOLUME 12

New College, Oxford, D 155, fol. 1.

Giovanni Conversini da Ravenna
DIALOGUE BETWEEN GIOVANNI
AND A LETTER

Edited and translated by
HELEN LANNEAU EAKER

Introduction and Notes by
HELEN LANNEAU EAKER
BENJAMIN G. KOHL

BX
3637
.G5613
1989

medieval & renaissance texts & studies
in conjunction with
The Renaissance Society of America
Binghamton, New York
1989

Generous grants from Pegasus Limited
for the Promotion of Neo-Latin Studies
the Salmon Fund of Vassar College
and the Dean of Humanities of Rice University
have helped to meet the publication costs of this book.

Library of Congress Cataloging-in-Publication Data

Giovanni Conversini, da Ravenna, 1343–1408.
  [Dialogus inter Johannem et literam. English & Latin]
  Dialogue between Giovanni and a letter / edited and translated
by Helen Lanneau Eaker ; introduction and notes by Helen
Lanneau Eaker and Benjamin G. Kohl.
      p.   cm. — (Medieval & Renaissance texts & studies ; v. 59)
(Renaissance texts series ; v. 12.)
  Text in English and Latin.
  Original title: Dialogus inter Johannem et literam.
  Bibliography: p.
  Includes index.
  ISBN 0-86698—043-1 (alk. paper)
  1. Franciscans—Italy—Early works to 1800.   2. Vocation (in
religious orders, congregations, etc.)—Early works to 1800.
I. Eaker, Helen Lanneau, 1922-   . II. Kohl, Benjamin G.
III. Title.   IV. Series.   V. Series: Renaissance texts series ;
v. 12.
BX3637.G5613 1989
255—dc19   88-25846
                                                                  CIP

This book is made to last.
It is set in Janson, smythe-sewn
and printed on acid-free paper
to library specifications.

Printed in the United States of America

To J. Gordon Eaker, Professor Emeritus
University of Houston

For his patient and generous help
with this book

Preface

WITH THIS EDITION AND ENGLISH TRANSLATION of the earliest long work by Giovanni Conversini da Ravenna, *Dialogus inter Johannem et Literam*, we continue our collaboration in making available integral critical editions of the previously unpublished works of this major early Italian humanist. The *Dialogus* lays claim to our notice for several reasons. It contains the first humanist biography of a major religious figure, in this case, the Franciscan prelate and cardinal, Tommaso da Frignano; it includes a psychological portrait of the author and rare insight into the daily emotional and professional concerns of a younger humanist in the last quarter of the Trecento; it demonstrates the enormous debt to Petrarch and the lesser one to Boccaccio of an Italian intellectual of the next generation for both ideas and themes; and it shows Petrarch and Bocaccio as cultural heroes who stirred men of Conversini's talents to advance in the world through a career in letters. The work derives inspiration from the Christian tradition, the Bible and Church Fathers, especially Saints Augustine and Jerome, as well the great authors of Latin literature and the Stoic tradition. It demonstrates also Conversini's knowledge of ancient medical works and the Aristotelian tradition from the library of his father, a physician trained in Bologna and Modena. Most significantly, it shows the

close affinities between early humanism and the more rigorous traditions of the Franciscan movement, with its praise of peace, simplici-
ty, and love. Hence, in the *Dialogus* we have a work inspired both
by Petrarch's militant classicism and Roman Stoicism and by the religious values of the Franciscan Order as represented by the life and
teachings of the author's uncle, Tommaso da Frignano, who was himself
for a time the Minister General of the Ordo Fratrum Minorum.

In editing, translating, annotating, and introducing this work we
have incurred some debts. Benjamin Kohl would like to thank both
Helen and Gordon Eaker for careful correction of earlier drafts of
his part of the introduction and his old friend, Professor Reinhold
C. Mueller of the University of Venice, for checking and correcting
his transcriptions of Documents 1–2 of the Appendix against the origi-
nals in the Archivio di Stato at the Frari in Venice. The accuracy of
the appendix, introduction, and notes has been much improved by
their help and that of the readers and editors for the Medieval & Renaissance Texts & Studies series, though Professor Kohl is of course fully
responsible for any errors that remain.

We are also grateful to the Warden and Scholars of New College,
Oxford, for permission to use MS. 155 as the base for our critical
edition.

Helen Lanneau Eaker would like first and foremost to thank her
husband, J. Gordon Eaker, Professor Emeritus of the University of
Houston, for his countless hours of help, both in improving the wording
of her translation and the introduction and in typing hundreds of pages.
Her thanks are due also to two good friends: Elizabeth Eikel Day,
who reviewed all the translation and made many good suggestions
for better use of English, and Goldie Jane Feldman, who turned the
four lines of Latin dactylic hexameter at the end of the manuscript
into English hexameters.

Helen Lanneau Eaker
Rice University

Benjamin G. Kohl
Vassar College

Contents

INTRODUCTION

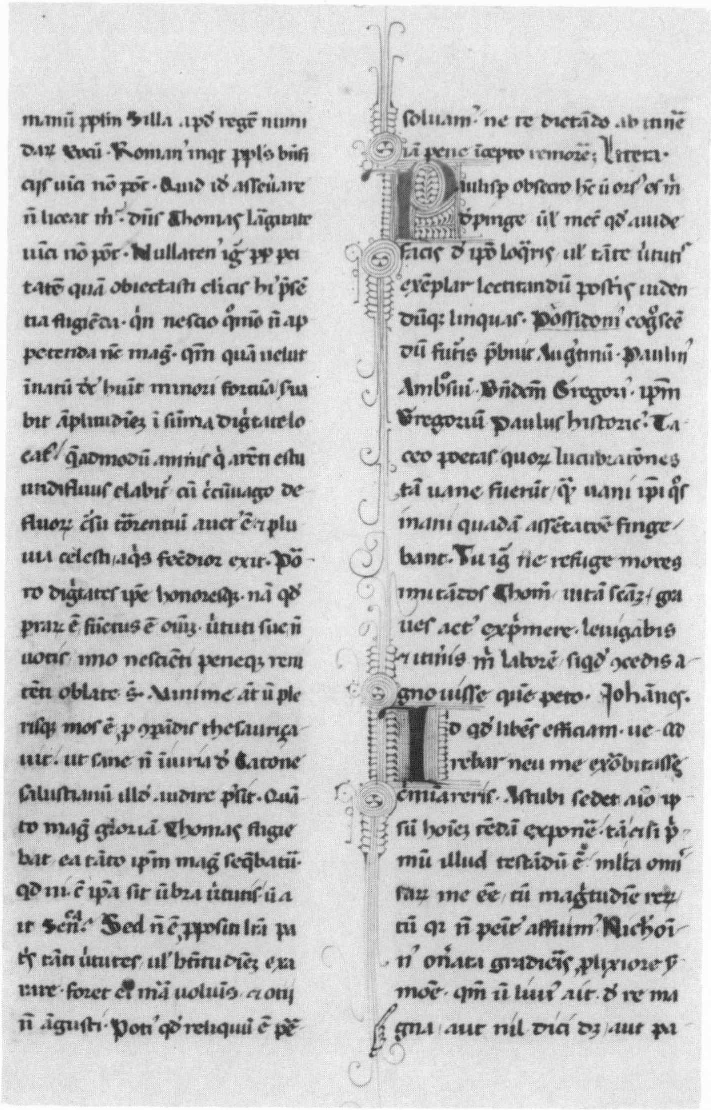

New College, Oxford, D 155, fol. 5.

Introduction

AMONG THE MOST ENIGMATIC and least studied humanists of the early Italian Renaissance stands the schoolmaster, statesman, and author, Giovanni Conversini da Ravenna (1343–1408). The author of a number of important treatises and dialogues, Conversini's first major work was the *Dialogus inter Johannem et Literam*, written during the Christmas season of 1378 upon the occasion of the elevation of his uncle, the Franciscan prelate and diplomat, Tommaso da Frignano, to the cardinalate by Pope Urban VI on 18 September 1378. The dialogue, cast in the form of a discussion between the author Giovanni (*Johannes*) and the epistle (*Litera*) and sent to the uncle in congratulation on receiving his red hat, has been little studied until now.[1] In fact, the existence of the dialogue was only surmised by the principal biographer of Giovanni da Ravenna, Remigio Sabbadini, and the principal manuscripts were noted for the first time only in 1963 by B. L. Ullman, the indefatigable student of Giovanni's famous humanist contemporary, the Florentine chancellor, Coluccio Salutati (1331–1406).[2]

This introduction aims at sketching in some detail the early life and career of the author of the dialogue, Giovanni Conversini da Ravenna, and of its recipient, Tommaso da Frignano; at providing background on the specific events mentioned in the dialogue; and at

assessing Giovanni's sources, and providing descriptions of the manuscripts used in this edition.

Giovanni, called da Ravenna from his first Italian home, was born in Buda where his father, Conversino da Frignano, was a physician at the court of King Louis of Hungary. After his mother's premature death, Giovanni was sent to Italy and entrusted to the care of his uncle Tommaso da Frignano, a rising priest in the Franciscan Order. He was the pupil of various schoolmasters in Ferrara and Bologna, as well as in Ravenna, where he studied in the 1350s under Donato Albanzani, who was to become a lifelong friend.[3] At the age of ten he was betrothed to the daughter of a physician in Ravenna, Margherita Furlan, and two years later the teenaged couple was married. But the early death of Margherita's parents deprived the young couple of close supervision, and Giovanni was forced to find employment as a waiter in the household of Michele de' Medici in Florence. Later he followed the more practical course of the notarial arts in Bologna, and in 1368 he was appointed one of the five foreign notaries working in the court of the podestà at Florence.[4]

After years of wandering in Italy, brief employment in Bologna lecturing and commenting on Valerius Maximus,[5] and a stint as a tutor at the Este court in Ferrara, Giovanni settled as a schoolmaster in the Veneto hill-town of Conegliano. There in the summer of 1372 he was visited by his young son Conversino and ailing wife Margherita. Both suffered from malnutrition and poor health because of the deprivations that Giovanni's wandering had caused, and his wife died soon after she arrived. The son Conversino was nursed back to health, but Giovanni himself was soon weakened by the arsenic poisoning which one Luigi da Ravenna, a kinsman of Margherita, had administered to his food, probably in a quest for revenge for the suffering that the wife had undergone. The arsenic did not prove fatal, but Giovanni was forced to remain bedridden for half a year. The next year Giovanni left his post in Conegliano and visited his uncle Tommaso at his palace on Campo San Silvestro in Venice, where he had been recently installed after his election as patriarch of Grado by Pope Gregory XI.[6]

In the third quarter of the Trecento, Tommaso da Frignano was one of the rising stars of the Franciscan Order in Italy. Born on the Panino River in the Apennines above Modena, probably at the end

of the first decade of the century, Tommaso entered the Order in Modena as a novice in about 1318. After a career as student of theology and letters in Modena and perhaps in Venice, he became the guardian of the Franciscan convent at Ferrara on 14 January 1349. In 1352, he was elected Provincial General of the Order at Bologna, a post he was to hold for the next fifteen years.[7] He became an important figure in the Bolognese Studium, serving as one of the nine reformers of the College of Theology appointed by Pope Innocent VI in 1360. By 1364, he was teaching at the University of Bologna as a professor of theology.[8] In this same year, the powerful papal legate in the Romagna, Cardinal Egidio Albornoz, named Tommaso as one of the executors in his will. The greatest recognition of his standing with the Franciscans came at the meeting of the general chapter of the Order at Assisi on 6 June 1367, when he was unanimously elected minister general of the Order overseeing more than 35,000 religious in more than a thousand convents.[9]

But Tommaso's success as administrator and apparent favoritism toward certain spiritual Franciscans aroused the envy and opposition of powerful members of the Order, especially from two conservative churchmen, Tommaso Racani, provincial general of Umbria, and the Cardinal Protector Nicolas Bellefaye. At a meeting of the chapter held at Foligno the following year, Tommaso was lavishly entertained by the lord of the city, Ugolino de' Trinci. In return for this hospitality, Tommaso offered him anything he wished as a gift. Ugolino promptly requested that his kinsman, Paoluccio de' Trinci, a leader of the spiritual branch of the Franciscan Order in Umbria, be given the convent of San Bartolomeo at Brugliano, which was in fact at the time under the direct supervision of Racani. There Paoluccio de' Trinci soon established a vital community of friars dedicated to the strict observance of the Franciscan Rule. But Racani and other Franciscan inquisitors saw this grant as evidence of Tommaso's favoring the heretical Fraticelli and supporting the condemned doctrine of absolute poverty.[10] Tommaso was then denounced as someone who favored the Fraticelli and came under suspicion of heresy. Late in 1368, in response to these charges, Pope Urban V removed Tommaso from his office as minister general and immediately established a commission to investigate the charges.

This persecution of Tommaso da Frignano came at a time when many communities of spiritual Franciscans were under attack from inquisitors, and Fraticelli were burned at the stake in these years in Perugia, Viterbo, and Rome.[11] But soon after Tommaso's suspension in late 1368, Pope Urban V appointed a commission to determine Tommaso's innocence. The commission was composed of several of Tommaso's closest friends and allies, including Phillipe de Cabassole, friend of Petrarch and a cardinal since 22 September 1368, as well as Pierre Roger Cardinal Beaufort, who was to become the future Pope Gregory XI. Moreover, no less a figure than Francis Petrarch took up Tommaso's cause in a letter (*Seniles* XI.12) of 1 January 1369 to Pope Urban V. There Petrarch praised Tommaso's virtues to the skies, writing:

> Speaking personally, most blessed Father, I know maestro Tommaso, whom I am discussing, as a fine and most honorable man, outstanding in his learning and even more outstanding in his virtue, one who is great and supreme, most famous for his distinguished faith and piety and as a beacon for the Catholic faith. . . . I can say at great length that the story of no other man can be told who is so full of gravity of mind, sweetness of manner, of sobriety, abstinence and austerity of life, of most fervid devotion, of humility, of contempt for himself and for the world, of unfeigned mercy and love, and of many other gifts.[12]

It is possible that Petrarch's words had some effect, for the commission meeting at Rome from November 1369 to April 1370 completely exonerated Tommaso of any charge of heresy, and at the annual meeting of the general chapter of the Franciscan Order held in Naples on 21 June 1370, Phillipe de Cabassole rehabilitated the Minister General and restored him to his office.[13] With his innocence definitely established, Tommaso took up again his duties, appearing at Bologna at the granting of the doctorate in theology to Bartolomeo da Milano, O.F.M., on 25 January 1371.[14]

But Tommaso's main duties during the early years of the 1370s were as diplomat in the service of his close friend, the new pope Gregory XI. For example, in October 1371 Gregory XI sent him to

Genoa to pacify the doge and factions of the nobility; this resulted in a peace within the city in the spring of 1372.[15] Gregory's greater plan was to form a defensive league against the Visconti in north Italy and thus to bring peace and unity among the pope's potential allies. This Tommaso accomplished by the fall of 1372, bringing Genoa, Savoy, Monferrato, and the Este of Ferrara together in a league directed against Bernabò and Galeazzo Visconti, lords of Milan. That same fall, Tommaso traveled to Germany to help make peace between King Louis of Hungary and the dukes of Austria, Albert and Leopold. By 21 November 1372, Tommaso had returned to Avignon to report to Pope Gregory XI on his success.[16] Earlier on 19 July 1372, Gregory had promoted Tommaso to be patriarch of Grado, resident in Venice, probably for several reasons. First, the pope needed an experienced diplomat on the Adriatic frontier to overcome any obstacles in mounting a crusade against the Turks. In fact, the pope hoped to turn the Genoese from war against the king of Cyprus and to urge them to fight against the Turks instead. Second, Gregory expected that Tommaso would be able to reconcile Padua under the Carrara lord and his allies, including the king of Hungary, who were engaged in a war with Venice to establish definite boundaries on the eastern frontier of the Padovano. Third, Gregory intended that Tommaso could prevent mercenary troops of the dukes of Austria and king of Hungary from reaching and aiding the Visconti that autumn. In other words, Tommaso's embassy to Germany hoped both to avert war with Venice and stop Hungarian and Austrian aid from reaching the great papal enemies, the Visconti of Milan.[17] After this embassy, Tommaso served on only one other diplomatic mission: as mediator to end the border war between Venice and the Carrara ruler of Padua in the summer of 1373.[18]

For the next five years, Tommaso mainly turned to the reform of monasteries and clerical abuses in Venice, as Giovanni himself notes in the dialogue. On 29 January 1374, he was commissioned in a letter from Pope Gregory XI to investigate and bring about monastic reform. In this letter, the pope called upon his friend in his office as Patriarch of Grado to make visitations and inspections of religious houses of both monks and nuns, and not just of the mendicant orders, but also of the Cistercians, Cluniacs, and Camaldolensians, using the

secular arm of the Venetian government to punish wayward religious of both sexes, if need be. The patriarch was further to provide the pope with the names of the religious houses that had been visited and the clergy and laity who had been punished or excommunicated.[19]

Shortly thereafter the patriarch turned to the problem of criminous clerics and improving relations between clergy and laity in Venice, appearing before the doge and his council requesting aid in reforming clergy and ending disputes between cleric and laity.[20] As a result of Tommaso's request, on 23 April 1374, the doge and Ducal Council recommended to the Great Council of Venice the creation of a committee of five *Savi*, one each chosen by the doge, his council, and the Three Heads of the Forty, and two elected by the Great Council, to confer with the patriarch and the vicar of the bishop of Castello to lay out a program of reform in writing within a month.[21]

A month proved too short a time, but less than half a year later, on 19 November 1374, three of the *Savi*, with the consent and agreement of both the patriarch of Grado and the vicar of the Bishop of Castello, placed before the Great Council an elaborate program for reform of treatment of criminous clerics and clearer definition of the roles of both clerical authority and the secular arm in bringing clergy to justice.[22] The reforms, which in general placed clergy who committed violent crimes, such as homicide, armed robbery, and thievery, more directly under the control of the Venetian state, were passed in the Great Council by a wide margin. Although clergy were not to be punished for serious crimes by death and mutilation as were lay criminals, clergy could be imprisoned and subject to perpetual exile from Venice and its dominions.

As Giovanni suggests in the dialogue, Tommaso's willingness to deal harshly with criminous clerics or lax monks brought sharp response from the clergy involved. But the pope stood by his reformer, squashing an appeal from the Benedictines of San Zaccaria against Tommaso's reforms in a letter of 25 September 1375.[23] Shortly thereafter, Tommaso had to deal with a counterfeiting bishop within his jurisdiction. Answering a complaint from the Venetian government on 31 December 1375, that the bishop of Cittanova and some of his clergy were minting false coins in both gold and silver, Tommaso seems to have had the culprit, a Venetian nobleman, one Niccolò of the Augustinian

Hermits, dismissed from his office, though it is not known what further penalty the counterfeiter might have suffered.[24]

During his term as patriarch of Grado, Tommaso continued his lively interest in the promotion of theological learning. On 27 April 1375, at the request of Pope Gregory, Tommaso redirected Bartolomeo Rinonchi of Pisa, O.F.M., a bachelor of theology, to any Studium Generale, where he might obtain a master's degree and the *licentia docendi* because he could not go to study at Cambridge or, due to war in northern France, to the Franciscan convent in Paris. On 28 June 1376, again on order from the pope, Tommaso sent the Franciscan theologian Giovanni da Menevia to lecture on Lombard's *Sententiae* in Venice instead of Bologna, because of civil strife and warfare in the latter city.[25] The next summer at the urging of Pope Gregory, Tommaso and his colleague the bishop of Castello asked the doge and his Council to elicit aid for the papacy in its war with Florence. But on 20 September 1377, the doge and Council, the Three Heads of the Forty, and the *Savi* of Istria and the Trevisano, proposed to the Senate that Venice turn a deaf ear to the pope's request for military aid against Florence. While professing love for the Holy Mother Church, the Senate voted to instruct Venice's ambassador at the papal court to beg off the proposed alliance against Florence, citing close economic and commercial ties with the Arno city and, most importantly, the need of Venice to defend itself at home from the threat of conquest by Genoa.[26] But Tommaso's failure to win over Venetian support in a clearly impossible diplomatic situation did not diminish the respect the patriarch of Grado commanded in the world of Italian ecclesiastical politics. When, some months after his election as Pope Urban VI, Bartolomeo Prignani of Naples sought to ensure that there was a College of Cardinals favorable to his remaining in Rome by creating on 18 September 1378 twenty-nine new cardinals, he included among his supporters the tested and trusted diplomat and reformer, Tommaso da Frignano.[27]

Returning to Giovanni's career, we find that the nephew made a visit to his uncle in the fall of 1373 hoping for a position as tutor in a patrician household. Learning of plots to oust him from the patriarch's curia, Giovanni fumed and even threatened to kill his uncle, but eventually he left Venice to visit Strà and Padua and spent Christ-

mas of 1373 at Arquà with his great hero Petrarch, before taking up
a post as head of the communal school at Belluno early the next year.
For the next five years Giovanni remained at Belluno, where he soon
remarried, this time to a wealthy widow named Benasuda, and in 1375
the couple's only child, a son named Israele, was born. At Belluno,
Giovanni essayed his first polished letter, one of consolation on the
death of Petrarch, written in the late summer of 1374 for his former
mentor, Donato Albanzani.[28] There followed fragments on the misery of human life and on the conception of Christ, and a short work
on the powerlessness of fate, *De fato*, addressed to his lifelong friend,
Paolo Rugolo, at Treviso in 1378.[29] And at the same time Giovanni commiserated with another friend, Paolo de Bernardo, on the
difficulty of schoolmastering at Belluno.[30] News of his uncle's elevation to the Cardinalate soon reached Giovanni, and he spent the Christmas season in Belluno composing and polishing the dialogue, finishing
the whole work on 5 January 1379. When on 13 February of that
year the commune of Belluno did not renew Giovanni's contract as
schoolmaster, he took the enforced leisure as an opportunity to travel to Rome to present a dedication copy (now Oxford, New College
D.155) to his uncle in the papal curia.[31] After a quarrel, perhaps over
the failure to gain employment in the papal curia, something hinted
at in the dialogue, Giovanni left Rome and settled in Padua where
he was soon hired as a secretary in the Carrara court and became a
confidant of the ruling lord, Francesco il Vecchio.[32] Tommaso meanwhile continued to be a busy and useful churchman during the three
years remaining to him, serving as chancellor of the Holy Roman
Church, a vicar of the Franciscan Order, and member of the commission for the canonization of Saint Bridget, and in 1381, while in Florence as apostolic visitor for the reform of the Camaldolensian convents,
he struck up a friendship with the Florentine chancellor, Coluccio
Salutati. Tommaso died at Rome on 19 November 1381 and was
buried in the Franciscan monastery of S. Maria d'Aracoeli on the Cam-
pidoglio.[33]

IN COMPOSING THIS FIRST LENGTHY WORK in the relative isolation of
the hill-town of Belluno, Giovanni was able to utilize comparatively
few works, but these he mined for anecdotes and quoted fairly fre-

quently. In a work designed to praise a great churchman and present the virtues of the religious vocation, Giovanni naturally turned to the primary sources of the Christian tradition. He quotes from the Bible often and his text is filled with allusions to Old Testament figures and anecdotes. For the lives of saints and the fathers, Giovanni used, most of all, the widely-popular thirteenth century collection of saints' lives, the *Legenda Aurea*, composed by the Dominican preacher Jacobus de Voragine, for use in sermons. But he also knew some of the works of the Church Fathers at first hand: he quotes both of Saint Augustine's most famous works, the *Confessions* and the *City of God*, as well as Saint Gregory the Great's *Pastoral Care*, a book he definitely had in his own library.[34] Giovanni's favorite Father, however, was Saint Jerome, whose *Against Jovinian* and *Life of Saint Hilarion* he cited on several occasions and whose letters of advice he mined to good effect.

For historical illustrations from classical antiquity, Giovanni relied most heavily on the first-century author, Valerius Maximus' *Factorum et dictorum memorabilium libri novem*, a text on which he had lectured at Bologna a decade earlier. No doubt he possessed his own copy of this text, which was clearly his favorite source of anecdotes and tales from Greek antiquity as well as Roman history. He also utilized the compendium of Greek and Roman history compiled by Justinus in the third century, and widely popular in the Middle Ages. These two authors he often called his common historians, as did his contemporary Coluccio Salutati.[35] His other principal source of classical sayings was a contemporary work, the *De vita et moribus philosophorum antiquorum*, compiled by the English Franciscan theologian, Walter Burley (1275–1345?), a text that he probably already had in his library and that he read carefully and annotated copiously.[36] Other Roman historians, including Sallust and Suetonius, are cited rather infrequently, and, except for one counterfeit quotation from Livy, Giovanni shows no knowledge of Petrarch's favorite historian and the greatest source for the history of early Rome.

Among other Roman prose writers that Giovanni knew best he often quoted the works of Cicero and Seneca. He clearly has read carefully Cicero's most popular treatises and dialogues, especially *De amicitia*, *De senectute*, *De officiis*, and the *Tusculanae disputationes*. He cites as well Seneca's letters and moral essays, especially the *De con-*

stantia and *De providentia,* as well as several of the tragedies. Among authors, both pagan and Christian, from late antiquity Giovanni quotes at one place or another from Macrobius' *Commentarium in Somnium Scipionis,* Cassiodorus' *Variae,* Boethius' *De consolatione philosophiae,* and one of the treatises of the sixth-century north Italian bishop, Ennodius. He probably shows as well some reliance on Aulus Gellius' treasury of classical anecdote, *Noctes Atticae.*

As a scholar who had earlier lectured at the University of Florence on Vergil's *Georgica* and was to make a reputation as lecturer on Latin poetry at the Paduan Studium some years later, Giovanni shows here a facile knowledge of the great Roman poets. At least once he quotes each of the five canonical poets of late medieval literary education—Vergil, Horace, Ovid, Lucan, and Statius.[37] He also shows intimate knowledge of the great satirists, Juvenal and Persius, and of some of the plays of Terence, although many of the quotations from Terence had no doubt long since become proverbial tags.

Finally, Giovanni shows some knowledge of the most common texts of Greek science and medicine, probably from books that he had inherited from his father's library earlier in the decade. He shows through quotation some acquaintance with Latin translations of Aristotle, *De generatione animalium,* Hippocrates' *Aphorisms,* and Avicenna's *Canon,* and the compendium from Galen known as the *Ars medica* or the *Ars parva.*[38] Among Latin scientific writers, Giovanni quotes most notably from Book 7 of Pliny's *Naturalis historia.*

It is also very probable that Giovanni had some knowledge of several of the Latin works of his revered and admired older contemporaries, Giovanni Boccaccio and Francesco Petrarca, both recently dead. Giovanni Conversini had known Boccaccio in Ravenna as a boy and at some time acquired a copy of his famous work on the fates of illustrious men, *De casibus virorum illustrium,* now Vat. Pal. lat. 970. Further, since so many of Conversini's examples of the great deeds of women are similar to those contained in Boccaccio's other important historic work, *De mulieribus claris,* he may have owned or had access to that work as well.[39]

Giovanni Conversini had first met Petrarch in Padua in 1364 on introduction from his teacher, Donato Albanzani, and as we have seen, he renewed acquaintance with his cultural hero at his home at Arquà

south of Padua during the Christmas season of 1373. It cannot be known with certainty which, if any, of Petrarch's works Giovanni had available to him in Belluno in the winter of 1378, but it is clear from his letter of consolation on the death of Petrarch addressed to Donato Albanzani in the late summer of 1374 that he did possess a developed sense of the Petrarchan Latin corpus. In the dialogue, many of his most striking ancient allusions and anecdotes were also among Petrarch's favorites, especially as found in the *De remediis utriusque fortune* and the *Rerum memorandarum libri*. It is just possible that he had access to at least some of Petrarch's treatises, including *De otio religioso* and *De vita solitaria* as well as the two just mentioned.

In any case, the similarities between Giovanni's *Dialogus* composed in 1378 and Petrarch's *De otio religioso* begun in 1347 are so striking in theme, sources, and argument as to warrant close comparison. Petrarch's work was begun as a thank-you note to his brother Gherardo, a monk in the Carthusian house at Montrieux in southern France that Petrarch had recently visited. Petrarch divided his examination of the repose of the religious into two parts: Book 1 on the need to combat sin and false doctrine and for monks to keep the faith, and Book 2 on the miseries of the world and the frailty of the flesh to be remedied by choice of the religious life and faith in divine providence. Likewise Giovanni's *Dialogus* arose from a communication to a relative, in the form of a dialogue between the author Giovanni and the Letter (Litera) he was sending to Rome to congratulate his uncle on his election as Cardinal of the Church. The dialogue structure permits Giovanni to profess his own sincere thought over the more specious and conventional arguments put forth by Litera.

In an important sense the *Dialogus* is an elaborate and rather self-centered effort by Giovanni to capture his uncle's good will and secure a post in Rome. In this effort Giovanni examines the love and conflict between generations, his own life as husband, father and layman, while giving a detailed portrait of Tommaso's career and character. Near the beginning of the *Dialogus* in terms reminiscent of a passage in Book 1 of Petrarch's *De otio religioso*,[40] Giovanni asserts that the best path to Christian living is the imitation of the lives of the great Latin Fathers, as handed down in biographies from the early Church: Possidius for Saint Augustine, Paulinus of Nola for Saint Ambrose,

Gregory the Great for Saint Benedict of Nursia, and Paul the Deacon for Gregory himself. Similarly, Giovanni promises to recount his uncle's biography to the best of his ability; his account of Tommaso's virtue will be "accurate and filled with love," because "the perfect way to virtue is to know who Tommaso was" (p. 41 below). Hence, most of the central part of the *Dialogus* functions as an account of Tommaso's virtuous upbringing and career as a Franciscan prelate. Giovanni describes the harsh conditions of Tommaso's early life in the Apennines, his early propensity for study and interest in the liberal arts, his avoidance of women, marriage, and frivolity, and his great services to the Franciscan Order and as a papal diplomat bringing peace to Christendom.

In this description of Tommaso's life and character, Giovanni dwells upon his virtues derived both from common Franciscan values of love of peace and acceptance of poverty, and from Stoic commonplaces as found in such works as Cicero's *Tusculan Disputations*. He describes his uncle's patience and long-suffering, his chastity, his learning, his piety, love of justice, moderation, and sobriety, and his activity for peace and church reform. Giovanni's account of Tommaso's bravery in facing death on storm-tossed seas during his embassies closely follows Petrarch's quotation and praise of the teachings of Pliny, Seneca, and Cicero in *De otio religioso* on the powerlessness of death. Giovanni is near to Petrarch's views also in his condemnation of sin and immoderation, especially drunkenness.[41]

In the second part of the dialogue, Giovanni examines and eventually asserts his own fitness for service in the papal curia. He realizes that, because of his two marriages and two sons, he cannot hope for an ecclesiastical living, but he does wish that "even if my father cannot summon me to a benefice, at least he can find me an office [in Rome]" (p. 103 below). Giovanni examines his other options and finds them wanting: King Louis of Hungary, his father's patron, is near death and his state is about to be racked by civil strife; Francesco da Carrara is a fine patron as demonstrated by his friendship with Petrarch, but the Paduan lord knows nothing of Giovanni; and, most of all, his present situation as schoolmaster in Belluno is difficult, onerous, and mean. Therefore, Giovanni hopes for the leisure and time for study that employment in Rome will bring. In fact, he gives as his

reasons for composing the *Dialogus* and travelling to Rome, not economic gain, but the wish to enjoy the patriarch's company, to deliver
the work personally, to find patronage worthy of a man of letters,
and to have time to study the books he had received from his father's
legacy through his uncle's good offices. To demonstrate his own seriousness as a scholar, Giovanni describes how he composed the *Dialogus* during nightly studies at the recent Christmas season, while others
were banqueting or sleeping.

In his conclusion on the misery and folly of most of humankind,
Giovanni shows close affinities with Petrarch's works in their common use of Book 7 of Pliny's *Natural History* on human frailty and
of Heraclitus on inevitable strife and conflict, and in their praise of
a life of solitude and scholarly leisure. In this last instance, Petrarch's
own love of solitude and rural living at Arquà is given as evidence.
In the end, Giovanni asserts that the purpose of his letter is not to
gain wealth, glory or power but to have from his uncle the gift of
leisure for his own studies. In the final analysis, Giovanni Conversini,
like Petrarch, sees no contradiction between his own way of life and
the religious vocation. Both admire the monastic calling and voice
regret that they cannot follow it, but both believe that a secular life
of scholarly leisure is appropriate to their own needs and characters.

THERE ARE, AS FAR AS WE KNOW, three complete manuscripts of the
Dialogus, and a small part of the beginning appears in a fourth. The
manuscripts are: MS D.155 of New College, Oxford, now kept in
the Bodleian Library; Vat. Pal. lat. 970, in the Biblioteca Apostolica
Vaticana; Cod. 3449, in the Österreichische Nationalbibliothek at Vienna; and fols. 179va–180b of Codex II.C.61 of the Yugoslav Acade-
my of Arts and Sciences in Zagreb.

The Oxford manuscript (O) is the presentation copy made by
Giovanni for his uncle and begins with a brief dedication to him. It
is written on vellum in two columns of twenty-eight lines in an elegant Petrarchan script and decorated with an illuminated initial depict-
ing a kneeling Giovanni presenting his book to Uncle Tommaso,
properly attired in a cardinal's hat. The initial and its marginal vine
decoration are colored in red, green, mauve, gold, and blue. The names
of the collocutors, Johannes and Litera, appear each time there is a

change in speaker and are colored in red. There is also an illuminated capital to signal each change of speaker; the name of the new speaker usually appears in red at the end of the line above the illuminated capital, but when there is not enough space, the name appears at the end of the line with this illuminated letter. In the manuscript, the color contrast keeps this from being confusing. Our identification of each speaker with capital letters in the current text is meant only as a convenience to the modern reader. The work is north Italian, very probably done in Padua or Treviso. It was finished by April 1379, when Giovanni took his dialogue as a gift to his uncle in Rome. Our edition is based almost entirely on the text of this fine manuscript, which is singularly free of errors. There are a few inconsistencies in spelling, most noticeably in the confusion of *ti* and *ci* before a vowel; we have not attempted to correct these.

The nearly contemporary Vatican manuscript (V) of the *Dialogus* is thought to be Conversini's own copy which later belonged to one of his pupils, the Venetian humanist and statesman, Francesco Barbaro. Manuscript V has blank spaces where the illuminated capitals should be, and no mention of either speaker's name. The original manuscript is very poor, not only because of many incorrect readings but even more so because of omissions, on nearly every page, of words, sentences, or even paragraphs. However, Barbaro has painstakingly corrected most of the errors and supplied the omitted parts, using the margins for the purpose. In referring to this manuscript, we have not attempted to distinguish between the original and Barbaro's additions, as the former without the latter presents an inaccurate and incomplete text. As it now stands, however, it is obvious that Barbaro had access to a manuscript very similar to O (but not identical with it) from which he took his corrections, thus creating a good text which is very useful for collation. It is his emended manuscript, therefore, to which we refer as V. In little more than a dozen instances the readings of V are adopted in our edition in preference to those of O. Most of the discrepancies between the two are in word order or in the use of synonyms; although in these cases V's readings are perfectly good, we have used those in O as a matter of course.

The third complete manuscript, that in Vienna (Vi), is mistakenly listed in the Nationalbibliothek's catalogue of dated Latin manuscripts

written before 1400, because of the composition date of 1379 found
at the end of the text. The handwriting of the Vienna codex is fifteenth-
century, and the spelling too is evidence of a late date, as it is quite
classical, even to the correct use of diphthongs. The manuscript is,
however, so full of careless errors that it does not present a readable
text. Its interest for us lies in its many agreements with V as opposed
to O in word order and use of synonyms; yet it is not a copy of V,
for it shares the dedication and many preferred readings with O. The
readings of Vi are indicated in the critical notes of this edition only
when they coincide with one of the two major manuscripts (almost
invariably V).

All variant readings of the Zagreb manuscript (Z) are given, mainly
as they are few in number because of the very small amount of material
presented. It is generally a good text.

It is clear that there are several manuscript traditions for the text
of the *Dialogus,* as internal evidence proves that none of those which
we possess is a direct copy of another. Without more detailed study
it is not possible to determine the exact relationships among them.
However, it is a fair assumption that the beautifully and carefully made
presentation copy, O, comes closest to what the author wrote, with
very few exceptions.

Notes

1. See brief discussions by B. G. Kohl in his Introduction to Giovanni
di Conversino da Ravenna, *Dragmalogia,* ed. and trans. H. L. Eaker (Lewisburg, Pa., and London, 1980) 19–20, and L. Gargan, "Per la biblioteca di
Giovanni Conversini," *Vestigia: Studi in onore di Giuseppe Billanovich,* ed. R.
Avesani et al. (Rome, 1984) 1:378–79.

2. See R. Sabbadini, *Giovanni da Ravenna, insigne figura d'umanista
(1343–1408)* (Como, 1924) 49, where there is mention of a letter *Ad Thomam Grandensem cardinalem de eius creatione,* in the form of a dialogue between the writer and the letter. B. L. Ullman, *The Humanism of Coluccio
Salutati* (Padua, 1963) 199–200, was the first to give a detailed description
of the Oxford MS, New College D.155, which belonged to Salutati, but
he cites the wrong shelf mark for the Vatican MS: Pal. Lat. 970. The third
MS of the dialogue, in Vienna, is late and of little value for this edition.

3. For convenient summaries of Giovanni's life, see, in Italian, L. Gar-

gan, "Il preumanesimo a Vicenza, Treviso e Venezia," *Storia di cultura veneta*, in vol. 2 of *Il Trecento* (Vicenza, 1976) 159–67, and B. G. Kohl, "Conversini, Giovanni, da Ravenna," *Dizionario biografico degli Italiani* 28 (Rome, 1983): 574–78, and in English, Kohl, Introduction to *Dragmalogia*, 11–30.

4. For records for this post in Giovanni's own hand, see Archivio di Stato, Firenze, Atti del Podestà, reg. 1970–72, 3 vols. of acts from September 1368 to January 1369, for podestà Guido Odone Fortebracci, and reg. 2073–75, three vols. from February to April 1369, for podestà Raimondino Danieli.

5. A fifteenth-century copy of Giovanni's commentary on Valerius Maximus was recently discovered by Paul Oskar Kristeller in Venice, Museo Corror, MS. 855, and is described by Dorothy Schullian in her essay on Valerius Maximus in the *Catalogus Translationum et Commentariorum*, ed. F. E. Cranz (Washington, D.C., 1984) 5:340–42.

6. See Sabbadini, 38–40, and B. G. Kohl and J. Day, "Giovanni Conversini's *Consolatio ad Donatum* on the Death of Petrarch," *Studies in the Renaissance* 21 (1974): 9–30.

7. See G. B. Tondini, *Delle memorie istoriche concernenti la vita del cardinale Tommaso da Frignano* (Macerata, 1782) 11 ff., and G. Pistoni, "Un modenese amico del Petrarca, il Cardinale Tommaso Frignani, con lettera inedita di Coluccio Salutati," *Atti e Memorie dell'Accademia di scienze, lettere ed arti di Modena*, 5th ser., 12 (1954): 84.

8. See Luke Wadding, ed., *Annales Minorum*, 2d ed. (Rome, 1731 ff.) 8:147, no. 1; and Tondini, xviii–xix, no. 7.

9. See Wadding, 8:200, and C. Piana, *Chartularium Studii Bononiensis S. Francisci (saec. XIII–XIV)*, Analecta Franciscana 11 (Quaracchi, 1970) 86*.

10. On this episode, see D. Nimmo, "Poverty and Politics: The Motivation of Fourteenth-century Franciscan Reform in Italy," *Religious Motivation: Biographical and Sociological Problems for the Church Historian*, ed. D. Baker, Studies in Church History, vol. 15 (Oxford, 1978) 172–73; C. Eubel, *Bullarium franciscanum* (Rome, 1902) 6:418; and Pistoni, 86–88.

11. See A. Callebaut, "Thomas de Frignano, Ministre générale, et ses defenseurs: Pétrarque, Philippe de Cabassol et Philippe de Maizières, vers 1369–70," *AFH* 10 (1917): 239–49.

12. See Petrarch's text in Callebaut, 246.

13. Wadding, 8:231, and P. Péano, "Jacques de' Tolomei, éléments de biographie," *AFH* 68 (1975): 293.

14. C. Piana, ed., *Nuovi documenti sull'Università di Bologna e sul Collegio di Spagna* (Bologna, 1979) 177.

15. Wadding, 8:234–35.

16. Wadding, 8:249–56.

17. On the Pope's use of Tommaso, the Patriarch of Grado, as diplomat,

see G. Mollat, "Thomas de Frignano, O.F.M., et la diplomatie pontificale," *AFH* 55 (1962): 521-23.

18. B. Gatari, *Cronaca carrarese*, ed. A. Medin & G. Tolomei, Rerum italicarum scriptores, n. ed. 17 (Bologna, 1931) 122-24; and Eubel, 6:509, no. 1272, peace of 28 June 1373 between Padua and Venice.

19. For Gregory's letter of 29 January 1374, see Wadding, 8:296, no. 15; Eubel, 6:522, n. 6; and full text in G. Cappelletti, *Le Chiese d'Italia* (Venice, 1854) 9:84-85.

20. See Wadding, 8:297.

21. Archivio di Stato, Venezia, Maggior Consiglio, reg. 19 (Novella), fol. 140v, 23 April 1374, published below as Appendix, Doc. 1.

22. Archivio di Stato, Venezia, Maggior Consiglio, reg. 19 (Novella), fols. 145v-147r, 19 November 1374, published below as Appendix, Doc. 2.

23. See Wadding, 8:297.

24. See R. Predelli, ed., *I libri commemoriali della Repubblica di Venezia*, vol. 3 of *Regesti* (Venice, 1878) 122; Eubel, 6:522.

25. Eubel, 6:551, no. 1379, 27 April 1375; ibid., 6:575, no. 1441, 28 June 1376; and C. Piana, *Chartularium Studii Bononiensis*, 40, where the number given from Eubel is incorrect.

26. Archivio di Stato, Venezia, Senato, Misti, reg. 36, fol. 42v, 20 September 1377.

27. Wadding, 9:14, no. 5; W. Ullmann, *The Origins of the Great Schism* (Hamden, Conn., 1969) chap. 5; and Eubel, *Hierarchia Catholica Medii Aevi* (Münster, 1913) 23-24.

28. Kohl and Day, "Giovanni Conversini's *Consolatio ad Donatum*," 14-30, and Sabbadini, 42-48.

29. B. G. Kohl, "The Works of Giovanni di Conversino da Ravenna: A Catalogue of Manuscripts and Editions," *Traditio* 31 (1975): 355, and Sabbadini, 48.

30. L. Lazzarini, *Paolo de Bernardo e i primordi dell'umanesimo a Venezia* (Geneva, 1930) 192-93.

31. On this manuscript, see Kohl, "Readers and Owners of an Early Work of Giovanni Conversini da Ravenna: New College, Oxford, MS D.155," *Scriptorium* 40 (1986): 95-100, and plates 6-7.

32. Sabbadini, 52-55, and for his own account of his years at Padua, Giovanni Conversini da Ravenna, *Two Court Treatises*, ed. & trans. B. G. Kohl and J. Day (Munich, 1987).

33. See Pistoni, 92-93.

34. See Kohl, Introduction to *Dragmalogia*, 24.

35. See Ullman, *Humanism of Coluccio Salutati*, 234.

36. See Gargan, "Per la biblioteca di Giovanni Conversini," 370-71, for a description of Giovanni's heavily annotated MS of Burley's collection, now Milan, Biblioteca Ambrosiana, S 72 sup.

37. On texts and poets in early Renaissance education, see E. Garin, ed., *Il pensiero pedigogico dell'Umanesimo* (Florence, 1958) 92–103, and B. G. Kohl, "Humanism and Education," in Albert Rabil, ed., *Renaissance Humanism: Foundations, Forms and Legacy* (Philadelphia, 1988) 3:5–22.

38. On the inheritance of books from his father, see Sabbadini, 157–58, and for his knowledge of works of Aristotle and Galen, Gargan, "Per la biblioteca di Giovanni Conversini," 368–69, 382.

39. For Giovanni's copy of Boccaccio's *De casibus virorum illustrium*, see Kohl, "Works," 354.

40. Petrarca, *Vita solitaria*, in vol. 1 of *Opere latine*, ed. A. Bufano et al., 2 vols. (Turin, 1975) 680, and on the genre of humanist treatises on the status of the religious, Charles Trinkaus's important essay in his *The Scope of Renaissance Humanism* (Ann Arbor, 1983) 195–236.

41. See, for example, Petrarch, *Vita solitaria*, in vol. 1 of *Opere latine*, 674.

DIALOGUS INTER JOHANNEM ET LITERAM

TEXT AND TRANSLATION

Omnis reverentie et sanctitatis cultu dignissimo patri domino Thome, titulato Sanctorum Nerei, Archilei, atque Pancracii Presbytero, Cardinali beatissimo. Integra subiectione devotissimus servus et affectu plenissimo filius.

Dialogus inter Johannem et Literam

JOHANNES: Quid agimus, Litera? Merendone tabescemus quod dominum, quod patrem, quod columen unicum spei nostre procul miserimus? Atque utinam non amiserimus! Arripimus iter an calamum? Illud arma scelesta, hunc negotiorum agminatim hinc inde obstrepentium numerus intercipit. Difficile utrumque sed optabile utrumque sed honestum utrumque. Quid obtices? Ibis prona libensque?

LITERA: Quonam liceat agnoscere? Nichil me piguerit utilitatem hec modo tibi allatura sit via.

JOHANNES: Nichil honestum quin continuo id utile existat, ut Stoycis placet. Honestum est autem ubi re nequeas gratificis saltem verbis pignus amoris integri dare. Eas itaque velim ad dominum meum et benefactorem unicum dominum Thomam, sacrosancte Romane Ecclesie cardinalem.

LITERA: Siccine vigilias et sudorem tuum existimas parvi, temporisque iacturam parum advertis ut me quoque nequicquam impingas, mox vel pleno periculorum itinere vel ipsius intenta maioribus maiestate

To my father lord Tommaso, most worthy of the honor of all reverence and sanctity, titular priest of the Churches of Saints Nereo, Archileo, and Pancrazio, most blessed Cardinal. In whole-hearted submission your most devoted servant, and in fullest affection your son.

Dialogue Between Giovanni and the Letter

GIOVANNI: What am I to do, Letter? Shall I waste away in grief because I have let go far away my lord, my father, the sole support of my hopes? If only I have not lost him! Do I start with a journey or with my pen? One is forestalled by the evils of war, the other by a host of business affairs assailing me on every side. Either course is difficult, but both are also desirable and honorable. Why are you silent? Will you be ready and willing to go?

LETTER: Where, I'd like to know? I do not mind, provided this trip will be useful to you.

GIOVANNI: There is no honorable thing which is not in consequence useful, as the Stoics say.[1] It is honorable moreover to give a token of sincere love at least by means of grateful words when one cannot do so by actions. Therefore I'd like you to go to my excellent master and benefactor, Lord Tommaso, Cardinal of the Holy Roman Church.

LETTER: Do you consider your wakeful nights and toil of so little value, and do you mind so little the sacrifice of your time, that you can urge me to a useless course where I am sure to fail, either because the journey is full of dangers or because his majesty is intent upon more im-

ruituram? Quonam me pacto inducat edituus manu vacua pulsantem, lacero amictu, illoto sermone, insipido etiam, ne dicam nonnullis ingrato? O te ineptum, tam altas inter curas atque beata fastigia, si vicem habere non desperas quo vel candidatis adire vix pervium est.

Atqui non ea nunc mundi constantia, non ea benignitas est ut summa felicitas respiciat in sorde iacentem. Potius humilitate necessitudinis° primitive ac veteris amicitie coinquinari se putant. Quin proprii° sic elatio nidi reddit immemores ut ipsos quoque parentes exhorrescant interdumque diffiteantur. Quodsi nec satis ipse didicisti, nusquam exempla non supersunt. Fallerer utinam mentireturque Satirus: "Quantum quisque sua nummorum servat in archa tantum habet et fidei." Quo fit ut solitaria et campestris pene virtus sit, et ultro sepe ignavi interdum etiam stulti paupertate ipsa qui prediti sunt virtute ferantur. Idcirco delite potius nudus opibus, inops amicis, hebes ingenio, et sordido tacitus pulvere serpe, ut meritus es et datum est tibi. Cum vero° mens evolandi fervebit, recordator Phetontis et Ycari.

JOHANNES: Sapis crude nimium, Litera! Nec succense, faris insipide. Non est ut° suspiciose priusquam experiare de hominibus iudices presertim bonis, quorum pectora ut non temere ingreditur difficile ita convellitur caritatis integritas, nisi forte illam Ciceronis sententiam inficiemur, quod "amicitie vere sempiterne sunt." Hominum vero temere diligentium est absque radicibus fidem alere, mox primo aure levioris impulsu arietantem. Quotidie hinc amicitie ille quas Anneus° temporarias appellat labefacte lapseque° deplorantur. Graves autem viri non sine delectu consilioque ita quemvis affectum complectuntur, ut confederata semel affectio quantavis fortunarum accessione numquam° labet. Verus nempe genitor eque hirsuta ac lacera in veste quam

portant matters? Why should the sacristan admit me when I knock with empty hand, in tattered cloak, with my "speech unwashed"[2] and even silly, not to say unwelcome to some? Oh how foolish you are, wavering between depths of anxiety and heights of happiness, if you do not give up the hope of having a chance where approach is scarcely possible even for privileged candidates.

Now the world does not possess the kind of loyalty or benevolence which causes men at the peak of prosperity to have regard for one in a mean position. On the contrary, they consider themselves contaminated by the humble estate of their early connections and long-ago friendships. What is more, pride in their own niche makes them so unthinking that they neglect even their parents and sometimes disown them. If you yourself haven't learned this well, you can find examples everywhere. How I wish that I were wrong, and that the Satirist did not speak the truth when he said: "A man's word is believed in exact proportion to the amount of cash which he keeps in his strongbox."[3] Consequently virtue is solitary and almost uncultivated; and moreover those possessed of virtue are often called lazy, sometimes even dense, because of their poverty. Therefore it is better for you to hide yourself, being devoid of wealth, without friends, and dull of wit, and to creep silently in the filthy dust, as you deserve and have had allotted to you. When indeed your mind grows eager to fly out, remember Phaethon and Icarus![4]

GIOVANNI: Your understanding is very immature, Letter! Don't get angry, but you are speaking foolishly. There is no reason why you should suspect men before you put them to the test, especially good men. It is very difficult for a sincere love to be dislodged from their hearts, as it does not enter there lightly. Or perhaps we are to reject Cicero's maxim, that "real friendships are eternal." But it is typical of men whose affections are casual to nourish a loyalty without roots, which then totters at the first touch of a light breeze. Every day those friendships which Seneca calls "temporary,"[5] (i.e., assumed for the occasion) grow weak, collapse, and are given up for lost. Serious men, however, embrace objects of affection with discrimination and forethought, so that an attachment once made never falters with any increase in fortune. A true father indeed welcomes his son as readily

variata auro bissoque natum acceptat, et quamvis obtutui honestior in trabea, non autem animo carior occursat.

Ita vir bonus ac sapiens tametsi conspicari mallet amicum fortune favore circumfluum, tamen non aspernatur e felicitatis gremio excussum. Quin nescio qua cordis humanitate susceptat avidius,° gratulans tacitus beneficentie sue locum superesse. Ut enim ille ait apud Anneum: "Fidem secunda poscunt, adversa exigunt." Quantum itaque necessarium utili prestat, tanto deiectis in rebus pulcrior quam in letioribus illata benignitas.

Et enim qui potest amicitia illa vel esse vel dici vere in qua cum omnia esse communia iubeantur, seu ex duobus potius animis unus fiat, fortunarum alter copia floreat, alter inopia tabescat? Plane huiusmodi ficta, vel nulla potius, iuxta Socraticum illud censenda: "Non est," inquit, "amicus qui fortune particeps non est." Amicatio nempe sincera leti sinistrive communione magis tamen sinistri deprenditur. Quoniam sicut gratari prosperis amicorum, tristiora sic demere vel saltem lenire debemus. Namque si fidem illustrant, cur non et beneficentiam ipsam adversa? Velut enim paupertati decus addit nescire precio corrumpi, sic fortunatissimis dum inferioribus mansuescunt predicatio debetur. Hinc Fabricium in auro Samnitum, inde Paulum in Persico rege, et Alexandrum in gregario milite claros historie commemorant.

Denique, ut animadvertas mendaciter collegisse, cuntam arctis amicitiam finibus stringis, imo ad ipsos quoque defunctos solidus amor extenditur, quodque nequivit auctoribus reddere, ipsorum heredibus supplet. Et hic extat amicitie honestissimus fructus. Id explicuit liquido Tullius, per amicitiam non imbecilles modo inopesque valere, verum etiam vivere mortuos asseverans, "tantus° eos honor, memoria, desiderium prosequitur amicorum." Porro tum benevolentie ac liberalitatis honor nitescit accrescitque cum eadem fides servatur extinctis.

in a torn and rough garment as in one embroidered with gold and silk. Although he presents a more handsome appearance in a dress uniform, he is not thereby dearer to the heart.

Just so, a good and wise man, even though he would prefer to see his friend surrounded with fortune's favor, nevertheless does not scorn him when shaken out of the bosom of prosperity. Instead, with a kindly heart he receives his friend all the more eagerly, silently rejoicing that he has an opportunity to do him a favor. For, as Seneca quotes: "Good fortune asks for faith but adversity demands it."[6] Therefore, as need takes precedence over what is merely useful, so kindness offered in adversity is superior to that offered under happier circumstances.

In fact, since in friendship all things are commanded to be shared, as if two hearts become as one, how can this relationship truly exist or even be said to exist when one man flourishes with abundant wealth and the other wastes away in poverty? Plainly such a friendship must be considered false, no friendship at all, according to Socrates: "That man is not a friend," he says, "who does not share his fortune."[7] It is true that genuine friendship is attained by the sharing of both good and bad, but more by the sharing of the bad. As we ought to rejoice in the prosperity of our friends, we ought also to remove or at least alleviate their misfortunes. For if adversity adds luster to loyalty, why not also to charitableness? As honor is bestowed upon poverty by a refusal to be corrupted by bribes, so commendation is due to the wealthy when they treat their inferiors with kindness. For this reason histories record the fame of Fabricius concerning the gold of the Samnites, of Paulus in the case of the Persian king, of Alexander in the case of the common soldier.[8]

Finally—so that you may see that you have come to a false conclusion—you restrict the whole of friendship to very narrow limits; but in fact complete love is extended even to the dead, and what it could not give to the parents, it supplies to their heirs. And here is the most honorable fruit of friendship. Cicero explained it clearly, asserting that through friendship not only are the poor and weak made strong but even the dead are alive, "so great is the esteem on the part of their friends, the tender recollection and the deep longing that still attends them."[9] Further, renown for benevolence and generosity grows bright and increases when the same loyalty is shown to the

Nil plane Blosium magis honestavit quam, publice damnato Gracco, publice ceso ac insepulto iacenti, minime defuisse. Strophilus fide quam tribuit amici filio habetur insignis. Inter clarissima Ligurgi opera predicatur tutela fidelis.

Quid per deos animo iocundius quam is qui gratiam ultro contulerit egenti, cum audire potest: "Perpendo michi te, non fortune mee, dilectorem. Persone non rerum amicus eras. Nunc patet quam sincere colueris cuius fidei possessor eras. Quam intaminato, quam vero, quam solido pectore complexus amicum sis! Dum florebam rebus parque fueram indulgentia fortune, non clarebat quali arderes amore. Habebas stimulum spei. Tota nunc bonitas tibi, laus tota debetur." Quem non iuvet hasce voces audire?

Oberras igitur tota spe, cum huiusmodi suspectibus angeris. Num° te preterit quali quantoque impendio rex sanctissimus et propheta amici filium suscepit Misboseth? Quis nesciat Barzelai filium ab eodem ipso rege incrementis auctum, que pater decrepitus acceptare non valuit? Pretereo quas lacrimas Phrix Hiulus parenti° indulsit Euriali. Angustares nimium quippe vinculum mundi, caritatem, si quidem° vel quantovis successu apud bene institutos animos vel etiam morte posset extingui. Certe cum plurimas et maximas commoditates amicitia contineat, tum illa nimirum prestat omnibus, quod bonam spem prelucet in posterum, nec "debilitari aut cadere animos patitur," ut Tullius ait.

Haud itaque dubium quin idem amor, eadem indulgentia humanitasque cum illo ipso patre, licet summis aucto beatitatis gradibus, mansura sit. Ad hec omnes pene Latii per angulos nepotem me suum indicantibus populis, sine proprie fame comminutione eum michi abrogare non posset honorem. Quandoquidem quem minore positus loco, tuum sponte feceris, summo functum apice aspernari turpissimum sit. Quippe circumspectantes desertum proferre possent: "Puerum hunc pontifex ille fortuna potitus minore susceperat habebatque

dead. Surely nothing did more honor to Blossius than that he did not
desert Gracchus after Gracchus was condemned and executed by the
state and was lying unburied.[10] Strophilus is deemed outstanding for
the loyalty he showed to the son of his friend. Among the famous
deeds of Lycurgus, responsible guardianship is praised.[11]

What, by the gods, is more pleasing to a man's heart than to hear,
after freely doing a favor to one in need, "I value you for loving me,
not my fortune. You were a friend of a person, not of his possessions. Now it is obvious how sincerely you have cherished the man
whose trust you possessed. With what a pure, true, and steadfast heart
have you embraced your friend! When I was in flourishing circumstances and was your equal through the kindness of fate, it was not
clear what sort of love burned in you. You had the encouragement
of expectations. But as it is now, all generosity and all honor is due
you." Who wouldn't be pleased to hear such words?

Therefore you are wrong in all your apprehension, in being trou-
bled by suspicions! Surely you do not fail to remember the great out-
lay of money with which the most holy king and prophet received
Mephiboseth, his friend's son. Who does not know that the son of
Barzillai was enriched by that same king with the benefits which his
aged father was not able to accept?[12] I need not mention the tears
which the Phrygian Hiulus shed for the parent of Euryalus.[13] You
would surely limit too narrowly that binding tie of the world, affection, if it could indeed be destroyed among right-thinking people by
great prosperity or even by death. Certainly not only does friendship
contain many very excellent advantages but this advantage surpasses
all others, that it shows the light of good hope for the future and
"does not suffer the spirit to grow faint or to fall," as Cicero says.[14]

There is, then, no doubt that the same love, the same lenity and
kindness will remain in my father, even though he has been exalted
to the highest degree of blessedness. Also, since in nearly every corner of Italy people point me out as his nephew, he could not deprive
me of this position of respect without a diminution of his own reputation. It would surely be very shameful for a man enjoying the highest
rank to spurn one whom he, when of lower status, had voluntarily
made his own. In that case, indeed, observers could bring attention
to the deserted person, saying, "When that bishop had a lesser for-

pro suo. Summum nunc culmen attingens deficit." Quid huiusmodi
susurratione viro perfecte virtutis indignius? Ergo si patrem meum Con-
versinum fratrem habuit, caro ipsa sanguisque benignum ac paternum
reddent. Si vero amicum verissimum ac utilissimum expertus est, quo
affinitatis genere nullum prius, amoris integritas prisci dulcisve memoria
propicium quidem tibi aditum vendicabunt.

Minime igitur laborem huiusmodi itineris fugias, nisi forte ut ais
ipsa te dissertitudinis confundit inopia. Sed hoc te quoque remorari
non debet. Affectum ipsum non rudem verborum structuram, il-
laboratorum quidem ac velut ab occupato manantium attendet. Neque te ullus item pudor mordeat vacuis palmis veritam proficisci. Eodem
censore tuta es. Intelligit enim quanta sit tibi domus, quam longe vires,
et non habere nos nisi que ipse contulisset. Non vales quicquam elargiri, reddere potes. Abito itaque plena spei. An usque adhuc cuntaris?

LITERA: Quid exponam? Agendum quid exigendumve iubes? Aurumne
fortassis? Maiores illud et acceptiores in usus mavult! Accepisti quoque exulare hactenus munificentiam a clero, pol, virtutem hanc ut ple-
rasque alias oblito, quorum contractis abuncisque manibus vix°
extorquere quid valeas. Mentiorne id? Esto sim mendax—quod quidem mallem! Tot circum se hiantes affectus videre videor ut suppli-
cem antistes ille attendere conetur incassum. Preterea secundis te nuptiis
subiugem beneficio compotire non potest, cuius nunc rei facultatem
habet quam ne quidem negaret opinor.

Quas ob res impetum huiusmodi legationis admoneo seponendum,
neu lassa nequicquam irrisave repetam limen tuum. Hec te magis con-
fusura quo spem ipsam, quantulacumque restat adhuc, extinctam frus-
tratamque cognoris.

tune, he took in this boy and looked upon him as a son. Now, upon attaining the peak of eminence, he turns his back upon him!" What could be more unworthy of a man of perfect virtue than such scandalous whispers? Since my own father Conversino was his brother, flesh and blood itself will make him kindly and paternal; and since indeed he found my father a most true and helpful friend — and there is no better kinship than this — the sincerity and the sweet memory of his old love will assure you of a favorable approach.

Therefore do not shrink from undertaking this journey; unless, perhaps, as you yourself say, your lack of eloquence embarrasses you. Yet even this ought not to hold you back. He will pay attention to the affection expressed, not to the ill-fashioned construction of words which come unpolished from a busy person. Neither likewise should any shame distress you in your fear of setting forth with empty hands. You are safe in his judgment here also. For he knows the size of your home, the extent of your resources, and that I have nothing which he himself has not given. You cannot bestow anything on him, but you can make a repayment. Go then, filled with hope! What — are you still waiting?

LETTER: What shall I tell him? What do you require me to do or to ask for? Gold, perhaps? He prefers to keep that for more important and agreeable uses! You know too that until now generosity has been living in exile from the clergy, by Pollux, who have forgotten this virtue like many others; from their tight-closed fists you wrench away what you can only with great difficulty. Am I inventing this? Suppose I am giving a false account — indeed I wish I were! I seem to see so many influences being brought to bear upon the bishop that he will try in vain to pay attention to a suppliant. Besides, since you are tied down by a second marriage, he is not able to put you in possession of a benefice,[15] a favor which now he has the ability to give and would not refuse, I believe.

For these reasons I recommend that the undertaking of this embassy be cancelled, lest I return to your doorstep ridiculed and worn out for nothing! Then you will be more upset, for you will learn that the little hope which still remains in you had been disappointed and destroyed.

JOHANNES: Avari est et peticii hominis meditatio ista, et magis rem ipsam quam diligentis amicum. An nisi accipiendi gratia non visendi sunt amici? Ac semper ut aliquid demas accedis, et non potius ut ipsius fruaris° presentia, colloquio, contemplatione, quibus quidem rebus vita dulcius nil habet? Deliras nimium siquidem excidit quam longi et toti sepe dies confabulantibus amicis non transierint modo sed fugerint. Minimene sapis id michi contigisse non semel? Profecto nulla mortalibus cura magis subducit tempus quam amatorum collocutio blanda conversatioque.

Legimus beatum Antonium ac primum heremitam Paulum, cum sese primo visere, dulces inter amplexus et sancta, seria, sobriosque narratus, noctem et diei plurimam partem non sensisse. Illustrissimam virginem Scolasticam, quo diutius sancti fratris presentia frueretur, idem ipse amor grandinem nymbosque, quibus remoraretur Benedictus, impetrare coegit. Taceo sanctos viros, divinis cum tedium in rebus nefas sit obicere. Non totam Phenissa noctem, si fabulis creditur, Enee narrantis ab ore pependit? Quidni avide amantes si sese revisunt, quibus presentia ipsa et commemorationis actorum dictorumque vicissitudo celestem quandam voluptatem parit.

Quandoquidem miro quodam igne fervoris absentium ac defunctorum quoque renarratio audientis mentem titillet. Scipionem Lelius dulci apud Ciceronem memoria commeminit, quantam familiaritas vera vel requirat vel debeat habere. "Sic," inquit, "recordatione nostre amicitie fruor ut beate vixisse videar, quia cum Scipione vixerim." Quem non accendat Ieronimus, Paulam clarissimam atque sanctissimam feminam scribens, ubi quicquid exprimit sanctam redolet caritatem? Oblitane es qua mentis abundantia, quam ignito sermone depingere nitatur Martinum Severus?

> Tecum etenim longos memini consumere soles
> et tecum primas epulis decerpere noctes.
> Unum opus et requiem pariter disponimus ambo
> atque verecunda lassamus seria mensa.

GIOVANNI: That sort of thinking is typical of a greedy and self-seeking man who cherishes possessions more than a friend. Are friends to be visited only for the sake of gain? Do you always seek out a person in order to come away with something, and not rather to enjoy his company, conversation, and attention? Life holds nothing sweeter than these things. You are very foolish if you forget how a large part, or even the whole, of a day can not only pass by but flee when friends are chatting with each other. Are you not aware that this has happened to me more than once? Certainly no preoccupation is a greater thief of time from mortals than pleasant discourse and association with loved ones.

We read that the blessed Anthony and the first hermit, Paul, at their first visit, passed a night and the greatest part of a day in loving embraces, talking of chaste, serious, and sober matters, without noticing the passage of time. The illustrious virgin, Scholastica, in order to enjoy longer the company of the holy friar Benedict, was compelled by a similar love to call down hail and cloudbursts by which he might be delayed.[16] I shall speak no more about holy men, since it is wrong to be tedious about divine matters. Did not Dido, if one believes the stories, hang on Aeneas' lips the entire night as he was relating his adventures?[17] And this was natural, for when ardent lovers meet they experience an almost heavenly pleasure from each other's very presence and from telling each other what they have said and done.

Indeed conversation about those who are absent or dead also stimulates the hearer's mind with a marvelously warm enthusiasm. Laelius, as reported by Cicero, thinks back upon Scipio with the sweet memory which true friendship requires or ought to possess: "Such is my enjoyment in the recollection of our friendship," he says, "that I feel as if my life has been happy because it was spent with Scipio." Whom would Jerome not inspire when, in writing of the very famous and holy Paula, everything he expresses is redolent of pure affection? Have you forgotten the exuberance of mind and the glowing words with which Severus strives to depict Martin?[18]

With you, I remember, did I pass long days, with you pluck
for feasting the early hours of night. We two were one in our
works, we were one in our hours of rest, and unbent together
over the modest board.[19]

Abunde hoc aperuit poeta carmine Cornuto suo, amorem sincerum non egere forinsecus vinculo, contentum se dumtaxat peti, se amari, se coli.

Omnino autem hesitationis plenas voces continuisses, beneficia si huius erga me pontificis, si favorem, si demum agnovisses quo quicquid sum inde est. Nam genitor meus ab Hunnorum finibus ubi regio ministerio salutis artifex maximus diu vacavit, tandem obiit, huius me vivens gremio mandat, moriens linquit. Suscipit unicum pater ille et infantulum clementissimo sinu indulgentia tanta, studio tanto, humanitate denique tanta quantam vix a parente sensissem, tum alendo, castigando, fovendo, honestissimis quoque artibus instruendo ad hanc usque provexit etatem. Sensi numquam defuisse michi parentem.

O me felicem, sua numquam° si decreta non obaudissem, unde libet sepius cum propheta clamare: "Exitus aquarum deduxerunt oculi mei, quia non custodierunt legem tuam." Sed res vana iuventus, ut sensus credula, sanis ita monitibus pervicax, queve non prius interdum resipiscit quam penitentia° frustra° sit. Non me piget illorum ascribi sententie qui huiusmodi etatem improbant cultis veluti sanctisque moribus repugnacem. Nec eam qui tantopere laudant, extollunt, optant quanti stat iactura temporis et quam periculosa erumnosave sit huius exilii nostri diuturnitas plane intelligunt. Quam nimirum moderari compositam sobriamque ducere, non id humane sed divine opis est. Ideo indulgendum innata quadam inscitia et nature infirmitate deliranti. Atque id propheta clamavit, equidem precatus omnipotentem pro adolescentie delictis continuo subintulit: "Et ignorantias meas ne memineris."

Assentior rursum minus apertas clericorum manus, forte quoniam intelligunt pauperum necessitatibus deberi vel ecclesie usibus fore dicatum omne quicquid stipem quotidiane vite superat. Quid respondebis si non tam eos abundare tenacia quam te fortassis aviditate recipiendi doceberis?° Ac plerique non habendi libidine cogunt, magis autem

In this poem to his friend Cornutus Persius has made it abundantly clear that sincere love does not need an external bond, being content only to be sought, loved, and cherished.

Moreover, you would have completely held back your doubting words if you had acknowledged the kindnesses of this bishop toward me, his favors, and, in short, the fact that whatever I am is due to him. For indeed my own father, from the land of the Huns, where for a long time before his death he devoted himself to the royal service as chief doctor, sent me, while he was still living, into Tommaso's care and, when he died, left me to him.[20] Like a father he took me to his kindly heart, an only child, an infant, with as much indulgence, devotion, and human feeling as I should hardly have experienced from my own parent. Then, nurturing, chastising, cherishing, and instructing me in honorable studies, he brought me up to my present age. I never felt I was lacking a parent.

Oh how happy I would be if I had never disobeyed his orders! It is well to exclaim often with the prophet: "My eyes have sent forth springs of water; because they have not kept thy law."[21] But youth is a vain thing, as confident in the emotions as it is resistant to sound advice, and sometimes does not come to its senses before repentance is too late. I fully agree with the opinion of those who criticize this period of life on the grounds that it is opposed to refined and virtuous habits. And persons who greatly praise, extol, and desire youth do not understand clearly how costly is the wastage of time and how full of danger and trouble is the duration of this exile of ours. Of course, to subdue, control, and soberly guide one's immaturity is not within human, but divine power; and therefore leniency should be shown to one who is deranged because of his innate ignorance and unstable nature. This the prophet proclaimed when he prayed to the Almighty on behalf of the sins of his youth and immediately added: "My ignorances, do not remember."[22]

I agree too that the hands of clerics are not open, perhaps because they realize that everything which exceeds their everyday expense is owed to the needs of the poor or has been dedicated to the uses of the Church. What will be your response if you are told that these men are not so much tight-fisted as you are perhaps greedy to receive? As a rule they amass wealth not from a desire to keep it, but rather

quatenus liberalitate donandi multorumque invisceratione plurimum
favoris ac nominis emant, et benefici liberalesque habiti dum efferun-
tur plausibus sublimentur. Quasi ecclesiasticus gradus magnificentia
et rerum profluxarum celebritate seu clientelarum favore et non potius
paupertate spiritus et rerum moderatione, nec non affluentia virtutum ac sanctitatis cuivis offerendus existat. Quo fit ut, dum acervant
ut ascendant, ruant plerumque dum ascendunt; ut nimirum illud
propheticum impleatur: "Deiecisti eos dum allevarentur."

Verumtamen presulem nostrum ubi omnem eius per etatem cu-
curreris, si clericorum ut ais parcitas est, haudquaquam de cleri sorte
comperies. Recense dum Bononie provincia eius ministerio fovebatur:
quis locus, que pars eius virtute non floret? Ubi non clarent amplis-
sime largitatis vestigia? Nemo fratrum privato illius ope fuit immunis;
munificentiam claustrum omne testatur. Ravenne monasterium cir-
cumspecta; quod auctum postquam decoratumque videris, pari existima-
tione singulos conventus agnoscito.

Sed his ne dicatur oratio deviasse supersidendum. Mannos ei preterea
frequenter a meo genitore donatos, non quemadmodum ceteri qui
vel domesticos servassent in usus vel eorum precia captassent, verum
elargiebatur Latii principibus, quibus ne quidem alter venerabilior pri-
orque fuit. Ast ubi totius Francisci gregis effectus est pastor, quanta
amplitudine gregem beatum rexerit, quid attinet referre? Quicquid
offerebatur, multis enim donabatur et multifariis quotidie opibus, vix
apud illum dies integra sentiebat. Adeo peculiare illi opus largitas erat
ut elargiendo iocundior quam suscipiendo ceteri° videretur. Age,
quam magnificus quamque munificus archipater Venetiis fuit! Erat eius
aula benignitatis officina quedam, occlusa nulli, cuntis pervia, etiam
e longinquo peregrinantibus. Sane altero anno tabe celi Bononia
laborante, plenam convalentibus eiusdem urbis civibus qui letificum
aerem° fugerant, plenam quoque languidis vidimus, necnon Grayos
homines hospitaliter ibi collectos diu. Quid multa? Hospitalis ita cun-

that, by giving generously and showing kindness to many, they may buy as much favor and reputation as possible. Then, being considered kind and generous, they will be exalted with praises. They act as if ecclesiastical rank should be offered to a man because of the magnificence and renown of his lavish possessions or the favors shown to his clients, rather than because of his humble spirit and modest way of life, his abundance of virtue and goodliness. This is the reason that, when they amass riches in order to ascend, they usually fall while ascending. Thus the prophecy is fulfilled: "When they were lifted up thou hast cast them down."[23]

However, if, as you say, clerics are parsimonious, in perusing the entire life of our bishop you will not find him among that breed of clergy. Think of the time when the province of Bologna was being cared for under his administration.[24] What place there, what area does not flourish thanks to him? Where are the traces of his ample generosity not famous? There was not one of the friars who did not share in his wealth in private; every cloister bears witness to his bounty. Look at the monastery at Ravenna: after you have seen its enrichment and ornamentation, compare it with other convents one by one.

But enough of these matters, lest my discussion be said to have gone astray! To continue: regarding the coach horses frequently presented to him by my own father, unlike other men who would have either kept them for use at home or tried to sell them for a profit, he donated these to the princes of Italy, who were more worthy of respect and more important than anyone else. And when he was made pastor of the entire Franciscan flock,[25] need I describe the great liberality with which he ruled that fortunate flock? Whatever offering was made (for he was presented daily with many donations from many places) stayed in his possession barely a whole day. Generosity was a trait so characteristic of him that he seemed happier in giving than others in receiving. See how generous, how beneficent he was as chief priest at Venice![26] His court was like a production-line of bounties, closed to no one, open to all, even to travelers from afar. In fact, in the second year of Bologna's suffering from the plague of the sky, he saw his court filled with healthy citizens of that city who had fled its deadly air, filled also with the sick. Even Greeks were hospitably gathered there for a long time. Why say more? He was so hospitable

tis propiciusque vixit, iuris ut publici eam domum censuisses. Penu
iusserat plurifario vino confertum esse, uti foret laborantibus sanisve
quid pro voluptate quisque inde reportaret. Pene magis ceterorum quam
usibus propriis promptuaria patebant. Quin usque Ferariam Bononiam-
que ac in Euganeos quoque fines atque piniferum litus, largitatis eius
veluti fecundissimi rivi e celesti quodam fonte munificentie defluxere.

Memini altero quidem anno, cum se videre Venetias perexissem
allataque illi Damascena poma forent, preciosum quidem condimenti
et electum genus, mox pronunciasse beatissimum presulem atque lar-
gissimum digna esse qui mitti Ferariam debeant militi strenuo domino Rizardo de Cancelleriis, veluti rem accommodissimam atque
utilissimam senibus; cum interim pater is grandevus adprime foret.
Cui tum ex apparitoribus unus "Cunta," inquit, "emittis, pater, nil usui
reservas." Tunc surridens ipse et modesta urbanitate famulantis vel in-
honestam spem vel assertionem insipidam arguens, "Malo," inquit, "fons
esse quam situla." O largitatis vocem et tenaciam nescientis, o vocem
sancto viro dignam, o non intellectam neque servatam a plerisque!

Ad hec, quod inter mortales nuspiam invenisti, domesticos numquam dispensatores accersivit ad computum,° nullam umquam cal-
culavit accessionem, expensas ignoravit, redditus proventusque nescivit.
Quos suppeditare tantis valuisse quotidianisque sumptibus qui ad-
mirarentur fuere, ampla adeo completa ac singulis hospitaliter edes
aperta erat, unde quisquam indonatus vix umquam abscessit. Laudavit
Romanum populum Silla apud regem Numidarum Bocum. "Romanus," inquit, "populus beneficiis vinci non potest." Quid idem asseve-
rare non liceat michi? Dominus Thomas largitate vinci non potest.
Nullatenus igitur propter parcitatem quam obiectasti clericis huius
presentia fugienda. Quin nescio quomodo non appetenda nunc magis, quoniam quam velut innatum decus habuit minori fortuna ser-
vabit amplitudinem in summa dignitate locatus, quemadmodum amnis

and gracious to all that you would have thought it a house belonging to the public. He had ordered the storehouse to be filled with all kinds of wines, so that both the sick and the well might find something there according to their taste. The storerooms were available almost more for the use of others than for his own. In fact, all the way to Ferrara and Bologna, to the Paduan lands and the pine-clad coast of Ravenna, the riches of his bounteousness flowed like copious streams from a celestial spring.

I remember, in another year when I had gone to Venice to see him, some Damson plums had been brought to him, a costly and choice type of delicacy. That most blessed and generous bishop announced that the plums were worthy to be sent to Ferrara for the vigorous soldier, Lord Ricciardo Cancellieri, being a very suitable and useful gift for old men; and yet the father himself was very old.[27] One of his attendants then said to him, "Father, you send everything away and keep nothing for your own enjoyment!" Smiling, and with modest amiability chiding the servitor for either an unbecoming expectation or a foolish statement, the father said, "I would rather be the well than the bucket." What an expression of generosity from one innocent of greed, a saying befitting a saintly man, though neither appreciated nor observed by most people!

In addition (and this is something which you have nowhere found among mortals!) never did he call for an accounting from his household stewards, nor did he reckon up his revenues; he ignored the monies paid out and knew nothing of income and profits. There were persons who marveled that the revenues were sufficient to cover such great daily expenditures, so spacious and well-equipped was his house, and hospitably open to one and all. Almost never did anyone leave there without gifts. Sulla praised the Roman people to Bocchus, king of Numidia, saying: "The Roman people have never been outdone in kindness."[28] Why can I not make the same claim: Lord Tommaso cannot be outdone in liberality. By no means, therefore, should you avoid his presence, fearing the stinginess of which you have accused the clergy. On the contrary, he ought all the more to be approached now; since after reaching his eminent position he will retain the greatness which he possessed as a natural distinction when his fortune was less. He is like a river which during the dry summer glides

qui arenti estu undifluus elabitur, cum circumvago defluorum cursu
torrentium auctus est, et pluvia celesti aquis fecundior exit.

Porro dignitates ipse honoresque—nam, quod perrarum est, func-
tus est omnium—virtuti sue non votis, imo nescienti peneque renitenti,
oblate sunt. Minime autem, ut plerisque mos est, pro comparandis
thesaurizavit, ut sane non iniuria de Catone Salustianum illud audire
possit. Quanto magis gloriam Thomas fugiebat ea tanto ipsum magis
sequebatur. Quidni, cum ipsa sit "umbra virtutis," ut ait Seneca?

Sed non est propositi, Litera, patris tanti virtutes vel beatitudinem
exarare, foret enim materia voluminis et otii non angusti. Potius quod
reliquum est persolvamus, ne te dictando ab itinere iam pene incepto
remorer.

LITERA: Paulisper obsecro hunc ut orsus es michi depinge, ut vel mecum quod avide facis de ipso loquaris, vel tante virtutis exemplar lec-
titandum posteris videndumque linquas. Possidius° cognoscendum
futuris prebuit Augustinum, Paulinus Ambrosium, Benedictum
Gregorius, ipsum Gregorium Paulus Historicus. Taceo poetas quorum lucubrationes tam vane fuerunt quam vani ipsi quos inani quadam assentatione fingebant. Tu igitur ne refuge mores imitandos
Thome, vitam sanctam, graves actus exprimere. Levigabis et itineris
michi laborem siquidem concedis agnovisse quem peto.

JOHANNES: Id quidem libens efficiam. Verebar neu me exorbitasse
criminareris. Ast ubi sedet animo ipsum hominem tendam exponere,
tametsi primum illud testandum est multa omissurum me esse, tum
magnitudine rerum, tum quia non penitus affuimus. Nichilominus one-
rata gradieris prolixiore sermone, quoniam, ut Livius ait, de re magna
aut nil dici debet aut parum dici non potest. Sed que maior uberiorve
materia quam exarare virtutes Thome? Preterea non ego Paulus aut

along in gentle ripples, becomes swollen from streams of inpouring torrents, and then with the rain from Heaven bursts forth teeming with water.

Furthermore, those high offices and honors—for, what is very rare, he held them all—were conferred for his excellence, not at his request; indeed, he was uncertain and almost reluctant. Also he did not, as is customary for most, build up a treasury for the purpose of acquiring possessions. Hence Sallust's words about Cato could rightly be applied to him: the more Tommaso avoided glory, the more it pursued him. And why not, since, as Seneca says, glory is itself "the shadow of virtue."[29]

But it is not my intent, Letter, to give an exhaustive narration of the great father's virtues and blessedness, as that would be material for a volume and for unlimited time. Instead, as to the rest, let us make an end so that I will not by my talking delay your journey, which you are now almost ready to start.

LETTER: Please, for just a little longer describe him to me, as you have begun, either merely to converse with me about him (which you are eagerly doing), or to leave a model of great virtue for posterity to read about and contemplate. Possidius made Augustine known to future readers, as Paulinus did Ambrose; Benedict was depicted by Gregory, and Gregory himself by the historian Paul.[30] (I omit the poets, whose labors were as insubstantial as those imaginary persons whom they created in foolish flattery!) Therefore, do not refuse to portray Tommaso's character, so worthy of emulation, his virtuous life, his important deeds. You will lighten the labor of my journey if you permit me to learn about the man I am to visit.

GIOVANNI: Certainly I'll be happy to do this. I was afraid you would charge me with getting off the track! So, as you have decided, I shall strive to sum up the man himself. However, first I must point out that I shall omit many things, not only because of the quantity of the material, but because I was not always there in person. Even so, you will go off laden with a rather copious discourse, since, as Livy says, concerning an important matter either nothing ought to be said or too little cannot be said.[31] But what is a greater or more comprehensive subject than the description of Tommaso's virtues? Besides,

Paulinus non ceteri abs te presignati, neque ea michi scribendi vena seu promptitas nec liberum ita otium, que duo prima sunt eloquentie fundamina. Tamen utcumque morem tibi geram, splendida licet non omnino absolutaque dictione, fideli tamen et amoris plena, queve tuo dumtaxat iudicio contenta sit, et ab ipsis quidem radicibus sumente inicium. Quia sicut de Antonio fertur, perfecta est ad virtutem via, scire Thomam quis fuerit. Qui si qua in his morbidis rebus fluentibusque beatitas inest, divinis ut ita dicam flatibus totam percensuit. Cui e beatis fortuna favoribus nichil invidit, sed omnes per felicitatis numeros circumduxit.

Est locus interiore ac medio pene Latii sinu inter Etruscos ac Ligurum Emiliosque fines, qua ad Appennini levam, e nubiferis Alpium iugis, torrenti Scultenna impetu petit Eridanum. Fregnanum incole vocant, viribus patientiaque rerum clara gens. Non luxus ibi seu delicie, non opes, fortasse minima etiam avaricia. Siquidem ut Justinus ait: "Ubi divitiarum usus est plurima ibi cupido." Non item illic cetera irritamenta luxurie animos gentis effetant nec cultus nitor operosus armos emollit. Sed ut in alimentum non in voluptatem esca sumitur, in hibernos ita rigores minime vero ad ornatum iactantiamve amictus est genti. Inde robusti animis, feri corporibus, laborum patientes in ferrum mortemque bellaces ruunt, quoniam° minus quidem formidat interitum qui vitam in deliciis non habuit.

Ex honesto hinc Thomas lare amplaque familia literarum primis imbuendus elementis Bononiam agitur, ubi puer senilem animum gestans, maturus, solitarius, tum preceptoribus obtemperans tum paribus obsequiosus vixit, nullis iuvente ludicris sed intento literis animo toto, cuius iam precox virtus germen indolis alte spondebat. Quippe vix fieri potest quatenus ab ipso quoque initio virtus innata sui omnino tacita servet indicia. Quin tenuibus veluti quibusdam surculis se infantilibus quoque explicat elementis, ut in Spartaco, Astiagis nepote,

I am not Paul nor Paulinus nor the others you previously mentioned, and I do not have their natural talent and ability in writing or have leisure time, the two basic elements of eloquence. Nevertheless I shall somehow comply with your request, though certainly not in a splendid, accomplished recitation. Still, it will be accurate and filled with love, and content with your judgment only. It will take its beginning from his very roots, because, as is said about Anthony,[32] the perfect way to virtue is to know who Tommaso was. If there is any blessedness in this sick and unstable world, he has experienced it all by, so to speak, divine good fortune. Fate has begrudged him nothing of her blessed favors; she has surrounded him with every sort of felicity.

There is a place in an inner recess of Italy, almost in the middle, between the Etruscan and the Ligurian and Emilian lands, where on the left side of the Apennines, from the cloud-covered ranges of the Alps, the Panaro River rushes into the Po in torrents. The area is called Frignano by the inhabitants, a race of people famous for their strength and capacity to bear hardship.[33] There is no luxury there, nor comforts, nor wealth, nor — perhaps least of all — covetousness. For as Justinus says: "Where there is need of riches, there greed is great."[34] Also, in that place there are no other incentives to extravagant living to weaken the minds of the people, nor does the studied elegance of culture soften their muscles. As they take food for nourishment and not for pleasure, so do they dress against the rigors of winter rather than for adornment or display. Thus vigorous in mind, tough in body, resolute under difficulties, they rush aggressively to meet the sword and death; since a man who has not passed his life amid comforts does not fear losing it.

From this place, from a respectable household and eminent family, Tommaso was taken to Bologna to be steeped in the first elements of letters. There, as a boy with the mind of a grown man, mature, retiring in nature, he lived obedient to his teachers and compliant to his peers, wholly devoted not to young people's amusements but to the study of literature. His precocious virtue was even then giving promise of the flowering of a lofty genius. Seldom even at its very beginning does innate excellence keep evidence of itself entirely hidden; but on the contrary, as if putting forth delicate shoots, it unfolds itself even in early childhood. Such was the case of Spartacus and of

aliis omissis; ut in Catone, quorum hic fastus regii tenellus in pueris, in Popedio Latino, virilis alter constantie spem puer dedit. Quis putasset tale pueri specimen ab indomitis crudisque sedibus emanaturum? Sed clarum natura testem protulit illius soli populis fortunam non virtutis ingenium defore.

Porro, velut ab eodem ipso in fluentis mee ac fervide iuventutis rudimentum audire crebro solebam, cum festis ceteri consodales diebus evagarentur, ab ineunte iam tum etate iacturam nullam esse maiorem quam temporis advertens seorsum sese recipiebat in cameram, et que vel didicerat ipse ruminabat vel discutiebat edocenda. Numquam a scola procul nisi adurgente necessitate divini seu causa audiendi verbi vadebat. Dein mox grammaticis institutis excultior redditus, minorum habitum induit. Idque primus ei nimirum prosperitatis limes extitit.

Quippe, quoniam ab initio mundum agnovit et fugit, et ipsum virginitatis florem perpetuamque latriam Christo dicans, non ornatum non voluptatem seu cultus iactantiam, non delicias non plausum seculi, non liberorum et coniugis blandum malum respexit. Quamquam non desint coniugatis admiratores sui, quos quidem miseratione dignos putet, quisquis aloes plenum, ut Socrates ait, plenum curis coniugium, inquietudinis plenum didicerit. Lites nempe, fastidia, turba mentis et animi supercilium grave, denique servitus pronube dotis sunt. Unde Satirus bene:

> Semper habet lites alternaque iurgia lectus
> in quo nupta iacet. Minimum dormitur in illo.

Volve Theofrastum, Jovinianum volve, Ieronymi quam° geniali thoro celebs vita prestet edisces, hancque sobriam, tacitam, sui compotem, illum anxium, solicitum, quodque deterius est, contemptissime fragilissimeque rei, femine, scilicet mancipium. Unde nec honestis serviri artibus potest vel cum immodica certe difficultate potest. Quo fit crebro virtutis ut intermissio fiat. Cicero id fortassis advertens cum rogaretur ab Hir-

Cyrus, the grandson of Astyages, omitting others; or of Cato, who as a very young boy showed his regal pride, or of Poppaedius Latinus, who in boyhood gave promise of manly steadfastness.[35] Who could have thought that such a fine specimen of youth would be produced from a violent and rough homeland? But his nature offered clear proof that what was lacking in the people of that area was prosperity, not native virtues.

Furthermore (as I was accustomed to hear frequently from him by way of a first lesson for my restless and impetuous youth!), when the rest of his companions used to ramble around on holidays, he felt even then at a very early age that there was no greater loss than that of time; and he would withdraw to his room and there ruminate over what he had learned or examine what was to be taught. Never would he go far from school unless under pressure of necessity or to hear the divine word. Later, after he had received further education from the grammarians, he put on the habit of the Franciscans.[36] This was for him the initial step on the road to success.

Indeed, since from the first he knew and fled the world, vowing to Christ both the flower of his virginity and perpetual service, he cared for neither adornment nor pleasure, nor the display of luxury, nor the charm and approval of the secular world, nor the attractive evil of wife and children. Although he does not lack admirers among married people, he would certainly think worthy of pity the man who, as Socrates says, has experienced a marriage full of bitterness, worries, and turmoil.[37] Quarrels, slights, mental distress, oppressive haughtiness of spirit, and finally, subservience follow in the train of a bridal dowry. Hence the Satirist says:

> The bed that holds a wife is never free from wrangling and mutual bickering. No sleep is to be got there.

Consider Theophrastus and Jovinianus: you will learn how superior Jerome's celibate life is to the marriage bed.[38] Such a life is sober, quiet, master of itself; but the married state is anxious, care-ridden, and, worse yet, under the control of a most contemptible, frail thing—a woman. In this situation a man cannot serve honorable arts, or at least only with extreme difficulty. Therefore frequently virtue comes to an end. Perhaps realizing this, Cicero, upon being asked by Hir-

tio° sororem eius in coniugium duceret, negavit omnino uxori affir-
mans et philosophie pariter operam dare non posse.

Hoc ipsum presul iste cum puer esset, iam tum Deo plenus, sensisse videtur Christo non posse et mundo pariter operam dare. Proinde
noxias mundi illecebras et Syrenarum pestiferos cantus adolescentu-
lus declinavit. A malorum procul strepitu quibus terra redundat pacis
habitum locumque legit, superbiam fugit humilis adeo ut non preciperet
prepositus fratribus, sed monstraret humilitatem — veluti de fratrum
capuciis memini puer. Namque prefecto eo provincie Bononie fratres
erant cucullarum capucia deorsum a tergo corda tenus, qua cingi regula iubet, vel ultra dependentia, gestantes, pompam fluxumve animi
in re tantula contra normam quidem ordinis professi. Enimvero sua
quoque iactancia claustrales habet, veluti sunt laxi prolixique° habitus quos quia nequeunt variare coloribus preciosiori vellere struunt,
idque cum cenobite huiusmodi secte institutoris iniuria. Qui ut venerabilem militiam suam, omnis eliminande causa superbie, minorem
appellari sanxit, cuntum ita successoribus iactantie cultum interdixit,
humilitatis et deiectionis preposuit et iussit; ut qui sciret tantum abiu-
rari a divinitatis consortio mentem quantum nos corporei solicitudo
honoris propensius vendicat. Contra eo fieri propiorem Deo quo lon-
gius cura nostra fugit a sensibus, quoniam difficillimum est humilitatem sine qua nequit ad superos tendi sub amictorio pompe tegi.

At vero presentes non modo lana quidem mollior effert sed defluentia
quoque capucia, candide operosisque distincte nodis ac tenuibus in-
texte filis cingibiles cordule. Item albicante vel luteo facte corio solee
et artificis ingenio cohercite, cura preterea ut albidi pedes eminent
mundioribus et tornatis ut ita dixerim unguibus, manus quoque poli-
to ac exquisito ungue et affabre circumciso laute. Taceo vestes precio-
so interdum varioque infectas odore. Quibus ut leves quidam intenti

tius to marry his sister, emphatically refused, claiming it was not possible to give attention simultaneously to a wife and to philosophy.[39]

This fact the bishop seems to have perceived in boyhood, being already filled with God, namely, that he could not give attention to God and to the world at the same time. Later, when a young man, he shunned harmful worldly enticements and the deadly songs of the sirens. Far from the turmoil of the evils with which the earth abounds, he chose a habit and place of peace, humbly avoiding a prideful demeanor so that he did not give commands to the monks in the manner of a prior, but displayed humbleness. I remember an instance of this from my childhood, concerning the monks' hoods. When he was provincial general of Bologna, there were monks who wore the hoods of their cowls down their backs as far as the cord with which the rule compelled them to be girdled, or even hanging below it, thus displaying ostentatiousness and a frivolous attitude in this small matter, which was nevertheless contrary to the rule of their order.[40] For cloistered monks too have their affectations, as for instance wearing their garments loose and full; and, because they cannot vary the color of these, they have them made of very costly wool. In this they do outrage to the monk who was the founder of this sect, for in order to eliminate all ostentation he decreed that his venerable order be called "minor," i.e., "lesser." Thus he forbade to his successors all practice of display, preferring and demanding humility and abasement; because he knew that the mind is alienated from fellowship with the divine in proportion as desire for material distinctions lays eager claim upon us. On the other hand, he knew that the farther our concern flees from the senses, the nearer the mind is to God; as it is very difficult to conceal under a cloak of ostentation the humbleness without which one cannot reach God.

But in fact the monks of today are adorned not only with soft woolens but with long, flowing hoods and encircling white cords which are distinguished by elaborate knots and woven from fine threads. They also wear sandals made of white or yellow leather, fashioned by skilled craftsmen, and see to it that their pale feet show clean, well-rounded toe-nails. Their hands too have elegant nails that are polished, exquisite, and finely trimmed. I need not mention that their clothes are often imbued with various costly perfumes. Since like frivolous men

sunt curis, ita ab his refelluntur ultro qui cum Apostolo dicunt: "Si hominibus placerem, servus Christi non essem."

Sed tum quid venerabilis° Thomas? Nempe sibi primum ipsi sic extremum seu° capucii conum amputari fecit, ut quaternis eminus digitis distaret a sede cinguli. Tum ita mutilato capucio vadere ac per fratrum ora sese talem obiectare studuit. Mox edixit quatenus parili omnes cultu et vellent et uti cogerentur. Quo factum est ut qui vanitate prius diffluebant, superioris humilitate monstrante, irreligionis puderet, nec iustis obiectare quicquam mandatis, imo nec rectis contraire exemplis auderent. Namque sicut mores prelatorum contorti subditis dilirandi propinant favorem, sic integritas vite pastoris maiestate virtutis audaciam reprimit diffluendi suppositis. Hinc esse reor illud Gregorii: "Scire," inquit, "debent prelati quod siquando adversa perpetrant tot mortibus digni sunt quot ad subditos perdicionis exempla transmittunt."

Taceo viri castitatem, quam emulorum quos ei multos virtutis invidia comes peperit nullus umquam vel tenui suspiciuncula labefactare valuit, illum ita sexum vitantis ut vix adigi posset pudicissimis ut matronis aurem confessoris accommodaret. Quid multa? Nulla carni parte consensit, sed paruit animo imperanti, denique liquit mundum, nactus est celum.

Posthac vero ubi literis curam applicuit nemo plenius ebibit, nemo facilius apprendit, nemo luculentius expressit, ita demum ut ipso divinitatis fonte scientiam hausisse videretur. Quasi nominationis vocabulum presagio sortitus, Thomas "abissus" vel "divisus" interpretatur utrumque illi facit. Si profunditatem scientie, si abissum sapientie metiris, Thomas est. Inde si ut° coherescens Deo a mundo seiungitur, utique Thomas est. Rursum de eius eloquentia quid disseram, qua omnium ferme convivorum ingenia preit? Ita nimirum quisquis illa ut

they are intent upon such matters as these, they are repudiated by those who say with the Apostle: "If I pleased man, I would not be the servant of Christ."[41]

So then what did the venerable Tommaso do? Why, first he had the point or cone of his own hood cut off so that it was four fingers' width away from the position of the belt. Then with his hood thus shortened he took care to walk about and show himself this way before the eyes of the monks. Next he declared that they all ought to desire and be compelled to wear similar clothing. As a result, those who previously were abandoned to vanity became ashamed of their irreligious acts as exposed by the humbleness of their superior; and they dared neither to make any objection to his just commands nor indeed to go contrary to his upright example. For as prelates of perverted habits give their inferiors the privilege of transgressing, so a pastor of uncorrupted life, by the majesty of his virtue, restrains in his subordinates their reckless tendencies to dissipation. This is the reason, I think, for that saying of Gregory: "Prelates ought to know that whenever they commit wrongs, they deserve as many deaths as there are examples of wickedness transmitted to their subjects."[42]

I pass over in silence the chastity of the man, which none of his rivals has ever been able to disparage by even the slightest suspicion, the many rivals who were created for him by envy, the companion of virtue. He so avoided the other sex that he could scarcely be prevailed upon to furnish a confessor's ear to the most chaste matrons. In brief, he yielded to the flesh in no way but obeyed the commands of his soul, finally withdrew from the world, and attained Heaven.

Afterwards, when he directed his attention to literature, no one drank more deeply, no one learned more readily, no one expressed ideas more clearly, so that, in short, he seemed to have drawn knowledge from the very font of divinity. As if he had acquired his own name by presentiment, "Tommaso" is interpreted as meaning either "depth" or "division." Both words describe him. If you measure profundity of knowledge or depth of wisdom, that is Tommaso. Then if, clinging to God, he is divided from the world, that surely is Tommaso. Again, what can I say about his eloquence, in which he surpasses the abilities of almost all his peers? In truth, everyone in that religious

in religione vel fandi gravitatem vel oris modestiam vel predicandi suavitatem vel sermonis ordinem velit exprimere, Thomam imitetur.

LITERA: Rara sunt et divina que narras. Quibus sequentia si consonant non habeo cur veluti a celo demissum terris oraculum negem.

JOHANNES: Fatereris hercule si doceri posses dictorum factorumve hominis singula. Sed accipis parva de maximis, pauca de multis. Non° enim usque interfuimus et maligna est semper invidia. Denigrat enim virtutis fulgorem et obtractando comminuit semper, vel quod saltem potest, tacet et occulit. Verumtamen velut ignis cum tegitur splendore vel fumo emittit indicia sui, sic mera virtus non ita circumscribitur ut non aliquid semper elucescat.

Atqui pervagatis et ut ita dixerim gignasiorum literis undique exhaustis, Theologie diademate Veneticorum in urbe nobilissima preditus, provincie Bononie preficitur. Quam miro ordine instruxit, moribus ornavit, sanctitate auxit et fratribus, ut totius orbis florentissima atque instructissima bonorum omnium provincia ferretur. Mox inde summum ad apicem nec absque miraculo trahitur. Nam pene moribundo tanti ordinis traditur summa regenda. Quem toto laborans corpore, spirituali dumtaxat vigore disponebat, consulebat, decernebat quid agendum sequendumve tanto gregi foret. Pastor vigil pro salute cuntorum intentus, cimbam ipsam tante religionis affectuum fluctibus variorum illisam moderans servansque clavo constantie. Cui tum fortune temeritas bellum indixit suasque vires pretentavit in illum.

LITERA: Quonam pacto? Quibus tandem iaculis usa? Aiunt fortunam semper imbellem esse contra virtutem. Falsone id? Expecto edisseras quale duellum. Eminueritne an ut solet terga dederit fugax illa?

•rder who wishes to display dignified speech, restraint in delivery, harm in preaching, or a well-organized discourse, should imitate Tommaso.

ᴇᴛᴛᴇʀ: Rare and god-like are the traits you describe! If what comes ᴀext is similar, I won't be able to deny that he is like a manifestation ᴏf divinity come down from Heaven to earth!

ɢɪᴏᴠᴀɴɴɪ: You would admit it, by Hercules, if you could learn all he details of the man's words and deeds. But you are hearing little ᴀbout his greatest deeds, and only a few things out of many. For I was not there at all times; and always spiteful envy blackens the bright-ᴀess of virtue and continually diminishes it by criticism or, what in ᴀny event *can* be done, omits any mention of it and thus conceals ᴀt. Nevertheless, like a smothered fire which by brightness or smoke ɡives signs of itself, true virtue is not ever so stifled that it fails to ᴀeveal some light.

Having completed and, one might say, totally exhausted the liter-ᴀry studies of the schools, Tommaso received the crown of Theology n the noble city of the Venetians and was made provincial general ᴏf Bologna.[43] This province he organized under an excellent system, ᴀrovided it with morality, and strengthened it by the holiness of its ᴀonks so that it was called the most flourishing province of the whole world and the best-supplied with all good things. Then from there ᴀe was assigned to the supreme position — and not without a miracle. For when he was almost on his deathbed, he was given the direction ᴏf that whole great religious order, which in spite of the suffering of his entire body, using spiritual strength only, he organized and cared for; and he determined what his great flock should do and strive for. He was a watchful pastor intent upon the salvation of all, using the ᴀudder of his firmness to guide and save that great religious body, a ship battered by the waves of conflicting passions. Then heedless for-tune declared war upon him and threw its forces against him.[44]

ᴌᴇᴛᴛᴇʀ: In what way, and using what weapons? They say that for-tune is always powerless against virtue. Or is this saying false? I am eagerly waiting for you to describe what sort of battle it was. Did fate win or, as usual, did it turn tail and run?

JOHANNES: Minime falso id, quin sole clarius patet virtutis expugnatri-
cem non esse fortunam. Haud usquequaque genus humanum licet multifariam miserum multisve calamitatibus obnoxium, sic natura
perstrinxit iniquior ut unam hanc eius portiunculam, virtutem loquor
inexpugnabilem denegaverit. Audet in illam casus, concutit, instat, laces-
sit; sed non deicit, non subicit, non vincit. Numquam enim trophe-
um retulit de probitate stulticia, quamquam aufert vel auferre putatur
interdum exuvias. Sed que vere virtutis non erant. Propius vero si manus
conserit, succumbit, tela demittit, dat terga, fugit. Sic nunc de Thoma triumphare nequivit, quin illam fede victam expugnatamque non
agnovit modo sed risit mundus.

Et enim, ut agnoscas quia, testante Gregorio, non erit Abel qui non
habuerit Caym, conspiravere in hunc ipsum e fratribus plurimi, Caym
quidem persimiles, quos in certamen impium fortuna multifariam instruxit. Plerosque successuum invidia, conscientia scelerum alios, malignitas quosdam ultronea, illos accendebat diffluendi amputata licentia.
Nonnulli ut fit cum universo raptabantur, non quia odirent verum
ut ceteris consonarent. Mundanus enim favor sic arietat ut plurima
pars mortalium cum fortune flatu decurrat, eo quidem leves quod re
tam levissima quam fortuna est agitari queunt.

Que tum animos usque adeo singulorum obliquavit° seu verius
cecavit, ut° cardinalium pars, ipse quoque Urbanus tunc pontifex
maximus, in participium calumpniantium traherentur. Ita plerumque
superiorum aures alioquin puras inquinat versuta malignitas. Quidni
multitudo tanta valuerit Urbanum cum solus Aman perverterit Assuerum? Referam inauditum priscis duellum: hinc pontifex, cardinales
plerique, illinc° religiosi (sed solo habitu plurimi), seculares inde
caterve. Quid multa? Hinc fortuna tota, mundus totus, illinc vir sapiens,
innocens, sanctus. Ut expediam verbo Annei: "Ecce par Deo dignum,
vir bonus et mala fortuna!"

GIOVANNI: No, the saying is not false. It fact, it is clearer than day that fate is not the vanquisher of virtue. Although the human race is wretched in many ways and subject to many calamities, nature has not limited it so unjustly as to deny it this one small, invincible portion—I mean virtue. Misfortune challenges virtue, shakes, attacks, and wounds it, but does not defeat, subdue, or overcome it. For folly never has taken the palm from righteousness, although it does take away sometimes (or is thought to take away) the spoils. But these were not a part of true virtue. Indeed if folly joins in battle too closely, it falls, loses its weapons, turns and flees. So now it was not able to triumph over Tommaso; in fact the world not only saw it shamefully conquered and beaten but ridiculed it.

And indeed—so that you may acknowledge the truth of Gregory's statement that there is no Abel who does not have a Cain—many of the monks conspired against this man, just like Cain; and fortune prepared them in many ways for the impious contest.[45] Many were incited by envy of his success, others by guilty knowledge of crimes, still others by deliberate malice; and some were angered by his curtailment of their unbridled self-indulgence. Some, as it happens, were borne along with the group, not because they hated him but just to be in agreement with the rest. For the approval of the world so compels men that the majority move with the winds of fortune, being so lightweight that they can be tossed about by something as light as fortune.

Then fate turned awry the minds of individuals or, more accurately, blinded them, so that some of the cardinals and even Urban himself, who was then pope, were drawn into the party of the slanderers.[46] Thus often clever spitefulness pollutes the otherwise pure ears of superiors. Why should so great a multitude not influence Urban, when Haman by himself perverted Assuerus?[47] Let me describe a battle unheard of in former times: here the pope and many cardinals, there the monks (yet most were monks in garb alone), and there the secular throng. In brief, on one side all fortune and all the world, on the other a man of wisdom, innocence, and uprightness. To use the words of Seneca: "Behold, a contest worthy of God, a good man matched against ill fortune!"[48]

LITERA: Impar nimirum certatio. Sed flagro vehementer id ipsum audire, quibus tantam humeris molem pertulit.

JOHANNES: Quibus utique mortalium nemo tulisset. Nec forte hactenus tulit, usus ea quidem moderatione in adversis qua prudens solet in prosperis quisque. Nemo tot illum hostibus impetentibus deiectiorem, nemo querulum, nemo turbidum vidit. Nulla e sacro illo pectore indignationis vox excidit, tristicie nullum in fronte vestigium. Accusatoribus lenis, iudicibus constans, omnia detractorum tela scuto patientie non illisit modo, sed reppulit velut undas certatim pulsantes eternus pelagi scopulus.

Sacerdotem nomine Peregrinum cum Romam ab ora Trevisina profectum ad Thomam causa compulisset, tandem ubi dicenda narravit: "Compatior," inquit, "religiosissime pater, et doleo tam sinistris tamque indignis laboribus tuis. Nichil periculi, pie sacerdos. Tres habebam," retulit,° "patientie sacculos. Sed tertius adhuc superest integer." O miram hominis tolerantiam, o miram virtutem! Circumfluebant fictis criminibus emuli, dolosis artibus, et fabricatis accusationibus e longinquo. Infremebant, imo infrendebant super eum dentibus suis peccatores, insultabant, calumpniabantur, detrahebant, et quod intolerabilius est, illi quidem ipsi quibus favore, honore, beneficiis presens dexterque fuerat. Ipse autem evangelico instituto mansuetissimus agnus iniurias alto corde premebat. Cum malediceretur non remaledixit, cum accusaretur falso non exarsit, cum damnaretur obticuit. Eum optimi omnes miserabantur, ipse vero accusantium inscitiam. Nam Rome cardinalium unus, ibi enim contra tantam virtutem certatum est, cum forte fortuna obviasset homini, inclamavit, rei quidem indignitate commotus: "Deus te," inquit, "liberet de manibus phariseorum." Verum quid arbitrer constantissimum virum quam dominicam illam vocem emisisse: "Ignosce illis, Deus, quia nesciunt quid faciunt." Hactenus obticeant Catonis constantiam quem, cum reiectus esset a foro et oris

LETTER: An unequal contest, to be sure! But I am very eager to hear what strength enabled him to endure so great a burden.

GIOVANNI: Not by mere mortal strength could anyone have borne it. Nor is it by chance that he was able to bear it thus far, but by using that self-control in adversity which a wise man customarily uses in prosperity. No one saw him downcast, in spite of so many attacks by his enemies. No one saw him complaining or put to confusion. Not a word of indignation fell from that virtuous breast, no trace of ill-humor was on his brow. Mild toward his accusers, steadfast before his judges, he not only struck away all the weapons of his detractors with the shield of patience, but he pushed them back just as an ageless sea-cliff repels the waves which vie in beating upon it.

A priest by the name of Pellegrino came from the coast of Trieste to visit Tommaso at Rome because of a legal matter.[49] When he finally had said all he had to say, Tommaso replied, "I sympathize, most reverend father, and am very sorry for your unfortunate and undeserved sufferings. Never fear, pious priest—I had," he continued, "three bags of patience, and the third is still left intact!"

Oh, the wonderful tolerance of the man, his marvelous virtue! Jealous men besieged him from afar with fictitious charges, crafty stratagems, and fabricated accusations. Sinners cried out angrily, gnashed their teeth at him, insulted, maligned, disparaged him; and (what is more intolerable) they were the very men whom he had willingly helped with support, privilege, and benefices. Yet he himself, a most gentle lamb in conformity to the Gospel's teaching, buried his wounds deep in his heart. When he was reviled, he did not revile in turn; when he was falsely accused, he did not flare up; when he was condemned, he remained silent. All good men pitied him, but he pitied the ignorance of his accusers. For at Rome, where there was strong opposition to his great virtue, one of the cardinals protested when by chance he encountered Tommaso; and in distress at the undeserved misfortune he said, "May God free you from the hands of the Pharisees!"[50] And what am I to think that most resolute man uttered except these words of the Lord: "Forgive them, God, for they know not what they do."[51] Hereafter no one need mention the steadfastness of Cato, who is reported to have kept silent when he was thrown

purgamento respersus, tacitum scribunt. Taceant Metelli exilium, taceant Rutilli. Socratem patiar quem nulla ut aiunt felicitas letiorem, nulla turbidiorem vidit adversitas, dum idem liceat de Thoma sentire, cuius nulla umquam vultus mutatio ubi colligi solet quicquid mulcet uritve mentem habitum cordis expressit. Sed velut tetragonus iuxta ethicam scientiam, quoquo fortuna compegisset, erectus integerque perstabat, id illi roboris ex integritate conscientie spes orta conferebat.

Fuisse possem memorare acres contumelias, dira supplicia perpessos, eius vocabuli archiepiscopum, expectata sapientia et sanctitate, expectata item constantia virum. Possem iniurias Ieremie, ignominiam Pauli. Pretereo contumelias Crisostomi, exilium, damnationem, quorum si grande illis patientia temporibus spectaculum dedit, nostro certe seculo clarissimum tolerantie speculum Thomas extitit. Tum vero vel Iudeos Christicole vel gentes infestas habebant. Sed fas fuerit partim legis diversitate, partim disproportione vite cultus, infideles odisse qui Christum colebant. Ast hic Christiani omnes erant qui Christianissimum adorti sunt.

Preter hec ea demum etate fuere quorum exemplis accendi possent. Ista vero ubi directiora omnia sunt incurvata, sopita vel potius extincta virtute et vulgo pubescentibus vitiis, mire quiddam virtutis divine fuit fervide pro iusticia decertasse et tantam inter morum malorum scabiem non traxisse contagium precipue° sediciosorum, et ut ait Apostolus "errantium hominum et in errorem mittentium" officina circumseptum.

LITERA: Vehementer expecto quales causa sortita sit exitus exequaris. Quonam modo a tot illaqueantium nodis pedem explicuit?

JOHANNES: Fiet quidem, ni longioris impatiens narrationis seriem iubes ad alia diverti. Scis me ut ita dixerim huius beati presulis rememoratione pinguescere.

out of the forum bespattered with spittle; let no one mention the exile of Metellus nor that of Rutillius.[52] I may allow Socrates, whom
they say no good fortune made happier and no adversity made more
anxious,[53] provided we are permitted to see the same traits in Tommaso. On his face, usually the reflector of whatever either soothes
or inflames the mind, no change of expression ever betrayed the condition of his heart. Like a square (according to the science of ethics),
however disposed by fate, he remained upright and intact. This strength
was conferred upon him by the hope born from the integrity of his
conscience.

I could mention men who have endured sharp insults, harsh punish-
ments: for instance an archbishop of this description, a man of gratifying
wisdom and sanctity and equally gratifying constancy. I could mention the injustices suffered by Jeremiah, the ignominy of Paul, or the
insults to Chrysostom, his exile, his condemnation.[54] If the patience
of these men gave a fine example in those times, certainly in our age
Tommaso has been a brilliant picture of forbearance. In those days,
to be sure, the worshippers of Christ had the Jews or the heathen
as enemies; but partly because of differences in their laws and partly
because of dissimilarities in their way of life, it was appropriate for
the infidels to hate those who worshipped Christ. But here all were
Christians who rose up against the one most Christian.

Finally, in this age there have certainly been men who could have
served as inspirational examples. But when all that was straight has
been made crooked, when virtue is lulled to sleep or even extinguished,
and vice is regularly flourishing, it is a quality of a wonderful, divine
virtue to have fought fervidly for justice and, in the midst of such
a rash of evil ways, not to have contracted the contagion of seditious
men, even when, as the Apostle says, surrounded by a training-school
of men "erring and driving into error."[55]

LETTER: I am impatiently waiting for you to reveal the outcome of
the situation. How did he free his feet from the snares of the hunters?

GIOVANNI: All right, I shall tell you—unless you become impatient
at too long a story and order my narrative to be turned to other subjects. You know that I (if I may say so) grow very verbose in talking
about this blessed bishop!

LITERA: Minime inquam. Ubi enim gentium certius patientie ac moderationis edes exemplum? Erit saltem, cum veteris prestantie aliquando obicientur indicia, ubi nostri quoque temporis attestari valeamus et indicare quod° non usquequaque huic etiam seculo germen probitatis aruerit. Quam rarum licet, enervato mundi vigore.

JOHANNES: Nempe simulac multum diuque improbitas in Thomam debachata est, lassata quidem nec saciata, aperuit tandem oculos verique medullam propicia mente respexit pontifex Romanus, emicante fulgore virtutis huius, tum delirantium quoque inclarescente nequicia, tum orbe toto miserante atque inclamante. Quem siquidem regum quemve principum, quos populos huiusce criminationis non° movit indignitas, ita quidem ut regna, tiranni, urbes, privato illustres, cunti supplicationibus celestem vicarium fatigarent. Imo procubuisse terrarum orbem sacros ante pedes constat, mestum, orantem ne unicum virtutis specimen et honesti exemplar impiorum diripi morsibus patiatur. In quo monstratur liquido quam splendida virtus hominis fuerit, pro qua mundus omnis solicitus fuit. Non est enim absque favore deorum in admiratione singulorum esse, utpote iratis agitur diis ut oderint omnes, boni presertim. Aperuit inquam summus pontifex oculos atque hunc ipsum, velut aurum fornace recoctum puratumque, innocentem ac integre sanctitatis virum declaravit. Ipsos vero delatores supplicia meritos et perniciem ut impostores et criminaces odio dignos confutavit.

Neque id protractum esset in tempora nisi summum locum sortiti retractarent dure proposita. Quippe ne quid minus consulte aggressi videantur, interdum pertinaces tentata defendunt, et dum verentur ne qua sententiam nota levitatis vel inscitie labefactet, plectuntur consciencie aculeis ipsi dum animadvertunt in alios. Detinetque studium pertinax quod debere sanior mens oppugnari decernit. In quo genere Photion est exemplo, qui Atheniensibus aliter quam consuluisset ipse agentibus, cum votis eventa° successissent, nichilominus quod suasis-

LETTER: No, indeed, I'll not stop you! For where in the world will you find a more positive example of patience and self-control? At least it will be an opportunity, whenever instances of traditional excellence are brought up, for us to produce a witness of our own time and to show that the off-shoots of righteousness have not altogether withered, even in this generation. But how rare it is, thanks to the enfeebled vigor of the world!

GIOVANNI: Of course, after evil—wearied perhaps but not satiated—had raged long against Tommaso, the Roman pontifex at last opened his eyes and looked with favor into the heart of the truth, because this man's virtue was radiantly shining, the wickedness of the mad-men was becoming clear, and the whole world was protesting out of compassion.[56] What king, what prince, what peoples were not moved by the unmerited calumnies against him? Kingdoms, tyrants, cities, men famous for their private means, all wearied Heaven's vicar with their supplications. In fact, it is known that the entire world fell before his sacred feet in distress, begging that he not allow so outstanding a model of virtue, an example of honor, to be torn apart by the vilifications of the ungodly. This clearly demonstrates how splendid was the virtue of the man, for which the whole world felt concern. To be admired by one and all is to have the favor of the gods, just as when all men hate (and especially the good) it is because the gods are angry. But as I say, the pope opened his eyes and declared this man, like gold remelted and purified in the furnace, innocent and completely blameless. Indeed, he denounced the informers as impostors and detestable criminals who deserved punishment and ruin.

And this would not have been so long in coming if, after attaining the highest rank, they did not continue to occupy themselves with their brutal schemes. In fact, lest they seem to have attacked ill-advisedly, they meanwhile obstinately defend their attempts; and fearing that some mark of capriciousness or ignorance may weaken their stand, they themselves suffer pangs of conscience when taking punitive action against others. A stubborn zeal grips them which saner minds perceive ought to be resisted. Phocion is an example of this: when the Athenians acted contrary to his advice and when subsequent events succeeded according to their wishes, he nevertheless extolled the ac-

set prelaudavit. Hoc ita fit ut errata continuentur sepe nec absque urbium plerumque detrimento. Capessuntur bella nonnumquam a quibus retrahi pudore vetante ipsis auctoribus exicium pariunt.

Nonne per deos immortales furendi genus est efficaci studio culpam sequi, cognitam presertim et dannificam? Que levitas maior, imo caligo profundior mentis quam furere ne ipse levis appareas? Plerique turpes quidem egritudines perferunt taciti quam curari malint. Cumque vel pudore obscenarum partium ostendendarum retrahuntur vel benevalentes ceteris ipsi credi volunt, occulta lue tabescunt. Qua simulatione si quid habes vanius finge!

Ut denique ad se redeat oratio, pontifex viri huius denigratam obloquiis ac ut ita dixerim laniatam invidorum morsibus extimationem, redintegravit et clariorem splendidioremque reddidit, tanto quidem quanto omnes per circumstantias etiam ab ipsis malivolis exquisito, quod nichil inquinationis, multum autem innocentie et sanctitatis inventum est. Ita dum adisset pontificem Thomas apostolice maiestati de sua liberatione gratias acturus, ut palam enunciaverit papa: "Minime gratias nobis debes, non munere quidem nostro sed iusticia et tua potius virtute de conventu sacrilegorum eductus." Quem mox ut integerrimum virum omnisque iusti capacem unice coluit, auxit honoribus, fama, dignitate. Nam quo tranquillior etati sue iam occidue et saluti quies prestaretur, aptissima quidem etate confectis, designavit sancte Gradensis ecclesie patriarcham.

LITERA: Quanti presulatus ille est? Pinguisne ut vulgo loquamur an sine suco, quique tanti amplitudinem viri non angustet?

JOHANNES: Ingentis plane fructus ac ponderis animas gregis salvare quam loculos farcire studentibus, cum asseverante Gregorio: "Ars est artium regimen animarum." Usibus domesticis, non autem avaris affecti-

tion which he had recommended.[57] Often wrong measures are continued and usually to the detriment of cities. Sometimes men initiate wars from which their sense of honor forbids them to withdraw, and which bring forth destruction upon the very instigators.

By the immortal gods, is it not a species of madness to pursue with energy and efficiency a mistaken course, especially when it has been discovered to be harmful? What is greater irresponsibility, indeed more profound intellectual darkness, than to act like a madman in order not to appear irresponsible? Many people endure shameful diseases in silence rather then be cured. As a result, because they hold back either from the embarrassment of exposing their private parts or from a desire to have others believe them to be in good health, they deteriorate from their hidden malady. Can you imagine anything more futile than such a pretence!

Finally, to return to our story, the pope restored this man's reputation which had been blackened by accusations and, so to speak, lacerated by the carping of the envious. And it was rendered the more brilliant and splendid for having been investigated in every detail by his ill-wishers themselves, because no corruption was revealed, only a great innocence and saintliness. So when Tommaso approached to thank the apostolic majesty for his deliverance, the pope publicly announced, "You do not owe thanks to us. It is not due to any gift of ours but to justice and to your own virtue that you have been rescued from the sacrilegious horde." Afterwards the pope cherished him as a most irreproachable man singularly possessed of all righteousness, and rewarded him with honors, fame, and high office. For in order that Tommaso's already declining years and health might be given a peaceful respite, suitable for those wearied by age, he designated him patriarch of the Holy Church at Grado.[58]

LETTER: How much is that prelacy worth? To put it in every-day language, is it rich or without juice? Is it one which would not diminish the prestige of so great a man?

GIOVANNI: Clearly that office has great rewards and importance for those who desire to save the souls of their flock rather than to stuff their own purses! As Gregory affirms: "The art of arts is the guidance of souls." It was sufficient for personal needs, but not however for

bus satis erat. Pro quo sane haud magnopere decertassent, qui ambitione coinquinari dignitates ignorant, illustrari accessibus putant. Quos
Osee vox fortassis increpuit: "Ipsi regnaverunt," inquit, "et non ex me;
principes extiterunt et ego non cognovi." Ceterum quisquis moribus
erigi non proventu querit insignem opulentumque extimaret.

Quippe in ora superi maris, Histriana videlicet, decus sibi primum
auctoritatemque vendicat, loco ut aiunt Alexandrini pontificatus, surrogata prelatio. Quid quod nunc Venetiis sedem habet que totius quidem Hesperie flos adornatissimus et fertur et est, imo singulare quidem
emporium omnis Europe? Ubi tanta claruit sanctitate, tanta virtutis
prestantia, tanta rerum omnium equitate ut dubitatum sit ipse dignitate an ipso dignitas facta foret illustrior. Nam solabatur merore
laborantes, levabat oppressos, dirigebat errantes, pater patronus pauperum, haud contentus erogari per ministros nisi sacratis ipse manibus
diariam erogationem centufariam egenis fluentibus propinaret. Ut in
summa hominis dotes absolvam, consulendo, exhortando, edificando
veluti salutare civitatis illius et clarissimum sidus erat. Oneris satis mehercule successuris liquit, modo id intelligant vehementer dedecorari
opinione quisquis precessorum virtutes non redolet.

LITERA: Ita est inquam. Sed age queso, in tanta civitate, in qua moribus non fore plerosque perditis vix fieri posse crediderim, veluti in
vasto quidem corpore obscene quedam partes insunt, precipue fatiscente
vitiis orbe terrarum, ullumne fuit tanto primati contra scelerosos bellum? Ubique enim mali bonis infesti sunt, quos nulla confederare vicissitudo potest, rerum natura dictante contraria sese invicem fugere vel
etiam invadere.

JOHANNES: Pol ingens ac ferme pari furore certatum est. Nullus extat
ita vitiorum locus impers ut uspiam suum probitati calcar desit. Quin

greedy appetites. It would certainly not be eagerly sought by the kind
of men who ignore the fact that self-interest pollutes high offices and
who think themselves enhanced by wealth. It was probably such men
who were chided by the words of Hosea: "They have reigned," he
said, "but not by me: they have been princes, and I knew not."[59] But
whoever seeks to be exalted by means of his character and not by
his income would consider the office distinguished and rich.

Indeed, on the coast of the upper sea, that is, the Danuvian (i.e.,
at Constantinople), a subsequent ecclesiastical power claims for itself
the first honor and authority in the place of, as they say, the bishopric
of Alexandria. What of the fact that now Tommaso has at Venice
a location which is called (and is) the most beautiful flower of the
whole west: indeed is the outstanding emporium of Europe? There
he was famous for such great saintliness, superior virtue, and righteousness in all matters that it is questionable whether he became more
illustrious because of his office or whether his office became more illustrious because of him.[60] For he consoled those burdened by grief,
relieved the oppressed, guided the erring. A father and patron to the
poor, he was not satisfied to have disbursements made by servitors
unless with his own consecrated hands he could present the daily con-
tribution to the needy who flowed in from a hundred places. To sum
up his attributes: by counseling, encouraging, edifying, he was like
a brilliant star of salvation to that city. He left a real responsibility,
by Hercules, to those destined to follow him, if they but realize that
public opinion holds in great dishonor the man who does not have
his predecessor's virtues.

LETTER: This is so, I agree. But tell me, in such a great city, where
I imagine it probable that there were many people of dissolute character,
just as there are certain indecent parts in a vast body, especially since
the world is being debilitated by vices—in this city was there any war
against the wicked on behalf of so great a nobleman? For everywhere
evil men are hostile to the good, and the two kinds cannot be united
by any set of circumstances, since nature dictates that opposites either
flee each other or even readily attack each other.

GIOVANNI: By Pollux, there was a great war, and it was fought with
almost evenly-matched fury. No place is so free of vices that it does

in maiore populo cum maiore temeritate certandum, nisi assertionem
Aristotilis abnegemus: "Quanto maior est populus," ait, "tanto remotior
intellectus." Igitur sancte memorie beatissimus papa Gregorius,
Veneticorum optimatum supplicatibus, Thomam ipsum censorem dis-
cussoremve delinquentium clericorum apostolica auctoritate firmavit,
onus quidem instantibus si moribus intervenissent, non Herculi dico
tantum molestum verum ipsi quoque Atlanti, quem humanis tulisse
polum humeris fabulosa Grecia mentita nobis est. Sed hunc sanctissimus imo pontifex Venetie finibus prepositum dedit peccatis, quod
noverat acutissimum vindicem delictorum ac recti equive amantissi-
mum, quem nec munus incurvare nec metus a iusticia valeret aver-
tere, que duo venena pretorum crebro censuras irritant vel strangulant.

Ergo sacri pastoris mandatum cepit obire, dare operam ne quid con-
torte ne quid vulgariter ne incontinenter a claustralibus tentaretur,
quatenus sancta, immaculata, sobria, ordinata, uti condecet, obtem-
peraret Christo religio. Inde monere virgines de sanctitate et corporis
integritate servanda. Hinc exhortatione clerum rudimentis, prece, dictis
factisve erigere, docere quoque eniterentur prestantia morum excellere
populum quantum gradibus anteirent, meminerintque se et appellari
et esse pastores, ob quam quidem nominationem necessitatis addi multum quatenus a plebe distare tantum discretione virtutis debeant quantum inter brutorum gregem interest et pastorem. Quoniam attestante
Gregorio decet nimirum decet dominicum sacerdotem moribus et vita
clarescere, quatenus in eo tamquam in sue vite speculo plebs commis-
sa et eligere quod sequatur et agnoscere possit quod corrigat. Tum
contumaces absterrere, fugare, plectere. Quid? Universa in celestem
quendam colorem vertere.

Primum quidem omnes admiratione sanctitatis divinorumque in-
stitutorum gravitate vereri imperium Thome, venerari maiestatem atque inde carnalia devitare ceperunt. Postquam recaluere vitia et diffluere
tramite solito vanitati collibuit, ausa libido est vel per decreta tanti
patris erumpere, ausa inquam numero honesti metas infreni prevarica-

not need to have a spur put to its goodness. In fact among a larger populace a battle must be fought with greater boldness, unless we dispute Aristotle's assertion that "The larger the populace, the more remote is its understanding."[61] Therefore that most blessed pope of holy memory, Gregory, at the behest of the noblest citizens of Venice, by his apostolic authority confirmed Tommaso as censor and examiner of delinquent clerics[62] —a great responsibility indeed, if they had obstructed him by their antagonistic attitude, a burden equal to that not only of Hercules, I say, but of Atlas himself, who according to the legends of Greece bore the heavens on his human shoulders. But the most holy pontifex gave him as provost to the region of Venice because of its sins, for he knew Tommaso was a very keen chastiser of misdeeds and devoted to fairness and impartiality, the kind of man whom no bribe could prejudice nor fear turn away from justice—the two poisons which frequently void or stifle the decisions of judges.

Therefore Tommaso undertook to carry out the mandate of the sacred pastor and to see to it that the monks ventured nothing perverse, vulgar, or intemperate, in order that a holy, immaculate, sober, and well-regulated religious body might fittingly obey Christ. He cautioned virgins about preserving the sanctity and purity of their bodies. Then he uplifted the clergy by exhortation, instruction, and prayer, in words and deeds. He taught them to strive to surpass the laity in excellence of character as much as they exceeded them in rank, and to remember that they were called—and were—pastors. Indeed, because of this title they had a great obligation to be as distinct from the common people in respect to virtue as is a shepherd from his flock of beasts. For, in the words of Gregory, it is fitting that the Lord's priest be exceptional in his character and in his life, so that from him, as if from the reflection of his life, the people entrusted to him can choose what to follow and learn what to correct.[63] Next he discouraged, drove off, or punished those who were defiant. In short, he converted all things into a semblance of Heaven.

At first then, through admiration of Tommaso's saintliness and the influence of his divine teaching, all began to respect his authority, to revere his dignity, and consequently to avoid worldly pursuits. But afterwards their vices flared up again, and in their folly they chose to go astray on the old accustomed path, wilfully daring even to leap

tione trasilire. Ac° non tantum quos accendebat luxuria impietate solita debachari, sed eorum plurimos in insaniam contagio implicuit qui boni clarique putabantur nec erant. Nemo clarus cui honestum oppugnari videtur debere, turpitudo defendi, quantumvis honoribus, genere, opibus fulgeat. Enimvero claritudini virtus ingenua, morum gravitas, animus invictus, eminens et conspicax intellectus insunt. Frustra se nunc itaque tam vana iactat quam vacua mundi nobilitas, cui quidem liceat audire quod simulacris gentium Abachuc insonat: "Ecce ipse coopertus est auro et argento, et omnis sensus non est in visceribus eius." Probe Solon unus is e septem atque Apollinis ore prelatus allusisse Lidorum regi Creso fertur. Cum namque rex auro, margaritis, ac ceteris humane vanitatis insignibus expolitus sederet philosophumque rogaret siquidem melioris quid pulcriorisve inspexisset, "Pavos," inquit, "et fasianos, qui veris et suis decoribus eniterent." Ita philosophus. Sed quid censeri absurdius potest vel debet quam splendescere foris, sordescere intus? Et summum esse fortuna moribus imum? Verumtamen hac de re hactenus uberrime dictum.

Illi inquam boni clarique viri° dum naturali vel alia quavis necessitudine coniunctis pietatem sevam, impudentem scilicet libertatem defendunt,impiissimi fiunt. Quasi non sit crudelitatis genus, quoniam ames, nolle cohercere languentem a noxiis, cum laborante stomaco devius identidem appetitus saluti adversa suspiret. Igitur inde cum improbis improborumque complicibus duellatum acriter,° statum contra est, dictum factumque. Hinc singularis hominis virtus, plurimorum illinc conspiratio facinorosorum in acie stabant. Dii boni, quas contumelias, quam comminationem subsannationemque, quas item insidias, que opprobria non audivit et toleravit miles Christi, que quidem omnia pia firmitate confutavit et fregit?

Quodam rursus tempore cum nonnulli huiusce temeritatis fautores

speedily over the bounds of honor, in unbridled transgression. And it was not only those incited by love of luxury who wantoned with their habitual impiety; but also many by contagion were drawn into the insanity, who were reputed to be good and noble yet were not so. No one is noble who believes it proper for honor to be attacked and baseness to be defended, regardless of how distinguished he is in position, family, or wealth. For indeed natural virtue, depth of character, an unconquered mind, and an eminently conspicuous intellect are innate in men of nobility. In vain now does the world's aristocracy vaunt itself, as haughty as it is empty. To such men can be applied Habakkuk's proclamation against the idols of the heathen: "Behold, it is laid over with gold and silver, and there is no spirit in the bowels thereof."[64] Solon, one of the Seven Wise Men and given precedence by the mouth of Apollo, is said to have properly derided Croesus, king of the Lydians. For when the king, sitting decked out in gold and pearls and other trappings of human vanity, asked the philosopher if he had ever beheld anything finer or more beautiful, Solon said, "Peacocks and pheasants, who are resplendent with their own genuine ornamentation."[65] So spoke the philosopher. But what can or should be considered more absurd than to be splendid on the outside and foul within? Or to be the highest in fortune and the lowest in character? However, by now more than enough has been said on this subject.

Those good and noble men, I say, who excuse a barbarous "piety," actually shameless wantonness, in persons connected to them by birth or some other relationship, are the most impious of all. It is surely a species of cruelty to refuse, on the grounds that you love someone, to keep him away from harmful foods when he is sick, when in spite of his unwell stomach his erratic appetite repeatedly longs for fare detrimental to his health. Therefore, then, Tommaso battled fiercely against the wicked and the confederates of the wicked, resisted them, spoke out and acted against them. On one side the virtue of a single man, on the other a conspiracy of many evil men stood in battle array. Oh good gods, what insults, what threats and mockery, what treacherous attacks and abuses did he not hear and endure, that soldier of Christ! But all of these he refuted and crushed by his pious resoluteness.

On one occasion some supporters of this audacious behavior were

in eundem insultarent et exquisito exprobrationis genere ut ita dixerim coaxerent, molirenturque iustum antistitem et incommutabilem in huiusmodi trahere factionem idque precum seu convitiorum ulla instantia minime consecutum iri cernerent, formidine flectine posset pertentare aggressi sunt. Tum minari pulsuros se esse de Veneticorum urbe, sibi ruinam machinaturos et suis, proferre item perditum ire, trucidatum ire. Quibus terrificis sermonibus atque furentibus immotus ipse nichil preterquam ait: "Faciat vos resipiscere Deus omnipotens." Ceterum convitia° postquam tanta celesti quadam equanimitate confutavit, minitanti pertinacius necem atque perniciem, "Ut animadvertas," inquit, "quam insultantem sevientemque liceor, his me exortum elementis velim intelligas ut dedecori sit in plumis extingui."

LITERA: Perpulcre edepol grassantis proterviam irrisit. Uberrimum sane constantie et per cunta quadri hominis documentum posse vel inter acerrima discrimina dicendi iocunditatem gravitatemque tenere.

JOHANNES: Perpulcre utique, sed nichil minus quod referam. Amotis namque delirantibus illis domesticorum unus, "Prestaret," consuluit, "divine pater, flectereris horum suggestionibus. Posset enim una tecum nos istic cesos membratim furor opprimere." In quem defixis Thomas oculis tacitus ac mox deinde surridens, "Putas," inquit, "his te sanctitatis muneribus functum martir ut fieri meritus sis?"

LITERA: Viro constanti et intrepido digna responsio, sed meticuloso admodum rudique illa suasio. Tamen id scire malim: licebat itane famulantibus insulse apud huius eminentiam ac temere profari? Cum apud nonnullos rumpere silentium tantus est elationis tumor, supplicio luatur, nedum impune transeat vernaculos dominis coniocari.

JOHANNES: Mansuetiorem inferioribus quam soleant paribus ceteri se prebuit. Equidem audivimus crebro procacitatem temerariam subdito-

scolding at him, croaking, one might say, with a carefully chosen type of reproach, in an attempt to draw the just and steadfast priest into such a faction. When they realized that they could not accomplish this by persistent entreaties or arguments, they proceeded to try whether he could be influenced by fear. So they threatened to drive him from the city of Venice and to contrive ruin for him and his household, even proclaiming that they would destroy and kill him. Unmoved by these frightful, frenzied words, he said nothing except, "May omnipotent God bring you to your senses!" And after he silenced their great abuse with his celestial equanimity, he replied to a man who was still stubbornly threatening death and destruction, "So that you may observe what value I put upon a man who reviles and rages, I should like you to know that I was brought up on the principle that it is a disgrace to be smothered to death by feathers!"

LETTER: By Pollux, how cleverly he made fun of his attacker's impudence! Certainly the fullest proof of steadfastness and of a man forthright in all things is his ability even in the most alarming dangers to retain both humor and seriousness in his words.

GIOVANNI: It was very cleverly said, to be sure, but what I am about to relate is no less so. For after those madmen had been removed, one of his household staff advised him, "Divine father, it would be better if you followed the suggestions of these men. For that anger of theirs could overwhelm us along with you and cut us apart limb from limb!" Tommaso, fixing his eyes upon him, at first was silent and then said with a smile, "Do you think you have performed your sacred duties so well that you deserve to become a martyr?"

LETTER: His reply was worthy of a strong and fearless man, and that advice was from an ignorant coward. However, I should like to know this: were his servants allowed to speak out so foolishly and boldly in the presence of his eminence? To some people, to break silence in their presence is so great a presumption that it receives punishment; and much less can house-servants with impunity make jokes with their masters.

GIOVANNI: Tommaso has shown himself more amenable to his inferiors than others usually are to their equals. In fact we heard that fre-

rum seu temeritatem procacem et risisse et humillime sustulisse.°
Quodque in eodem astantes vel dolebant vel indignabantur, gaudere
potius ipse videbatur. Quotiens assistentium effrenem ac mordacem
nimium dictionem equanimiter patienti presens illi, Socratem iurgia
Xantipes, convitia, aspersionem liquoris impuri tolerantem memini.
Libertatis ibi Decembris arbitrium numquam defuisse iuravisses. Minime dominator sed pater imo veluti comes singulis erat. In qua re
indicium efficax est quod vernarum nullum umquam alternavit sicuti
plerique faciunt, stomacatio quorum superbiaque perpeti novit men-
struos servientes. Contra hic radicatos una atque inveteratos continuit.
    Taceo de corporis cultu quo indiscretus a ceteris, fortasse etiam in-
ferior erat, ut sui nescios plerumque raperet in errorem, utpote Silvestrum quendam Coneglanicum civem. Dum quodam me tempore
in aula patriarchali a Coneglano hospitem alloqui ventavisset, tunc
humilis presul forte solus meridie, estas enim erat, in atrio sedebat.
Quem adit Silvester velut religiosum hominem non autem sicut patrem
patrum salutans. Acceperat enim famam viri magnam valde, nequa-
quam arbitratus humilitatem posse parem esse. Rogat et, "Ubinam,"
inquit, "Iohannes, bone frater, is inquam qui patriarce nepos est?" Tum
patriarcha, "Scitare," ait, "interiore domo. Nusquam michi locorum
nuper visum." Inter hec ego seorsum e cella prorumpens patrem in-
tuor, procumbo pedibus, veneror, adoro. Mox inde Silvestrum occu-
po, confestim quisnam ille sit percontantem, sacrum antistitem esse
doceo. Qui deinde erroris admonitus, rubore plenus ac stupore simul,
miris apud ipsum modis, tantam mentis caliginem excusavit. Atque
eodem asserente michi post, "Deprendebam," ait, "alte quiddam et sancte
maturitatis in viro. Sed coniectabam ratiocinans mecum, 'Tante prela-
tum amplitudinis circumstant domestici tales. Quoniam vitia virtutesque

quently he both laughed at and meekly endured the bold sauciness
(and saucy boldness!) of his subordinates. And situations which caused
either distress or indignation to the by-standers seemed rather a source
of amusement to him. How many times, when in my presence he
endured with equanimity the uninhibited and carping words of those
attending him, did I recall Socrates tolerating from Xanthippe abuses
and taunts and a drenching with foul liquid![66] You would have
sworn that the capriciousness of the Saturnalia was always in full sway
there. He was not at all like a master, but like a father, or even a
comrade, to each individual. A real proof of this is that he never had
a succession of house-servants, as many do whose bad tempers and
arrogance barely can put up with servants for the space of a month.
He on the contrary retained his until they were deeply-rooted and
grown old.

I need not mention his bodily attire, in which respect he was no
different from others, or perhaps even less concerned; so that frequently
he caused those who did not know him to make a mistake, as for
instance one Silvestro, a citizen of Conegliano.[67] On one occasion
Silvestro had come from Conegliano to visit me when I was a guest
in the patriarchal court. At this time the humble bishop happened
to be sitting alone at midday in the courtyard, for it was summer.
Silvestro approached him, greeting him as a monk and not as the Father
of Fathers. He had heard, of course, of the very great fame of the
man, but never realized that his humility could be equally great. He
asked, "Where is Giovanni, good brother, I mean the one who is the
patriarch's nephew?" Then the patriarch replied, "Inquire inside the
house. I have not seen him anywhere recently." In the midst of this
conversation I came out from my cell, caught sight of the father, fell
at his feet, venerated and adored him. Then I took hold of Silvestro,
who immediately asked who the man was, and I informed him that
it was the holy bishop. Then, being apprised of his error, he was filled
simultaneously with embarrassment and amazement that he was in-
credibly in the bishop's very presence, and apologized for his mental
obtuseness. Afterwards, in defending himself to me, he said, "I did
perceive something of a lofty and virtuous maturity in the man. But
I conjectured, reasoning with myself, this is the sort of servitor who
attends a prelate of such great eminence. Since the vices and virtues

dominorum etiam in subditis elucescunt, ac vix fieri potest ut regentis formam domestica membra non redolescant.'" Addebat preterea consentaneum non esse humane arrogantie temporis nostri presertim ut solitudine tanta et induminum moderatione contenta esset. Ita Silvestrum huius humilitas, ita complures par ignorantia fefellit.

Quantum in se erat contendebat esse pro Christo, opprobrium hominum et abiectio plebis. Parvipendit adeo corporis cultum in quo nimirum plerique nimium anxiantur, ut stamine famulari ceteris cum domesticis fratribus, patriarcha existens, tegeretur. Quin evenit ut a sutore quodam tempore unus ministrantium fratrum laicus quidem refelleret scapulare, querereturque admodum impatiens quod aliquanto arctius capuciive minoris ac optasset ipse factum esset, moribus homo et forma incompositus satis. Cui Thomas, "Obsecro," inquit, "ne ob hoc ipsum insanias. Alternemus. Tuum ego, tu meum vestiamus." Valet huiccine mansuetudini quicquam comparari? Nichil ornatus unquam sibi passus est apponi nisi quatenus maiestati dignitatis iniuria non fieret. Imo de vestitus decore identidem monere solebat preciose cultos vestium servos esse. Neque id falso quidem, nam ut pompa sine servitute numquam est, sic absque libertate mediocritas numquam. Si exigis in re tam apertissima testem, "Contemptus persone libertas est," Seneca dicit.

Sed par huic quoque exemplum accipe. Nam memini puer ego patrem olim ipsum cum Bononie minister esset Ravennam venire. Atque tum corporis lassitate tum ineptitudine quoque viarum in equis ventabat ipse cum sociis (nisi me fallit memoria, binis), in quibus erat qui asino insideret. Huiusmodi namque iumentum corpore precellens ac robore, doctum quoque modestioribus vadere gradibus, sacer archiepiscopus Ravenne, ni fallor Thome donaverat. Ceterum cum urbi propiores fierent, asini sessor immurmurans furentique similis, "Pudet," inclamat, "ceteris equo sedentibus me asino urbem ingredi." Huic minister, "Desine," respondit, "molestus esse. Dabo equum tibi, asinum ego supersedebo. Num indigner id ipse quod rex Israel, imo totius mundi formator regnatorve, Christus, fecit?"

of masters are displayed also in their subordinates, surely the members of the household reflect the likeness of the one who rules them." He added besides that it was not in keeping with human arrogance, especially in our time, to be content with such great solitude and modest attire. Thus Silvestro was deceived by Tommaso's humility, and thus also many others through a similar ignorance.

With all his power he strove to be for Christ, though scorned by men and rejected by the common people. He cared so little for physical adornment, about which most people are over-anxious, that although he was patriarch he dressed in servants' clothing along with the other monks of his household. It happened once that one of the serving friars, a layman, refused a scapular from the tailor, complaining quite impatiently that it had been made a little too narrow and with a smaller hood than he had requested. He was a man rather uncouth in manner and appearance. To him Tommaso said, "I beg you, don't rant so about this matter! Let us exchange—I'll put on your garment and you put on mine." Can anything equal such mildness? He never allowed any adornment to be placed on him except to avoid affront to the majesty of his office. In fact, concerning elegance of apparel, he frequently reminded that those who dressed expensively were slaves of their clothes. And this was truly said, for as slavery always accompanies ostentation, so freedom accompanies moderation. If you require proof for so obvious a fact, Seneca says: "To despise our bodies is freedom."[68]

But now hear an example equal to this one. I remember that once in my boyhood the father came to Ravenna when he was minister at Bologna.[69] Not only because of physical fatigue but also because of the poor roads, he was traveling on horseback along with his companions (two, if my memory does not fail me); and one of these men was riding an ass. This beast of burden, being exceptional in bodily strength and also trained to walk at a rather moderate pace, had been given to Tommaso by the holy archbishop of Ravenna, if I am not mistaken. But when they drew nearer the city, the man seated on the ass, grumbling angrily, cried out, "I am ashamed to enter the city on an ass when others are on horseback!" To him the minister answered, "Stop being a nuisance. I shall give my horse to you and I shall mount the ass. Surely it is not beneath me to do what the King of Israel Himself did, Christ, the creator and ruler of the whole world."

Volve, Litera, nostri temporis animarum duces, paria si quem daturum ostendis exempla. Totus iste conformari Christo gliscebat, cum ab evangelice nuper doctrine vestigiis tanta quidam quanta potest diversitas delirent. Quo quid potest enormius inveniri, confiteri voce Christum, negare moribus? Sed ut tandem revertar unde digressus eram, divina quedam maiestas Thomam ignorantibus, ex maiestate vero gravis emicabat severitas. Propius autem tractantibus sobria ac dulcis tractabilisve reperiebatur humanitas.

LITERA: Indicas abunde huiusmodi oratione tua quantum amoris homini feras. Quippe ignita adeo verba depromis ut audientem accendas ad amandum colendumve tot hunc beatitudinis dotibus descriptum. Haud enim fieri potest quod tanta scriptura tantoque laudum referta preconio ingenti absque amore prodeat. Ceterum unum id miror, si familiam eius nullum umquam dissidium inquietavit, ubi precipue servis usque adeo libertatis freni laxabantur. Nam quorum tum inscitia ipsa, tum ex animi imbecillitate scaturiente invidia mobilis pronaque est passionibus agi. Sed absolve, rogo, tanto libidinis periculo lacessitum in tanta errantium hominum coniuratione quisnam eventus excepit.

JOHANNES: Qui solet nesciam expugnari virtutem. Sunt quippe res que ipso usu atque exercitatione fatiscant deicianturque, plus quedam laborando sudandoque° nitescunt. Rubiginascit ferrum situ ipso, contractatum agitatumque splendet. Idem virtuti accidere auctoritate doctorum hominum, imo veritatis licet opineris. Atqui excelsus virtute animus ubi mala cum fortuna bellum conserit, tantum decoris vendicat quantum admirationis quid valeat ipsa probitas ignaris addit. Et si magnam ad felicitatem cautione magna opus est, tum certe potissimum quid animi vigor ingens queat asperitur quando his non frangitur rebus, imo ne concutitur quidem, que toleratu aspera formidolosaque mentes ceterorum non territant modo sed deiciunt. Atque id proprium est virtuti, non cedere duris.

Consider, Letter, the leaders of souls in our time: do you see anyone who can furnish comparable examples? Tommaso longed to be
wholly conformed to Christ, at a time when certain men were stray-
ing from the paths of the Gospel teaching, in as many different ways
as possible. What greater enormity can be found than this, to confess
Christ in words and to deny Him in deeds? But to return to the point
at which I had digressed, a certain divine majesty was apparent even
to those who did not know Tommaso, and, as a result of this majesty,
a stern austerity. However, to those who had a closer relationship
with him, he revealed a sober, sweet, amenable kindness.

LETTER: By your very speech you show abundantly how much love
you bear him. Indeed, you utter words so glowing that you inspire
the hearer to love and cherish this man who is portrayed with so many
blessed endowments. Certainly it is impossible for such a description,
replete with celebration of his praises, to come into being without
great love. But I do marvel at one thing, that no discord ever dis-
turbed his household, when the reins on liberty were so relaxed, especially for servants. For not only their ignorance itself but also the
ill-will arising from the weakness of their minds is easily influenced
and prone to be led by the passions. But please tell me what the outcome was for him, when he was challenged by the dangers of the
wanton behavior within that great conspiracy of sinful men.

GIOVANNI: It was the usual outcome for virtue, which cannot be van-
quished. There are of course objects which through use and handling
wear out and are discarded, but others grow brighter with manipula-
tion and exercise. Iron rusts through disuse, but it gleams when frequently handled and worked with. You can imagine that the same
thing happens to virtue, from the testimony of learned men, indeed,
from the testimony of truth. When a mind of lofty virtue joins battle
with evil fortune, its acquired glory is as great as is the astonishment
of those who do not know the true worth of goodness. And if to
attain great happiness there is need of great prudence, then certainly
the remarkable strength of a vigorous mind is revealed when it is not
broken, indeed not even shaken, by circumstances which, harsh and
fearful to endure, not only terrify but destroy the minds of others.
This is the property of virtue, not to give way before adversity.

Non mehercule Socratis virtus usquam melius quam hauriendo venenum claruit. Alcides non describeretur inter divos si non posse malis
succumbere dura laborum perpessio non monstrasset. Claruit in harena
Libies Cato, Regulus inter clavorum aculeos, paupertate Fabritius,
Aristides exilio. Neve honor suus negetur codicibus sanctis: Iosep post
venditionem, post servitutem, post compedes preficitur Egipto. Pretereo
Machabeos quos multi sudores, multa malorum tolerantia, multus denique sanguis effusus reddit insignes. Quorum probitas, quo sevior fuit
emulorum malignitas, eo magis emicuit et certior fuit. Quid Tobie
cecitatem? Quid erumnam sancti Iob? Quid Eustachii tentationem, uxore ablata, liberis, honoribus? Quid inquam attinet recolere? Post ie-
iunia, peregrinationes, verbera, naufragia, catenas, vas electionis dictus
Paulus. Supervacuum in hac quidem re subicere multos testes, presertim clarissima.

Adversantia nempe que integris viris obiciuntur probitatis examen
illustratioque plane sunt. Que vero impiis ac sceleratis hominibus, siquidem erigunt° vel emendant, noxe precedentis abstersio; si vero ob-
durant impatienti vel obstinatione quadam excecant, tam reprobationis
indicium quam supplicii iam inicium futuri sunt. Igitur si quis adver-
sitatem radicitus intuetur, boni quidem multum, mali parum afferre
mortalibus inveniet, nam instruit, emendat, homini experimentum sui
prebet. Quoniam "qui non tentatus fuerit quid sciet?" ut Ecclesiasticus
ait. Quam bene Demetrius apud Anneum: "Nichil," inquit, "infelicius
eo cui nichil umquam advenit adversi." Id multi riderent et ita esse
inficiarentur. Sed invitis deliciis verum esse constat quia secundis semper
labi successibus "alteram est rerum partem ignorare," ut ait Seneca.
Preter hec formidolosiora haberentur fortune tela, si nulla umquam
viri fortis patientia docuisset a natura ipsa accepisse nos arma quibus
adversum fortunam stari possit. At si nil aliud certe "amicorum certos
ambiguosque vultus decernit," ut ille ait. Quid quod a fedis volupta-
tum catenis non solvit modo plerosque sed erigit ad meliora?

The virtue of Socrates, by Hercules, nowhere shone brighter than in his drinking poison. Hercules would not be enrolled among the gods if the harsh ordeal of his labors had not shown it was impossible for him to succumb to evils. Cato achieved fame in the sands of Libya, Regulus among sharp-pointed nails, Fabricius through poverty, Aristides through exile.[70] And not to deny honor to the sacred books, after Joseph was sold, enslaved, and fettered, he became prefect of Egypt. Not to mention the Maccabees, distinguished by many labors, great endurance of misfortunes, and finally the shedding of their blood. The more savage was the malevolence of their antagonists, the more resplendent was their virtue, and the more sure. What about the blindness of Tobias, the suffering of holy Job, or the temptation of Eustachius after he had lost wife, children, and position? But why recall these? After hunger, long wanderings, beatings, shipwreck, and prison, Paul was called the chosen vessel.[71] Indeed it is superfluous to add numerous examples, when we have this particularly famous instance.

To be sure, adversity which befalls upright men is obviously a test and illustration of their probity. But that which comes to sinful and wicked men, if it improves or reforms them, wipes away previous wrong-doing. However, if it makes them hard and blind with a stubborn refusal to endure, it is not only a sign of condemnation but also a beginning of future punishment. Therefore if one studies adversity thoroughly, he will find that it brings much good and little evil to mortals; it teaches, improves, and furnishes man a means of testing himself. For "what doth he know that hath not been tried," as Ecclesiasticus says. How well Demetrius put it, according to Seneca: "No man seems more unhappy than one who has never met with adversity." Many might ridicule this saying and deny its truth. But despite the opinion of those dedicated to pleasure, it is an established fact that always to glide along in prosperity "is to remain ignorant of half of life," as Seneca says. Besides this, fortune's weapons would be considered more formidable if the endurance of a brave man had not proved that nature herself has given us armor by which we can withstand fortune. Yet, if nothing else, surely adversity "shows the friends whose smiles are true and those whose smiles are false," as the famous man says.[72] And what of the fact that it not only frees most men from the foul chains of lust but inspires them to better things?

Quid multa? Exornat celum adversitas, mundana felicitas implet infernum. Audi literam Sapientie: "In paucis vexati, in multis bene disponentur, quoniam Deus tentavit illos, et invenit dignos se." Ergo Deus ut innotescat electorum prestantia, obicit plerumque adversa uti videlicet experimentum sui captent, documentum aliis preponant aptum esse mundum qui vincatur. Clamat Apocalipsis: "Ego quos amo, arguo, castigo." Et Seneca: "Bonum virum non habet in deliciis Deus, experitur, indurat, sibi illum preparat." Quod quidem si mortales adverterent, non tantopere successus laudarent improbarentque que sinistra habentur, vel saltem formidarent delicati isti evangelicam illam vocem: "Fili, recepisti bona in vita tua." Que vox quantum plena terroris existat, satis patet exponente Gregorio. Hac fortassis opinione sancti viri non modo dura queque non metuebant sed ne quidem fugiebant, scilicet illustrati mentes beatifica luce, quod apostolus Corynthios instruit: "Id quod in presenti est momentaneum et leve tribulationis nostre, eternum glorie pondus operatur in nobis." Atque spes huiusmodi fecit martires, patrimonia amplissima refutari, delicias, potentatus, divicias, voluptates ceteras contemni. Fecit conteri corpus, demitti, persecutionem equanimiter suscipi.

Quemadmodum virum hunc cuius impresentiarum laudem versamus, persecutionem cuius atque constantium, diuturnitas ipsa, tum indignitas accusantium atque protervitas tum iudicum examen, nescio lentius an contortius dixerim, eius denique mira patientia tante calumnie reddidit insignem. Preterquam quod vite dimissus est, martirium certe passi. Sed omnipotens Deus ita cunta cognoscens, sic regens atque distribuens, haud ita omnino peccantem orbem deserit, ut integros quosdam et sanctos viros; sed perraros quidem, ex hominum cetu patiatur extingui, ne velut eclipsato sole virtutum vitiorum mole terra funditus tenebrescat. Atque ob hanc ipsam causam eternus artifex rerum de laqueis venantium presulem nimirum liberans decrevit superesse, quatenus opportuno tempore inter sacrosancte columnas

In brief, adversity honors Heaven, earthly bliss fills Hell. Listen to the letter of Wisdom: "Afflicted in few things, in many they shall be well rewarded: because God hath tried them and found them worthy of himself." Therefore God, in order that the excellence of His elect may become known, often causes them affliction so that they may make trial of themselves and show others a proof that the world can be overcome. Apocalypse proclaims: "Such as I love, I rebuke and chasten." And Seneca: "(God) does not make a spoiled pet of a good man; he tests him, hardens him, and fits him for his own service." Indeed, if mortals heeded this, they would not praise success too highly and would disapprove of acts which are held to be immoral. At least those persons addicted to pleasure would dread this Gospel saying: "Son, thou didst receive good things in thy lifetime."[73] Gregory explains clearly how frightening this saying is. Perhaps because of the holy man's opinion, not only were no hardships whatsoever feared, none were even avoided by men whose minds had been illuminated by the blessed light. As the Apostle instructed the Corinthians: "That which is at present momentary and light of our tribulation worketh for us an eternal weight of glory."[74] Such hope created martyrs, caused rich patrimonies to be refused, and luxuries, power, wealth, and all other pleasures to be scorned. It produced contempt and scorn for the body and the acceptance of persecution with equanimity.

So it was with this man whose honor we are now discussing. His persecution and his self-restraint were distinguished by their long duration, by the unworthiness and the impudence of his accusers, by the judges' examination (I do not know whether to call this too long-drawn-out or too distorted), and finally by his remarkable patience in the midst of so many unfounded accusations. Except that he was allowed to live, he surely suffered martyrdom. But omnipotent God, who knows, directs, and arranges all things, does not so entirely desert the sinful world that He will allow certain upright and saintly men (admittedly very few) to be exterminated from human society. Otherwise the earth would be wholly darkened by the mass of iniquity, as if the sun of virtue were in eclipse. And for this very reason the Eternal Creator, by freeing the bishop from the hunters' snares, decreed his survival in order that at the opportune moment he would be among

ecclesie futurus, impulsibus impiorum laborante piscatoris fidi navi-
cula, gubernatori summo propius assisteret.

Itaque nunc beatissimus papa Urbanus Sextus, Christiane fidei unicum decus, hunc° ipsum cum aliis quos ex omni mundo veluti flores
prestantiores excerpsit curavit habere cardinalem, ut altis de rebus agenti,
de mundi gubernatione, de pace populorum, deque propositis animarum, pastori beatissimo atque pro cuntorum salute vigilanti tante
sapientie consilium adderetur.

LITERA: Summum providentie magni pontificis argumentum est et item
laborum levamen immodicum absolutissimos quidem viros ex omni
cetu mortalium collegisse. Aut enim divina quedam revelatio aut sanctus
in papa residens spiritus horum delectum edocuit. Vix factivum aiunt
humana sapientia ut prudentem adeo sufficientem, utilem, iustam delec-
tionem dederit. Quippe quicquid erat ubique gentium virtutis ac doctrine ferunt exhausisse. Et o felicem tranquillumve populum Christi-
anum, Romanum si presulem tantum semper doctissimorum atque
gravium virorum collegium circumfulgeat! Quid aliud dixerim con-
sistentem in illa sancta patrum acie Christi vicarium, quam inter sidera solem in terris?

O utinam radios pietatis atque providentie sue ad hunc infelicem
inquietumve angulum Latii clementissimus papa deflecteret, ut pacem aliquando populi miseri, incognitum nobis bonum, degustarent.
Quamquam Auxonia pene bellicis tota furoribus langueat, iste nimirum angulus ad novissimum flatum est. Essetne divinitus Hesperie luc-
tuose in hoc ipso pontifice Urbano quam ariolantur gentes, et aviditate
ipsa vel somniant vel fingunt, pacis future ac fugate diu libertatis im-
pleta promissio. Quo tandem auctore reliquie misere laceratarum
provinciarum ac urbium respirare queant. O tempus est, quisquis genus curas humanum, singultientes ut hoc ipsum populos patiaris impetrare! Quandoquidem armorum furens cruditas Christianam plebem
devorat ut micam panis. An forte ut vaticinatus est Isaias: "Iniquitates

the pillars of the Holy Church and could render ready assistance to the chief helmsman when the ship of the faithful fisherman was suffering under the blows of the wicked.

Therefore now the most blessed pope, Urban the Sixth, the outstanding glory of the Christian faith, has undertaken to appoint as cardinal this very man, along with others whom he has plucked like choice flowers from all the world. Thus the counsel of their great wisdom will be available to him, the blessed pastor vigilant for the salvation of all, when he acts upon lofty affairs for the guidance of the world, the peace of the people, and the conduct of souls.

LETTER: It is the best testimony to the foresight of the great pontifex, as well as an immeasurable lightening of his labors, that he has collected the most accomplished men out of the whole society of mortals.[75] It was surely either a divine revelation or the Holy Spirit residing in the pope which dictated the choice of these men; for it is scarcely possible, they say, for mere human wisdom to have made a selection so prudent, satisfactory, useful, and right. Indeed, it is said that he drew off all the virtue and learning from the whole world. Oh, how fortunate and peaceful the Christian people would be, if so great a body of learned and serious men should always surround the Roman bishop with its light! What better name can I call the vicar of Christ, standing in that holy line of fathers, than an earthly sun among the stars?

If only the most clement pope would send the rays of his piety and wisdom to this unhappy and unquiet corner of Italy, so that its wretched peoples might at some time enjoy peace, a boon unknown to us! Although nearly all of Italy is wearied with the madness of war, that corner is feeling the most recent blast.[76] And if only, by divine agency, there could be fulfilled for the suffering west, in the person of Pope Urban himself, the promise of future peace and of freedom long fled, which the people foretell and with great longing envision in their dreams. Finally, under his protection the pitiful remainder of the shattered provinces and cities could draw a fresh breath. The time has come for you who care for the human race to allow the weeping peoples to obtain their request. The ravening greedy maw of war is devouring the Christian race like a piece of bread. Or perhaps,

nostre diviserunt° inter nos et Deum nostrum; et peccata nostra absconderunt faciem eius a nobis ne exaudiret." Verumtamen quoquo modo plectamur, mortales certe ad imum sunt. Hec hactenus spe mixta dolore.

Sed adhibe obsecro si qua restant opera viri. Nam avide sic haus narrata, sic splendida rerum series mulcet, ut nichil supra.

JOHANNES: Esset amodo tempus. Nec umquam sospitatore sic habuit opus Italia, vetus quondam imperatorum ac regum parens, unicum et eternum mundi caput, et sanctitate pastorum et illustratione doctrine. Quid agam de armorum arte industriaque, quibus ceteras tantum antecellit provincias "quantum lenta solent inter viburna cupressi," ut Maro ait, imo esse invincibilem armis Tullius prodidit. Anthioco adversum Romanos bella meditante, Hannibal, nominis Romani hostis acerrimus, Italiam absque Italicis copiis vinci posse negavit. Quid de soli fecunditate ac nobilitate sponte nascentium, arborum, frugum, metallorum, animalium? Quid de feracitate varietateque vitium, de moribus, de vite policia, de veneratione sacrorum, de comitate urbanitateque gentium. Dixerim pace carminis eius qui dum se iactaret amice, "Tenet," inquit, "septra parens Asie, qua nulla beatior ora est." Nuspiam certe oritur quod Hesperie negatum est, omni circumfluentia, omni celi salubritate ac temperamine, omni apricitate collium saltuumque, fluentorum commoditate, omni denique aminiculo vite dotate, ita ut videatur opera fuisse nature gaudentis, ut Plinius edit. Sic tamen innasci cunta propicius nature favor iussit, ut noxia quedam ac inimica reptilia ab hominum procul commerciis abesse vellet.

Utinam et opes scelerum semina, ut Naso ait, cum quibus pariter forte emigrassent cupiditas ipsa luxusque unde primorum virorum, quibus honestum virtusque magne opes erant, degeneravit indoles vivida, et abierunt probitas, fides, amor, pax, libertas, et dictorum

as Isaiah foretold: "Our iniquities have divided between us and our God, and our sins have hid his face from us that he should not hear."[77] Nevertheless, however we are punished, mortal men are certainly at the lowest point. Enough of this—hope is mingled with our suffering.

But please tell me if there are any additional accomplishments of Tommaso. For I have drunk your words so eagerly and found your splendid narrative so charming that nothing would please me more.

GIOVANNI: There just might be time. Not ever has Italy had such need of a savior, Italy once the mother of emperors and kings, the unique and eternal head of the world through the holiness of her pastors and the brilliance of her learning. Why need I mention her competence in the craft of weaponry, in which she towers over the other provinces "as cypresses oft do among the bending osiers," as Vergil says; even more, Cicero portrays her as invincible in arms. When Antiochus was planning war against the Romans, Hannibal, fiercest enemy of the Roman name, said that Italy could not be conquered without Italian troops.[78] What about the fertility of the soil and the excellence of things that are produced naturally—trees, crops, metals, animals? What about the productivity and variety of the vines? And the character and government of life, the veneration of what is sacred, the sophistication and urbanity of the people? I might say, with all due respect to the poem of the one who boasted to his mistress: "My father wields the sceptre over Asia, land than which none has more wealth." Certainly there is nowhere anything which has been denied to Hesperia, endowed with every advantage: a mild and healthful climate, sunny hills and groves, an abundant supply of flowing streams, in short, everything which sustains life; so that Italy seems to have been the handiwork of rejoicing nature, as Pliny writes.[79] And the favoring grace of nature arranged all things to be so created that harmful and dangerous reptiles are far removed from contact with human beings.

If only wealth too, the seed of crime, as Ovid says, were removed![80] For along with this came, as it happened, greed and love of luxury, which caused degeneration of the lively, natural quality of the first men, for whom honor and virtue were great wealth; probity disappeared, and trustworthiness, love, peace, freedom, and confidence

conventorumque constantia. Sed ex omni mundo divitie cumque divitiis
avaricia plurima, servitus, perfidia, bella, imperandi rapiendique libido, simultates, odia, invidie, huc velut in sentinam quandam conflux-
ere. Quamobrem dissipata omnia confusaque aliquando restrui posse
lugubris Italia desperat, cui denique, si quid superest spei, annixum
illud et annexum est Urbano Sexto, vero Christi vicario. Nempe consentaneum, ornata pastore Auxonio, Auxonicis quoque vallata cardini-
bus, principe urbium orbis Roma, quatenus Italicus papa, Italici
cardinales pro quiete gentium Latii quisque pro sua parte pervigilent.

En, quo miseriarum ventum! Sapientia, viribus, ingenio strenua gens,
quam olim metuebat honorabatque mundus, barbaros supplex ac be-
luinas ut ita dixerim gentes, pacisque nescias, concordie sequestros ac
feciales et rogent esse et faciant. Pro pudor Italice maiestatis, tot dudum triumphis insignis! O ingenua generatio degenerans, sine fronte,
sine mente, non pudet triumphatos ante populos genua demittere? Siccine plus intestina cupiditas quam debitus pudor valet? Non solum
ea viles demissione sed hactenus victis animos auges.

Quid putas dicturam intra sese barbariem cum tantis se quotidie
legationibus exorari fatigarique cernit? Nisi ridendo atque ludendo in-
opiam animi tui et item insaniam: "Agamus per morosa responsa, afficia-
mus ignominia, contractemus diu stultam et infelicem gentem. Bene
habent; digna luunt. Lacerantur dissidiis suis. Irrisione nostra tabes-
cant, saturemur opprobrio suo. Quid nos inquietant cum eos ipsos
nec requiramus nec egeamus? Feruntur sapere; desipiunt certe. Imo
nos sine literis, sine legibus, sine studiis, pacem libertatemque et habemus et servamus illesam, sua isti sapientia furunt. Verumne fortasse,
propter nimis multa scire, fieri quempiam insanum posse? Sed 'dimit-
tamus putrescere iumenta in stercore suo,' ut propheta ait, nec extin-
guamus, nutriamus potius, fomenta bellorum ne quando caput tollant."

in words and compacts. From all the world money and, with it, great greed, slavery, treachery, war, lust for dominating and plundering, feuds, hatred, and envy have flowed together here as into a cesspool. Therefore sad Italy despairs that all which has been dissipated and destroyed can ever be restored. If any hope at all remains, in the end it relies upon and is bound to Urban the Sixth, true vicar of Christ. Indeed, since Rome, the prince of the world's cities, is honored by an Italian shepherd and surrounded by Italian regions, it is fitting that an Italian pope and Italian cardinals keep watch over the peace of the races of Italy, each for his own area.[81]

See what a depth of misery has been reached! A race vigorous in its wisdom, power, and genius, once feared and honored by the world, is now a suppliant to barbarians, even, I might say, to bestial nations, unacquainted with peace, asks them to become intermediaries and ambassadors of concord, and makes them such. Oh, the disgrace to the majesty of Italy, once distinguished by so many triumphs! Oh, highborn generation now degenerate, without modesty, without thought, are you not ashamed to bow your knee before the peoples over whom you have triumphed? Is your national greed so much more powerful than the shame you ought to feel? Not only are you cheapened by this debasement, but you are encouraging boldness in those who until now were subdued.

What do you think uncivilized races will say among themselves when they perceive that daily they are being opportuned and wearied by so many embassies? Laughing and making fun of your spiritlessness and madness, what else will they say except: "Let us be unaccommodating in our responses to them, humiliate them, and drag out lengthily our dealings with them, stupid and unhappy race! It serves them right to suffer. They are being destroyed by their own dissensions. Let them be worn down by our mockery, let us sate ourselves with their shame! Why do they disturb us when we neither seek nor need them? They are reputed to be wise, but certainly they are fools. Indeed, we, without literature, laws, or intellectual pursuits, have peace and freedom and keep it unbroken, while they with their wisdom act like madmen. Is it true, perhaps, that because of knowing too much one can become mad? 'But let us permit the beasts to rot in their dung,' as the prophet says.[82] And let us not extinguish but rather feed the fuels of war lest at some time they may lift up their heads."

Cui non pingat talis et tam vera convitiatio rubore confusioneque frontem? Ah misere gentes Itale, barbaros arbitramini vestris accomodare fidem sermonibus, cum uno quoque vallo contentos intestinis discindi odiis intelligant? Illud forte Ciceronianum admoniti: "Qui suis rationibus inimicus est, quomodo alienis amicum fore speres?" Fallimini. Eque male vestris de moribus credunt quam bene vos eorundem levitatem debetis habere suspectam.

LITERA: Malorum est iners remedium fletus et lamenta. Que si levare clades possent, iam dudum tot continuatis populorum lacrimis questibusque vocata libertas afforet. Ceterum cum in manu Dei sint omnia humanoque idem generi amicissimus habeatur et sit, iniurius erit quicumque rerum eventus arguet. Quoniam ab optimo dispensatore nisi bona, a iustissimo nisi iusta, a sapientissimo nisi convenientissima necesse non permitti. Verumtamen oberrantem diu ac fluitantem dictionem reduc et da si quid habes ultra de Thoma.

JOHANNES: Habeo plane, ac numerosa quidem nec clara minus viri officia. Tametsi multa sed pro virtutis amplitudine pauca notaverim. Erunt autem omittenda multa, aut si omnia complectendi mens est, sicut hunc ipsum pro dignitate virtutis pingi coveniret, in sarcinam opus evadet, onerosam tibi et damnosam forte precipue viam grandem iture. Tuis tamen votis obsequar.°

Tenes ut arbitror que conclusa sunt. Namque paucula de Thome liberalitate narravimus, eius quoque constantiam patientiamque utcumque cucurrimus. Etiam non preterivimus tacite castitatem. Memoravimus, strictim licet, de profunditate scientie; sed nec de vite gravitate ac pietate pretermissum. Nec de iusticia quidem amplius esse dubium reor, cuius amore summo sepe discrimini ultro caput obiectavit.

Pretereo de sobrietate ac moderamento vivendi, cum didiceris ipsa in apparatione alimonie neminem minus intentum, escas neminem par-

Whose forehead would not be painted with the blush of embarrassment at such well-deserved insults? Oh, wretched races of Italy,
do you think the barbarians have any confidence in your words when
they know that although contained by one wall you are split apart
by internal hatreds? This saying of Cicero's is a warning: "How should
you expect one who is hostile to his own interest to be friendly to
another's?"[83] You are deceived. You ought to suspect their fickleness
as much as they mistrust your character.

LETTER: Weeping and wailing is a useless remedy for troubles! If dis-
aster could be relieved that way, we would already have freedom,
summoned by the long-continued tears and complaints of the people.
But once all things are in the hands of God, who is considered, and
is, the best friend of humankind, whoever finds fault with the final
outcome will be too unfair. For necessarily only good is allowed from
the best Giver, only justice from the most Just, only what is fitting
from the most Wise. Nevertheless, resume your meandering and drift-
ing discourse, and give, if you can, some further information about
Tommaso.

GIOVANNI: I surely can. His services are numerous and no less distinguished. Even if I were to recount many of them, they would be few
in proportion to the greatness of his virtue. However, much will have
to be omitted. Otherwise, if you desire everything to be included,
as a proper description of him in accordance with the high quality
of his virtue, this opus will become a burden, weighty, and perhaps
injurious to you, since the journey you are about to go on is a very
long one. Still, I shall comply with your request.

You remember of course what has been related. For we have mentioned a few instances of Tommaso's generosity and have also described
as best as possible his steadfastness and patience. We have touched
upon his chastity, and have spoken, although cursorily, of the depth
of his knowledge, not omitting the dignity and piety of his life. And
I think there is no longer any doubt about his justice, for the love
of which he often voluntarily thrust his head into a highly dangerous
situation.

I need not mention the sobriety and temperance of his mode of
life, since you have learned that no one was less interested in the prepa-

cius accepisse. In anno quadragenas bis terque sacro ieiunio celebrabat. Altero namque anno cum sancte memorie pape, Gregorii, conviva esset, cuntis vescentibus carne, ovo, ceterisque absolutorum dierum epulis, tam preciosis quam multifariis, solus illiusmodi cibi continentiam patriarcha servabat. Similansque nichil minus de apposito mandere, sodalem pia simulatione fallebat. Sed dum id papa circumspectus vel advertisset ipse vel alio indicante didicisset, mox confertum carnibus quem coram habebat ei discum apponi iubet. Nec alia verborum iussione monitus intellexit humilis Thomas voluntatem beati pastoris cui refragari nec iuste poterat nec debebat. Atque sic auctoritate apostolica lautiori prandio refectus abscessit. Certe si ad alimenta quibus corporalis infirmitas sustentatur meditationem flectas, integro reperies anno sanctum presulem ieiunare, de allato sic parce gustillat. At illam quidem vite austeritatem que obtutui hominum negata negandaque est, novit scrutans renes et cor Deus.

Palam illud, cum absolutum regule vinculis assumpta dignitas redderet, ita cuntos eius ordinis nodos observare curavit, ut mutavisse locum non gradum videretur. Mollius certe conventuali quivis e fratribus cella quam in palatio hic presul accumberet.

Fratres quoque ordinis sui, quamquam si meminisse velit eorum sevitatis in eum, male meritos, quidem sic vidit, tractavit, recepit, iuvit, collegit ut bonus pater vel pastor carum filium aut utilem gregem, sine his esse vel stare nesciens. Illius aula non patriarchalis eminentie sedes sed fratrum claustrum poterat eorum frequentatione censeri. Omnes illo cogitatus sui, cure omnes, vigilantia tota pendebat. Illic consulendo, iuvando, monendo, increpando, cumulata denique caritate visitando, totus semper erat. Quanta vero humilitate in cena pascali suorum pedes fratrum sacer patriarcha et venerandus antistes, ac humiliatione ipsa maior, lavabat, tergebat, osculabatur, quid attinet dicere?

ration of food or took nourishment more sparingly. Within a year he used to celebrate Lent two and three times with a holy fast. For in another year, as a dinner guest of Pope Gregory of sainted memory, when everyone was eating meat, eggs, and other delicacies of the days of absolution, as costly as they were varied, the patriarch alone abstained from that sort of food. Pretending, however, to eat something from what he was served, he tried to deceive his companion with this pious trick. But when the observant pope either noticed the fact himself or discovered it from someone else, he then ordered a plate which he had before him to be filled with meats and to be served to Tommaso. Though not chided in words, the humble Tommaso acknowledged the will of the blessed pastor, whom he could not, and should not, justly oppose. And so through apostolic authority he departed refreshed by an elegant repast. Certainly, if you think about the food by which his frail body is sustained, you will find that throughout the whole year the holy bishop fasts, so sparingly does he taste of what is served. At least God, who looks into the kidneys and heart,[84] is aware of that austerity of life which is kept, as it should be, from the eyes of men.

When the high position which he attained made him free of the restrictions of the Rule, it was publicly known that he took care so to observe all the restraints of his order that he seemed to have changed only his location and not his status. Certainly any one of the friars could sleep more luxuriously in his convent cell than this bishop in his palace.

As for the friars of his order, although deserving ill of him if he should care to remember their cruelty toward him, he regarded, handled, received, helped, and gathered them just as a good father or pastor would a beloved son or valuable flock, unable to be or to exist without them. His court could be considered not a site of patriarchal eminence, but a cloister of friars, because so many of them thronged there. On him rested all plans for his dependents, all the responsibilities, all the care. There he was wholly devoted to counseling, helping, advising, chiding, visiting with his abundant love. Need I indeed even mention with what great humility at the Easter feast the saintly patriarch and venerable priest, the greater because of his very humbleness, washed, dried, and kissed the feet of the brothers.

Denique vero quam obtemperans sacrosanctis ecclesie mandatis, quam fructifer mundo fuerit, presenti quidem oratione dici opus non est. Predicationem eius papa iubente adversum ecclesie contumaces ubique gentium opido accepisti vulgatam. In qua nimirum disciplina, de predicandi loquor, nullus ornatior, fervidior nullus, plenior nullus, planior nullus, neque verior, neque demum utilior; ut illi non iniuria quod de Luca Ieronymus attestatur dici possit: "Erant verba eius languentis anime medicina." Nam divinus quidam in verbis lepos gravitasque facundie, nectareum nescioquid, ipse dum loqueretur audientium mentibus instillabat, quo certe in amorem simul stuporemque raperentur, adeo ut dicendi finem quisque metueret nec ullus umquam audiendi satur abscederet.

Rursum mandata Romani pontificis ad regem Hunnorum perferre iussus, quanto regie maiestatis honore susceptus sit, letus ac dexter impetrationis effectus explicuit, dum completam requisitionem beatissimi pape retulit, regio favore honestatus et munere.

Age, quid memorem pacem tali mediatore partam Etruscis, dum Florentina Pisanaque civitas alternis cunta odiis laniarent? Seditionem vero civilemque Ianuensium discordiam eiusdem virtus media consopivit. Recens historia est quo labore quove senectutis sue discrimine Venetos Euganeosque furores medius extinxerit. Quod cuius rei premium reportarit sine alterutrius iniuria dici nequit. Sed grande sat bene gestarum rerum ipsa sibi virtutis consciencia premium est, cum sapientis omnino sit fructum virtutis in consciencia constituere, ut Macrobius ait.

In qua re accipe indolem claram firmitudinis animi, ut indeiectam sinistris ita secundis immobilem. Nam referente illo Venetias ab Euganeo principe compositionem fedusque pacis contractum iam et solidatum, nemo commeantium tanti operis successum in fronte deprendit,° nemo vel minimam iocundiore verborum prolatione suspicionem collegit. Sed unus in sacro ipse pectore expectationem gaudiumve populorum et gloriam suam clausam tacitamque reservabat,

Finally, I need not in our present discussion speak of his obedience to the sacred commands of the Church, his productiveness for the world. You have surely heard that his preaching, at the pope's command, against those who defied the Church was talked about everywhere in the world. In this discipline, that is, of preaching, no one is more elegant nor more fervid, no one is broader in scope, clearer, sounder, or more helpful. Hence Jerome's observation about Luke can justly be applied to him: "His words were medicine for a sick soul."[85] The divine charm in his words and his majestic eloquence distilled a kind of nectar into the minds of his hearers whenever he spoke, which swept them away into love and amazement at the same time. Each person dreaded the end of his speaking, and no one ever left sated with listening.

Again, after he was ordered to deliver the mandates of the Roman pontifex to the king of the Huns,[86] the happily successful outcome of his embassy showed the great honor with which he had been received by the royal majesty, when, enriched by royal favor and gifts, he returned to the most blessed pope with his mission accomplished.

Do I need to mention the peace which he obtained as mediator for the Tuscans when the cities of Florence and Pisa were ripping everything to shreds by their mutual hatred?[87] Indeed, the sedition and civil discord of the Genoese were also allayed by virtue of his intervention. It is recent history that, with effort and danger, in his old age he as mediator extinguished the madness of the Venetians and Paduans. What he received as a reward for this service cannot be told without disparagement to each of them. But the consciousness of virtue is in itself a sufficiently great reward for deeds well done, since, as Macrobius says, it is entirely in the character of a wise man to find the profit of virtue in the consciousness of it.[88]

In this regard, hear now about the outstanding quality of his strength of mind, which remains undiscouraged in adversity as it is imperturbable in good fortune. For when he brought back to Venice from the Paduan prince a settlement and peace treaty already agreed upon and ratified, not one of his fellow travelers detected in his face the success of that great accomplishment, not one received even the slightest hint from his rather jocular utterances. He alone kept back in his saintly heart the expectation and joy of the people and his own glory, held

nescio cur non preferendus Metello, quem, revocantes ab exilio tabellas perlegentem, nemo considentium hilariorem factum valuit advertere. Sed privatam ille leticiam, iste gentium ac propriam claudere potuit.

Omnino autem simile annectam quod ab aliis didici, pertinet enim ad integram viri veramque fortitudinem. Porro dum Ionio Mari patriarchalem ad sedem properaret, contra Neptunnus, ne quis virtutis eius index locus non esset, aciem ac impetum movit. Namque sub noctem omnia repente conturbari ac fremere celo marique cepere. Tum ab Eolio dimissi claustro pugnare inter sese venti, Circius in Eurum, in Chorum "madidis Nothus evolat alis," ut ait poeta, in Austrum Aquilo, in Africum Boreas. Magna vi pontus in aquarum montes attollitur, furentibus procellis ac impetentibus navigantes ipsos. Mugit omne celum, nymbis horridum minaxque fulminibus et opaca sevem caligine et imbribus infestum. Insidiantes inde scopulis, illinc oppugnaces, unde territant "presentemque viris intentant omnia mortem," ut Maro ait. Sed nec spes attingendi° litoris adest. Inde confragosum litus, vetant inde Tirrhene cautes.

Tanto igitur rerum turbore consternatus ipse arcis puppisque rector mentis ratisve moderamen amisit. Ita rapacium fluctuum ac flatuum circumvolitantium arbitrio, ceca nocte raptantur. Ergo amentes dissolutosque metu cuntos cerneres, tam mehercule prestolantes iam iam° venturam mortem quam metuentes. Cumque lacrimis alii indulgerent, hi lamentis, votis illi supplicibus accirent deos precarenturque. Nonnulli ceca ope, sed qua poterant, fluctibus certatim obsisterent; pars remos obicere, antennas obvertere, firmare rudentes vel amplustre moderari, omnibus vicissim pro salute solicitis, pertentarent. Plures quoque metu ac periculi magnitudine dissolverentur, plures enim navis illa vectabat, et patris illius comites et vernas.

Solus ipse inconcussus, integer, inperterritusque° manebat. Putavisses hactenus naufragantem Paulum videre, immotum, inqueru-

close and hidden. I do not know why he is not more to be esteemed than Metellus, who, upon reading the letter which recalled him from exile, did not appear happier before any of his companions: one was able to conceal a personal joy, but the other a joy both his own and the nation's.[89]

Furthermore, I can add a similar story which I heard from others, which pertains to the complete and genuine courage of the man. When he was hastening to the patriarchal see on the Ionian Sea, Neptune threw the force of his battle-lines against him, so that there might be no place which would fail to reveal his strong character. For at nightfall there suddenly came a roaring turbulence of all the sky and sea. Released from the barriers of Aeolus the winds fight among themselves. Circius flies against Eurus, "Nothus with wet wings flies," as the poet says, against Corus, Aquilo against Auster, and Boreas against Africus. Violently the sea is lifted into mountains of water, and the raging blasts attack the sailors themselves. The whole sky roars, bristling with storm clouds and menacing thunderbolts, ferocious with black mists and turbulent with rain. Reefs lie hidden on one side, on another they jut out terrifyingly, and "All forebodes the sailors instant death," as Vergil says.[90] But there is no hope of reaching land: here the broken shoreline, there the Tyrrhenian cliffs forbid.

Then, thrown into confusion by the great tumult, the helmsman at the stern of the ship himself has lost control of both his mind and his craft. So at the whim of the rapacious waves and swooping winds they are swept along in the blind night. You could see them all mindless and paralyzed by fear, as much expecting, by Hercules, as fearing that death would come at any moment. Some gave way to tears, and some called on the gods and prayed to them with lamentations, others with prayers of supplication. Still others resisted the waves with blind strength as best they could; some strove to thrust the oars against the waters, to turn the sails, to tighten the ropes and regulate the stern-post, each concerned for the safety of everyone else. Many too were paralyzed by fear and by the magnitude of the danger, for that ship was carrying a great number of people, companions and house servants of the father.

He alone remained unshaken, strong, fearless. You would have thought at this point that you were seeing Paul being shipwrecked,

lum, indeiectum animo. Nempe sentiebat eam boni animi esse naturam conditionemque, corporeis ut vinculis et carneo solutus carcere primum illum sempiternum rectorem motoremque ac summi boni verum et unicum fontem indefessa mox celeritate deposcat, unde tam illi vigor est quam origo. Nec posse rem tam levem et citam quam anima est fluctibus subrui, partem vero terrenam ubicumque fata vocarent ultro iocundeve rependendam a possessore fido presertim. Interesse nil quoque quanam° terrarum parte quove mortis genere emigrent electi, quibus evangelica veritas firmat: "Ne capillus quidem capitis vestri peribit."

Haud facile monstravero quid metui magis debeat ne pisces cadavera minime sensurorum quam vermes exedant. Tirannus mortem et insepultam minabatur Theodoro. "O te," inquit, "ineptum si mea putas interesse supra terram an infra putrescam." "Apponite bacillum dextrorsum istic quo ferarum morsus abigam," amicis Diogenes ait cum dilaniandum se vorandumque volucribus ac feris dimitti iussisset. "Sed nichil," aiunt, "persentisces." "Quid igitur mea?" respondit. Atque sic amicorum enervem femineamque sententiam illusit, in ipsos imo retorsit.

Qui vero sese vel peccatis deprimi teste conscientia deprendunt, que reprensibilis timidum reddit animum, ut ait Seneca, vel unum hominis bonum commercio corporis esse constituunt, non subter fluctibus detineri modo verum etiam interiore inferno recipi timent. Nec aliunde mortis formidinem causari hominibus extimo nisi quod vel nesciunt ipsi quonam profecturi sunt exituri, quoniam pavoris ignorantia nutrix est, vel quod delictorum conscientia penis proscribit eternis. Porro qui virtutibus armantur ac meritis, seu iuxta Virgilianum illud, "qui sui memores alios fecere merendo," ita ut in hominum celebratione deorumve cultu ac religione constiterint, qui fieri potest ut metuenda his magnopere mors luctuosaque sit? Sic apostolus dissolui et esse cupiebat cum Christo, asserebat item mori sibi lucrum esse. Sic Andreas

unmoved, uncomplaining, undiscouraged.[91] To be sure, he felt that
as soon as a good mind is loosed from the bonds of the body and
the prison of the flesh, because of its nature and character it at once
with tireless alacrity seeks out the eternal Helmsman and Mover, the
true and unique fount of the highest good, which is not only its origin but the source of its energy. And he knew that so light and swift
a thing as the soul cannot be destroyed by waves, but that the body's
earthly part, wherever the fates have summoned, must voluntarily and
cheerfully be paid back, especially from a loyal owner. Also it does
not matter in what part of the earth or with what kind of death the
elect depart, for whom the Gospel truth affirms: "But a hair of your
head shall not perish."[92]

I cannot easily explain why it should be more frightening for fish
instead of worms to eat the corpses of those who do not feel anything. A tyrant threatened Theodorus with death and denial of buri-
al. "How foolish you are," Theodorus replied, "if you think I care
whether I rot above the earth or below it." "Place beside me a stick
there on the right, which I can use to ward off the attacks of wild
beasts," said Diogenes to his friends, after commanding that his body
be given to birds and beasts to be torn to pieces and devoured. "But,"
they said, "you will be without consciousness!" "What then will it matter
to me?" he replied; and he ridiculed the weak and womanish senti-
ment of his friends, in fact even turned it back on them.[93]

But men who either find their sins weighing upon them, being
charged by their conscience (which, as Seneca says, makes the mind
of the guilty fearful),[94] or who believe that a man's one good is the
possession of his body, fear not only to be kept under the waters but
also to be received in the depths of Hell. And this I think is the very
reason why men complain of the fear of death—namely, that they
themselves do not know where they will go when they die, since ignorance nourishes fear; or else it is that the consciousness of their sins
condemns them to eternal punishment. On the other hand, those who
are armed by virtues and merits, or, according to Vergil, "they who
by service have won remembrance among men," and have settled in
a gathering of men in worship and adoration of the gods—for such,
how can death be very fearsome or distressing? Therefore the Apostle desired to be set free and to be with Christ, affirming that to die

expediri tantopere mole corporea perorabat. Sic beatissimus quoque Gregorius huius erumnifere vite novissimam agi suspirat ad metam. Nam egregie mulieri atque patricie Rusticane, "Ego autem in tanto," inquit, "gemitu et occupationibus vivo ut ad dies quos ago me pervenisse penitet solaque michi in consolatione sit mortis expectatio. Unde peto ut pro me orare debeatis quatenus de hoc carnis carcere citius educar." At si unquam odiosa presens vita gravisque fuit et expectatio future iocunda, huius plane temporis nostri obsitam miseria, sceleribus, imo quotidianis obrutam mortibus, rumpi finirique indesinenti voce orare optareque debemus.

Huiusmodi autem meditatione sacer extimo patriarcha, mors licet ante oculos esset, omnem e sinu terrorem excussit. Quos sic iactatos ubi portu petito (ita Deo placitum) sicca desiderataque accepit harena, cuntis illicet primevus pater, urbanitate dicendi qua ne quidem alius curiosior maturiorque fuit, vel increpitare vel surridere metum et tantam animi deiectionem occipit. Et erant qui divine Scripture et haberentur eruditi et essent magistri. "Siccine," inquit, "imbellem animum a theologia vendicatis ut debellari inani re levique valeat? Sed quid levius vento, quid timore mortis inanius? Itane parum literis constat mortem ipsam non magnum malum vel non parvum bonum esse, imo quidem muneris loco prebitam ne hominis esset in penam peccati culpa ruentis sempiterna miseria? Quam Plinius quoque si neque Cicero satis neque Seneca inter prima nature beneficia et scribit plene et probat acutissime. Num infructuose adeo impureque dies egistis, aut votorum hic tam compotes omnium et mortalium expertes angustiarum degitis, novissimam ut vocationem sic muliebriter formidetis vel trepide infirmeque vite continuos esse hospites gaudeatis? Unde sapiens quisque vel non metuit vel optat eici."

LITERA: Pape, quam magna viri fortitudo! Quidni delirantium contentionem° subsannationemque contempsit, qui celi fragorem, pelagi bel-

was for him a benefit; Andreas begged earnestly to be released from the burden of his body;[95] and the most blessed Gregory also longed to be brought to the end of this trouble-filled life. For to the distinguished patrician woman Rusticana he said: "I live amid such great distress and worry that I regret having reached the days of my present existence. My only consolation is the expectation of death. Therefore I ask you to pray for me that I be led more swiftly out of this prison of the flesh."[96] If ever our present life has been odious and burdensome and the expectation of a future life pleasing, clearly we ought to beg and pray with unceasing voice that our existence be broken off and ended, beset as it is with the misery of this our time, with crimes, indeed inundated daily with deaths.

It was by this sort of reflection, I believe, that the holy patriarch, even with death before his eyes, shook from his heart all terror. When the harbor was reached (for so it pleased God) and the longed-for dry sand received the storm-tossed travelers, at once the youthful father, using that smooth manner of speaking in which he showed an unequaled meticulousness and maturity, began to chide them all and to smile at their fear and mental depression. There were some who were considered learned in Divine Scripture and who were teachers. "Do you," he said to them, "acquire so feeble a mind from theology that it can be defeated by a vain and light matter? What is lighter than the wind, what is vainer than the fear of death? Do your studies fail to teach you that death itself is not a great evil, nor even a small boon, but on the contrary is offered as a gift so that a man incurring punishment because of his sin may not suffer eternal misery? If neither Cicero nor Seneca is sufficient, Pliny too writes extensively and proves most acutely that death is among the primary benefits of nature.[97] Surely you haven't passed your days so uselessly and sinfully, or lived here so fully-possessed of all desires and free of mortal troubles that, woman-like, you dread the last summons or enjoy being constant guests of a weak and fearful life! No wise man is either afraid or reluctant to be cast forth from it."

LETTER: Oh, what great courage! Naturally he scorned the wrangling and sneers of madmen, being the kind of man who, invincible, could behold with wide-open eyes the uproar of the heavens, the battles

la furentis, oppugnacem vim flatuum, qui imo ipsius mortis imminentiam oculis tam apertis intueri potuerit invictus!

JOHANNES: Magna profecto et sapientie et virtutis plenitudo, cunta si quis digerere valeat. Verum ne angustia temporis calami cursum infesta irritatione detineat (hora est quo iam dimitti queas), quod superest enodemus. Memini abs te obiectam fore coniugem michi, que beneficiorum capescendorum facultatem et spem adimat. Inficiari non possum iterum me maritum, quod quidem iugum absque singultibus nec fero nec recolo, sepius hoc ipsum cum ceteris quibus aggravor peccatis meis tam magnis quam multis ingemiscens. Quantis vero suspiriis hactenus luerim testis est Deus, testes omnes dictatus mei, testes amici, presens testis oratio. Et quamquam non usquequaque ubi habenda talis erat sarcina infauste cesserit, mecum stomacor tamen perditam libertatem, adauctas curas, irruptum otium quod unum pro literis apprendendis omni accessione carius habebam.

LITERA: Sine iniuria lamentatur nemo condicionem quam ultro sciensque subivit. Cur libuit non ignaro tibi incommodi coniugalis? Quasi illa Micionis sententia excidisset: "Quod fortunatum," inquit, "isti putant, uxorem numquam duxi." Satis admonitionis satisve cautionis adhibuisse primus himen debuit, vel si tua te mala minus erudire aliorum saltem ruina potuit. Sensit Iob in illa immodica tentatione infestam uxorem, in cecitate Thobias. Quid Micol, quid Besabee, quarum irrisit altera virum, fuit altera necis occasio? Ioram filium Iosaphath regem Iuda prevaricatorem legis factum esse ab uxore didicisti. Numeraretur in sanctis electis Salomon nisi° dum obsecundare contendit uxoribus conditorem offendisset. Precursoris sacratissimum caput sceleri coniugis donavit Herodes. Tullia Servii regis nata summa virum Aruntem perfidia necavit, Candualem Lidie regem uxor, Deianira Alcidem, Agamemnonem Clitemestra, Sansonem Dalida. Amphiaraum Eriphile

of the raging sea, the smashing force of the winds, and even the im-
minence of death itself!

GIOVANNI: Great indeed is the scope of both his wisdom and his virtue, if one could enumerate all the manifestations of them. But lest
shortness of time, with annoying frustration, check the course of my
pen (it will soon be time for you to be sent off), let me answer the
remaining points. I remember that you cast my wife up to me, claiming that she would destroy my opportunity and hope of receiving benefits. I cannot deny that I am married again, a yoke which I have
resumed and am bearing not without sorrow, often regretting it along
with the other sins which weigh me down, as great as they are many!
With what anguished sighs I have atoned for this one, God is my
witness—all my writings, my friends, my present discourse are witnesses. And although it has not proved entirely unfortunate for me
to have assumed such a burden, still I resent my lost freedom, my
increased responsibilities, and the interrupted leisure which alone I
held dearer than every other aid for my literary studies.

LETTER: No one has a right to complain about a situation which he
has entered into voluntarily and consciously! Why were you willing,
since you were not ignorant of marital disadvantages? That sentence
of Micio's must have gone out of your mind: "A thing which men
consider fortunate," he said, "is that I have never taken a wife." Your
first marriage ought to have given adequate forewarning; or if your
own misfortune couldn't instruct you, at least the downfall of other
men should have![98] Job suffered a wife's hostility in his sore trial, Tobias likewise in his blindness. What about Michal, what about Bathshe-
ba, one of whom mocked her husband and the other proved a cause
of death?[99] You know that Joram, king of Judah, son of Jehosaphat,
was made a perverter of the law by his wife. Solomon would be count-
ed among the holy elect if he had not offended his Maker by striving
to please his wives. Herod offered up the most holy head of John,
the forerunner of Christ, to the wickedness of his wife.[100] Tullia,
daughter of King Servius, through extreme treachery killed her husband Aruns. Candaules, king of Lydia, was killed by his wife, Hercules was killed by Deianira, Agamemnon by Clytemnestra, Samson
by Delilah. Eriphyla betrayed and destroyed Amphiaraus. If I should

prodidit perdiditque. Quas omnes si tangere calamo pergerem, que
ruine calamitatisque virorum occasio fuerunt, quemadmodum Cen-
sonia Caligule, Agripina Claudii, Aridei regis Euridice, quisnam ex-
arationis modus fiet?

Sed quid exempla vertimus cum hoc ipsum quotidie genus luat humanum? Imitari saltem bruta debuisti que, ut Cassiodorus ait, "itinera
illa non repetunt ubi in foveam concurrerunt." Et "semel piscis fallaci
lesus ab hamo omnibus unca cibis era subesse putat," tradit Naso. Tu
si hebetior quadrupedibus ineptiorque esse maluisti, quid ingemiscis?
Quid latras? Tu te precipitasti, sauciasti proprio telo. Ne queraris ergo
vulnus tuum vel communi cum sorte° tacitus perfer. "Nostrum enim
et nostra causa susceptum dolorem modice ferre debemus," ut Cicero
sonat. Debuisti apostolicam sequi doctrinam: "Solutus es, noli querere uxorem. Vel nunc saltem alligatus es uxori, noli querere
solutionem."

JOHANNES: Vera inquam nimium resonas. Sed que ipse commemorem
fuisse item vetustis illis patribus Abraam et Ysaac coniuges periculo,
fuisse Romanis quo tempore clxx veneficii dannate sunt. Verum ur-
banam hanc redargutionem tuam tum cum erat profectura° maluis-
sem! Impresentiarum quando morbus in statu° est, non amaris verbis
sed salvificis herbis opus habeo. Haud solide primis ita facibus cesse-
rat ut non statutum firmatumque foret degere vitam ab huiusmodi
iugo perpetuam. Cum sit indomitum animal et unice noxium homini
femina, doli capax, erudiri nescia, impatiens impetus proprii, que ubi
regnaverit vix adire virtuti licet. Tantum illi morborum animi, tantum insolide insolentisque meditationis nature imbecillitas addit. Testor
in oculis omnia cognoscentis Dei hanc michi non voluptas aut voluntas connexuit. Si dixerim "necessitas" an mentiar ignoro, nisi ut aiunt
sequatur thalamus fata sua. Cum id potissimum videamus unam ut
mille procis petitam solicitatamve divisim ac improviso adventans pene
invitus alius quispiam occupet. Quasi non in catholicum sit Senece

proceed to write down all those who caused ruin and calamity to their husbands, as Caesonia to Caligula, Agrippina to Claudius, Erydice to King Arideus, what end would there be to the list?[101]

But why cite ancient examples when the human race faces this type of suffering every day? You should have at least imitated the brute animals, which, as Cassiodorus says, "do not retrace the paths where they fell into a pit." And "a fish once injured by the deceptive hook thinks there are bronze barbs in all bait," as Ovid relates. If it suited you to be more dull-witted and foolish than animals, why do you groan, why do you complain? You took the leap, you wounded yourself with your own weapon. Therefore do not protest at your wound, but endure it silently as a fate that is common to all. "For our own grief, and grief felt on our account, we ought to bear in a spirit of moderation," as Cicero proclaims. You should have followed the Apostle's teaching: "You have been set free. Seek not a wife." Or now at any rate, "Thou art bound to a wife. Seek not to be loosed."[102]

GIOVANNI: What you say is all too true. And I myself could mention that also for those ancient fathers, Abraham and Isaac, their wives were a danger, and for the Romans, when one hundred and seventy women were condemned for poisoning.[103] However, I would have preferred your witty criticisms at a time when they could have done some good! Now, when the disease is established, I need not bitter words but healing herbs. My first marriage was so inconclusive that it did not result in a firm determination for me to pass my whole life free from this yoke. Since a woman is an untamed animal and singularly harmful to man, capable of trickery, impossible to train, unable to control her own impulses, virtue is unlikely to approach where she holds sway. The frailty of her nature gives her so many diseases of the mind, so many unsound and unrestrained ideas! I testify before the eyes of God, who knows all things, that neither my desire nor my will united this woman to me. If I should say it was fate, I do not know whether this would be untrue—unless, as they say, marriage follows its own destiny.[104] We see this particularly when a woman being courted and wooed by a thousand suitors is captivated by some other man who comes separately and unexpectedly, almost against his will. Seneca surely states a general principle

dictum: "Agimur fatis, credite fatis." Quicquid facimus mortale genus, quicquid patimur venit ex alto. "Non solicite possunt cure mutare rati stamina fusi," primusque dies dedit extremum. Et cetera que haud disparia subicit.

Et non potius illud affirmandum dispensari lege divina vicem hanc quoque pro congruentia cuiusque mortalium. Et obvenire bono infestam plerumque vel pessimo bonam quatenus hinc ille quodam quasi tortore exerceatur° mundeturque, altera ut viri veneno temperamentum ac moderamen existat. Permitti vero interdum improbis vitiosam et impiam, digno tacito licet Dei iudicio, quatenus° duabus veluti simul concertantibus beluis, alteram altera oppugnet infestetque semper. At iustis prudentem integramque, Salamonica auctoritate, in meritum ab Omnipotente elargiri putandum.

Verumtamen sive digerens cunta Deus sive quodvis astrum, seu casus aut meum potius crimen ita mulctandum mole me vinxerit, reluctanti certe animo vinxit. Qui cuntas hactenus huiusce rei et titillationes blandimentaque sensus et suasus forinsecus adventantes eminus reppuli, fortassis quoque haud inferioris fortune comitem° sortiri cum possem. Sed tam mediusfidius hec ipsa copulatio, quam in has crepidines accessus improvisus, ingratus, ac prope coactus fuit. Memoriter ipsa cognoscis quam invitus a Coneclano discessi ubi tranquille, sobrie, inter bonos amicosque viros degebam, quam fideliter huic patri famulaturus accessi Venetias. Unde quam turpiter detrusus, quam miserabiliter° alienatus, ne dicam ingratissime pulsus ac ne meo quidem modico detrimento. Qui labores meos per diversoria vagus expendi, quid attinet replicare? Cuius indignitatem rei mecum dolitura sepius agitasti. Tenes quoque ut desperatus inconsultusve dolor his me terris ascripsit, ubi quo ingenio, quibus laqueis, quibus denique artibus sim delapsus in nuptias admonere necessarium non est. Notum per se est, predicatum est, dictatum est, scriptum plenius atque uberius est, in eo quidem loco ubi de coniugii commodis atque incommodis agere constituimus.

in his observation: "By fate are we driven; yield ye to fate." Whatever we mortals do, whatever we experience, comes from on high. "No anxious cares can change the threads of its inevitable spindle,"[105] and the first day has given the last. He also adds other similar statements.

And one should not assert that divine law deals out destinies in proportion to their suitability to mortals. A bad destiny often overtakes a good man, or a good one a wicked man, in order that by this means the former may be disciplined and purified by a tormenter, so to speak, and the poison of the latter may be tempered and moderated. Indeed sometimes a depraved and wicked role is permitted to evil men, through a proper, though concealed, decision of God, so that, like two wild beasts fighting, one constantly attacks and harasses the other. But for the just, we should believe, with Solomon, that a wise and good fate is granted by the Omnipotent for merit.[106]

Nevertheless, whether it was God, who directs all things, or some star, or chance, or punishment for my sins, which fettered me with this burden, assuredly it was done against my spirit's protests! Before that I kept at arm's length all the stimulations of this condition and its sensual enticements, as well as the advice coming from outside. Perhaps I was caught by the opportunity to acquire a companion of a not inconsiderable fortune. But so help me God, not only this union itself but also my arrival at this pass was sudden, disagreeable, and almost forced. You yourself know well how unwillingly I left Conegliano, where I was living peacefully, soberly, among good friends, and how conscientiously I went to Venice to serve this father.[107] And how basely I was expelled from there, how miserably alienated, not to mention most ungratefully driven off and with no slight pecuniary loss to myself! Why repeat the hardships I suffered roaming from inn to inn? You have quite often discussed the indignity of these circumstances, in commiseration with me. You remember also how my despairing and injudicious grief assigned me to these lands where (I do not have to remind you) as a result of cleverness, well-laid snares, and craftiness I fell prey to marriage. That fact is known through itself; it is public knowledge, it has been spoken and written of quite fully and copiously in the place where we agreed to discuss the advantages and disadvantages of marriage.[108]

LITERA: Nescio cuinam ea ipsa materia proprie magis aut plenius exaranda sit atque tibi iam bis id ipsum experto!

JOHANNES: Ideo id sumus orsi, nota via currimus. Artem ab infantia perceptam fato stringente versamus, quoniam probabilissimum uniuscuiusque de notissimis iudicium est. Sed licet agnoscas quod illud unum iterum me traxit in rete, quia primas idcirco tedas° minus acceptas arbitrabar quod infirmis annis et quid lex maritalis exigeret ignaris, quo item moderamine quibusve frenis coartari regique femineus possit aut debeat animus, incidissent. Infestationem vero tantam iuventuti mee non sexui ascribebam. At experto assenti omnes feminas feminas esse, omnes uno morbo laborare. Quemadmodum vulgatum illud habet, fore pili unius lupos omnes, sic eiusdem fore° mulieres omnes, eque omnes deliras, nisi pudor alias, metus has cohiberet.

Verumtamen iudice Christo, quem huiusmodi occasione crebro peccator ego lacrimabundus oravi, ipsa scis habere me non voluptatis loco seu complende libidinis coniugem, uti plerique faciunt quorum vita nescio quid a pecudum distet; sed in fragilis potius vite commodum laborumve iugium opem. Quemadmodum salubrior Christicolarum norma docet, cum recens apostoli instrepat auribus michi sententia: "Qui in carne vivunt, Deo placere non possunt." Sed in carne servit uxorem quisquis non ut comitem amat. Quin miror magis cur non ipso desiderio virgo sim ego. Agnoscis ipsa tacitum mentis mee et votum et habitum. Taceo quam religiose, quam munde matrimonii iura colo, quam immaculate ac sobrie thalamum servo, eque illam dilecturus absentem quam ea me patienter pieque ferret abesse. Tu nichilominus mordaciter adeo matrimonii vinculum obiectasti, quod esset impedimento ad beneficium capessendum. Siquidem me dominus meus et pater ille ad beneficium nequit accersere, saltem ad officium potest.

LITERA: Ad quod aut quale? Virium tuarum oblitusne es? Alis implumibus evolare moliris? Quenam tibi prudentia callidissimos ut intus

LETTER: I do not know anyone who can handle this material more fittingly and fully than you, since you have had the experience twice!

GIOVANNI: That is the reason I have undertaken the task, since I am traveling a familiar road. I am discussing a skill I have known under pressure of fate from childhood, since every person is most credible when he assesses matters he knows well. But you must realize that what alone drew me again into the net is the fact that I believed my first marriage unpleasant because it occurred in my tender years, when I was ignorant of what the marital law required and also did not know the restraints and reins by which the female mind can and must be controlled and guided. In fact, I ascribed my great troubles to my youth and not to the feminine sex. But now that I am experienced, agree with me that all women are women and all suffer from one disease. As the common saying has it, all wolves are of the same pelt, and so are all women; and equally they all would be deranged if shame did not restrain some and fear others!

Nevertheless, with Christ as my judge, to whom I, a sinner, have often tearfully prayed on such an occasion, you yourself know that I do not keep a wife as a source of pleasure or to gratify my lust, as do many whose lives differ little from those of animals; but rather as a comfort to a fragile life and a help in constant hardships. Thus the wholesome rule of Christians prescribes, when the Apostle's saying sounds anew in my ears: "They who are in the flesh cannot please God."[109] Whoever does not love his wife as a companion serves in the flesh. Indeed, I wonder more why I am not a virgin, from my own preference. You know yourself the hidden wish and habit of my mind. I need not mention how religiously, how purely, I cherish the laws of matrimony, how immaculately and soberly I preserve the marriage chamber, expecting to love her when she is absent, just as she would endure my absence patiently and dutifully. You, however, have sharply reproached me for my matrimonial bond, on the grounds that it has prevented me from receiving a benefice. If indeed my lord and father cannot summon me to a benefice, at least he can to an appointment.

LETTER: To which one, or what sort? Have you failed to consider your capabilities? Are you struggling to fly on featherless wings? What kind

constare scias? Ut Flaccus ait: "Non isto vivitur illic quo tu rere modo;" sed labore multo, sed cautela magna, sed vigilantia integra, patientia dura opus est, nam oculatos cordatosque exigit curia. Cuius si vocabulum recolis ortum a cura, intelliges tuis nimium otiis fugiendam. Denique tua contumacia huiusmodi loco apta non est, nec homini libero atque in labiis argumenta ferenti frequentanda sunt solia, presertim hoc tempore. Non perpendis a quibus quibusve studiis regnatur in aula, ubi ferme pium est impietatem monere, ubi "prosperum ac felix scelus virtus vocatur," ut ait Seneca. Nempe adulari, mentiri, calumpniari, dependari plerisque regnantium° domesticis prima sunt ornamenta, cuius doctrine numquam fuisti discipulus.

Quin sic natura liber es ut rerum quamvis a facto° quidem tuo alienarum indignitate stomacheris, et loquaris interdum licet iuste, mordaciter nimium. Quotiens inde° scis bella tibi cum improbis extitere, quotiens adversum te invidia succensa, quotiens emolumenta subducta. Haud semel audisti. Increpas libere nimis, homo! An tu unus sufficis arma pro virtute capessere? Verum enimvero Terentianum illud constat: "Veritas odium parit." Minime sapis magnatum limina quo sint argumento calcanda, immemor Lucani docentis: "Exeat aula qui vult esse pius." Cum Satiro nescis alienum induere vultum, quemadmodum Terentianus ille ganneo: "Aiunt, aio; negant, nego. Persuasi michimet assentari omnia." Rursum tam fraudare quam fraudari doles. Honorandi, preterea, frequentandi, colendi multi, quorum mores ut aiunt pistrilla digni sunt. Numquam adolescentia usque adeo labasti, quin semper arbitrareris indignum immeritis inclinari. Has siquidem igitur artes vel doceri vel perpeti vales, nichil° te moror, perge.

of wisdom do you need in order to know that the most clever men
are in residence there? As Horace says: "Life is not lived there in the
way you suppose."[110] Much effort is required, great caution, unbroken vigilance, and endless patience; for the papal court demands
men with keen eyes and intelligence. If you recall the derivation of
the word *curia* ("court") from *cura* ("worry"), you will realize that it
ought to be completely avoided in the interests of your literary en-
deavors. And lastly, your stubbornness is not adaptable to a place of
this sort; a free-spirited man with a mouth full of arguments ought
not to frequent thrones, particularly at this time. You are not con-
sidering carefully what men or what interests rule in the court, where
it is almost a pious duty to recommend impiety, where "prosperous
and successful crime goes by the name of virtue," as Seneca says.[111]
Of course, flattery, lies, false accusations, and currying of favor are
prime ornaments for most staff members of rulers—and this is a doctrine of which you have never been a disciple!

On the contrary, you are so free by nature that you become indig-
nant at instances of unworthy treatment in matters which have nothing to do with you; and sometimes you speak out much too caustically,
though with justification. You know how often as a consequence you
have done battle with unprincipled men, how often hatred has flared
up against you, how often your privileges have been withdrawn. Not
once did you listen. You protest too freely, my man! Or are you sufficient by yourself to take up arms on behalf of virtue? Indeed this saying of Terence remains true: "Truthfulness is the mother of
unpopularity." You do not at all understand what motivates men to
cross the threshold of the great, since you are heedless of Lucan's teaching: "If a man would be righteous, let him depart from a court." With
the Satirist, you do not know how to "take your expression from
another man's face," like Terence's parasite: "They say yes, I say yes;
they say no, I say no. I have given orders to myself to agree in everything."[112] Again, to cheat distresses you as much as being cheated.
Furthermore, many people have to be honored, sought after, and cul-
tivated whose character is, as the saying goes, deserving of a work-
house. Never were you so flighty in your youth that you did not always
believe it beneath you to be influenced by unworthy actions. However,
if you are able to be taught these skills—or to endure them!—I won't
stand in your way, so go right ahead!

JOHANNES: Itane otiose viximus, et nichil vigilie nostre, nichil volumina que totiens inter pernoctamus, nichil patris illius rudimenta, exempla, nichil adiecit oratio? Sic omnino studia vacuos remisere ut per omnia simus inutiles? Non sunt fides et veritas artes contemnende, que licet ab hoc eminus seculo fugiant tamen apud quos perstiterint magnipenduntur. At hoc quidem polliceri queo. Sane licet invitus dolensque fateor hodie tecta regnantium, omnia sic occupante avaritia, vel dedicisse virtutem vel eam ipsam qualitercumque sed pavidam sed elinguem adhuc superesse; non autem ita in atrio summi pastoris quem fides Christi, evangelica veritas, scientia divina collustrat. Ibi homines seculi vel secularibus instituti, hic longe discolor milicia, uti gradu, moribus, habitu, ita scientia ac virtute immodice distans.

Pontificante Urbano Sexto presertim, sub quo pax, sanctitas, fides, libertas, clara studia, denique artes honeste reflorebunt. Mira cuius iusticia, divina virtute, saniore doctrina, extirpatis noxiorum radicibus, et equitatis rective amore circumfuso mentibus hominum erit aureum seculum. Quandoquidem in hoc celesti pontifice Baruc vaticinium aut implendum esse aut iam potius impletum ambigit nemo: "Imponet Deus," inquit, "capiti tuo diadema honoris eterni. Deus enim ostendit splendorem suum in te, nominabitur enim nomen tuum a Deo in sempiternum: pax iusticie et honor pietatis." Id Auxonia, imo totus id orbis et sperat et fatetur.

Ergo michi optanti recta nitentique vicem ibi omnem vel minimam intercludis? Siccine cunta illic ad virtutis extremum provecta ut mediocriter bonis non supersit locus ullus? O celitibus libeat, quatenus ita virtute precellant omnes dum si quid inest prestantie michi perseveret, si non datur auctari. Haud ego ambitionis altum culmen seu lucri plenioris augmenta requiro, que ferme numquam sine melioris animi usurpatione proveniunt. Sed opto, si quid optando mereor impetrare, ope domini et patris mei Cardinalis Thome sortiri calamo et literis

GIOVANNI: Have I lived so idly? Have my midnight vigils and the volumes on which I spend whole nights meant nothing, nor my father's teachings and examples, nor this discourse? Have my studies made me so completely detached that I am altogether useless? Loyalty and truth are qualities not to be scorned; and although they flee far away from this age, still they are considered of great value by those in whom they have endured. These things, at least, I can promise! To be sure, I do admit, though sadly and against my will, that today in the palaces of rulers, where avarice dominates everything, virtue is forgotten; or else if it still survives in some manner, it is timorous and speechless. But the situation is not thus in the halls of the chief shepherd, who is illuminated by faith in Christ, the truth of the Gospel, and divine knowledge. In the one place there are secular men or those interested in secular matters; in the other, there is a military service of very different color, as dissimilar in knowledge and virtue as in rank, character, and habits.

This is especially true in the pontificate of Urban the Sixth, under whom peace, holiness, loyalty, freedom, distinguished studies, and honorable arts will flourish again.[113] Through his marvelous justice, divine virtue, and sound doctrine, after evil has been pulled up by the roots and the love of equity and righteousness has embraced the minds of men, there will be a Golden Age. Certainly no one doubts that in this celestial pope the prophecy of Baruch is to be fulfilled, or, rather, has already been fulfilled: "God will set a crown on thy head," he says, "of everlasting honor. For God shows his brightness in thee, for thy name shall be named to thee by God forever; the peace of justice and the honor of piety."[114] Italy and indeed all the world both hope and confess this.

Therefore, because I desire and strive for what is right, do you cut off from me every position there, even the least? Has everything there been advanced to such a peak of virtue that there is no place left for the moderately good? May it please the gods for all men so to surpass me in virtue, provided that whatever excellence is in me may endure, if not allowed to increase! I do not seek a lofty pinnacle of ambition or increments of great wealth, which are almost never produced without the misuse of a good mind. But I do desire (if I deserve to obtain something by desiring it) with the help of my lord and father Cardi-

otium ab his sordidis ingratisque laboribus. Quod apud illum eo plenus fiducie spero, quod ipse mecum una tali deteri pulvere crebro stomacatus est.

Opinabar omissum iri° huiusmodi curam, spe nuper iniecta regis Hunnorum. Quamquam non paternis quidem auspiciis, cum laborante et sene rege quique mox eclipsari posset magnis lacerandum dissidiis regnum omnes ominantur. Quamobrem a Deo omnipotente factum reor, cui agendum regendumve huiusmodi eventum, ut omnia mea, supplex devotusque tradidi, quod monstrata occasio minus sortiretur effectum, ne profectus in barbaras ipse gentes hoc si quid habeo quietis amitterem.

Quod si non omnes bellorum animos cura mordacior et obumbraret et honestis a conceptibus retraheret, forte memet ultro principi obtulissem Euganeo. Cuius sub munificentia et presenti favore floruerunt ingenia et honos literis semper est habitus. Deinceps autem una michi spes in sanctissimo cardinali viget et superest, qui aliquando tandem paterne miserationis obtutum ad erigendum me componendumque deflectat.

LITERA: Conclusa sunt hactenus sua in te benignitatis officia. Sensisti olim non in te modo indulgentiam eius sed in nato quoque fructuosam. Nunc ablatus est, amotus est, ad maiora vocatus est. Vilent minora intento sublimibus.

JOHANNES: Nullo extimaverim° modo ut, quantavis rerum accessione, parentis mei Conversini memoria sic omnino queat extingui ut ullo id tempore futurum timescam. Non est enim incipere constantie sed incepta consumare. Profecto curatum hucusque dilectumve sponte nunc° abici, quid foret nisi quod de tanto quidem viro dictu nefas est? Enimvero meminit ut cum verecunda° humilitate ac simplici affectu pronunciem, quotiens me videt, parentis mei perseverans erga se studium ac ultra fraternas pene metas trasilientem caritatem. Meminit inquam labores, curas, impendia que in alendo, fovendo, instruendo

nal Tommaso to secure leisure for my pen and literary activities, away from these degrading and thankless labors. I confidently hope he will grant my request, because he has frequently been angered on my behalf that I am being worn out by such trifling occupations.

I used to think my problems would be solved by my recent expectations of the king of the Huns. However, I did not have my father's approval; since all predict, because of the sick old king who could soon be eclipsed, that his kingdom will be torn by great dissensions. Therefore I think that almighty God (to whom I as a devout suppliant entrusted the management and guidance of this situation, as all my affairs) caused the suggested opportunity to produce no result, lest by setting out to foreign lands I should lose what little leisure I have.

If sharp anxiety over the wars were not overshadowing the minds of all men, distracting them from honorable thoughts, I would probably have voluntarily presented myself to the Paduan prince, through whose bounty and ready favor talents have flourished and honor is always accorded to the study of letters.[115] From now on, however, my sole hope lives and rests in the most holy cardinal, who may soon at last out of fatherly pity turn his attention to reviving and restoring me.

LETTER: His previous services of kindness to you have been cut off. Once you enjoyed his indulgent favors, shown not only to yourself but to your son; but now he has been taken away, removed, called to great things. For a man intent on lofty matters, lesser ones hold small interest!

GIOVANNI: I could not possibly believe, regardless of the improvement in his circumstances, that I need fear such a thing would ever happen. The memory of my parent, Conversino, will never be so utterly extinguished. For loyalty is not characterized by beginning but by completing what has been begun. Certainly if a person who was heretofore loved and cared for should now voluntarily be cast off, how could that act be anything but what is sacrilegious to say about so great a man? For surely he remembers how, whenever he sees me, I declare with modest humility and simple affection my parent's constant devotion to him, and his love which almost transcended brotherly limitations. He remembers too the effort, care, and money which he himself

me suum posuit dulcis et optimus pater, qui me pro suo voluit, suscepit, habuit. Haud enim volet frustra laborasse meque ad absolutam
nunc et exoletam productum etatem abigere, dummodo precipue in-
telligere pervium sit qui impenso in me studio comparaverit, cum suus
cuique labor preciosus appareat.

Intuemur adventicios quosdam vernaculos, a dominis non modo
non desertos sed conditione, sed honore, sed incrementis rerum provec-
tos.° Absque diligentia nostra domesticos canes minime° patimur.
Quam accuratissime vidimus illi Sturnum haberi! Numquid ei abiec-
tior bruto sum ego? Genitor nempe meus quoad vixit hunc amavit,
coluit, veneratus est, nec amorem officiumque pium nisi cum vita
deposuit. Posse mallem officiis ego meis huic patri laudari. Sed quid
puer alumno, quod servus domino, quid postreme sortis fortunatissi-
mo conferat? Omnino tamen haud sterilis fui. Quippe amavi, fidem
servavi, cupivi salutem. Quibus quidem rebus avarus nimium est, plura
quisquis ab amato requirit.

Quod si in beneficiis collocatis "imitari debemus fertiles agros, qui
plus quam acceperint reddunt," ut ait Cicero, nonne, si me lentius
aspiciat asperneturque (quod absit!), actionem habeam in eum? Et
proferre quidem potero: "Conversinus novissimum ad usque spiritum
amicum te unicum,° venerande pater, te fratrem, te anime sue dulce
lumen, te fidei carissimum pignus, te inquam inter mortales primum
habuit, putavit, ostendit. Tu vero, clemens domine, vivis, viges, vales
adhuc. Nec Conversini respicis natum, tuis in ulnis dimissum, abs te-
que ultro susceptum?" Arbitrare, Litera, animadverti hoc idem a cir-
cumspectissimo presule, atque hinc indesinentem eius hucusque favorem
sensimus et sensuri, ni fallor, sumus. Ergo amplius cessa diffidere, hesita-
tio cuntatioque omnis absit, amplexare bonam spem. Tantam apud
sapientiam atque constantiam nullus umquam ingratitudini, nullus ob-
livioni locus fiet. Sed veluti ad uberrimum largitatis fontem spem dirige,
accingere igitur, et vade.

expended on nurturing, cherishing, and instructing me, like a fond
and good father, who wanted, received, and considered me as his own.
Surely he will not wish to have labored in vain, to cast me off now
that I have reached full manhood, especially if it is possible for him
to learn what he has acquired through investing his interest in me;
for to each man his own labor appears precious.

We see certain foreign house-servants not only not deserted by their
masters but advanced by them in rank, honor, and wealth. We do
not allow our family dogs to go without attention. I saw Tomasso
have Sturno treated with the greatest of care—surely I am not more
lowly to him than an animal! My own father, of course, as long as
he lived, loved and cherished and honored Tommaso, and did not
cease in his love and pious duty until he died. I would like to be able
to receive praise for my services to this father; but what can a boy
bestow upon a foster-parent, or a servant upon a master, who is so
fortunate in his most recent circumstances? Yet I have not been wholly
unproductive, for I have loved him, kept the faith, desired his salvation. Whoever asks more than this of a loved one is indeed exceedingly greedy!

But if in conferring benefits "we ought to imitate the fruitful fields
which return more than they have received," as Cicero says,[116]
should I not have a claim against him if he were to look upon me
coldly or spurn me (God forbid!)? Indeed I shall be able to put forth
a plea: "Conversino up to his last breath considered you his special
friend, venerable father, his brother, the sweet light of his soul, the
dearest pledge of faith. Truly he held you first among mortals, thought
and demonstrated it. You, clement lord, are still alive, strong, and
well. And do you have no regard for Conversino's son, who was left
in your protection and was received by you of your own free will?"
Consider, Letter, that this fact is appreciated by the very wise bishop,
so that I have until now enjoyed his unceasing favor and, unless I
am mistaken, will continue to enjoy it. So do not lack confidence
any longer, away with hesitation and delay, welcome hope with
open arms! In the presence of such great wisdom and loyalty there
will never be a place for ingratitude or forgetfulness. Direct your expectations as if to an abundant fount of generosity, gird yourself therefore, and go!

LITERA: Sic usquequaque confutas obiecta ut, tametsi supersit quod valeam ac velim opponere, silere duxerim, neu te labore supervacuo detineam et tu me longiore dictione mittas onustam. En maturo vadere. Sed quid dicam?

JOHANNES: Eas utinam, preduce Deo, me felicior, Litera. Quo simul perveneris sospes, serva ne sacris aut magnis de rebus disserentem adeas importuna. Sed delige vacuum tempus vacuumque extrinsecis pectus, quoniam haud utiliter exprimitur occupatis oratio que in pectore nequit radicare ubi negotiorum tenacior cura repullulat.

Non te pransum manere consulo, quamvis aiunt solere homines esse presentiores a mensis. Verum id de his quidem hominibus quos merum esculentiave turgidat, imo vincit et opprimit, ut rationis quoque lumen extinguat. Qui ut liberales persepe beneficique comperti sunt, ita crudeles nimium molestissimive plerumque. Clitus Alexandri Macedonis temulentiam luit, dum paternas illi virtutes approbare certat. Scortum a Flaminio, cum numquam decollari hominem inspexisset idque cupisceret, inter epulandum impetravit tam scelerate ac detestabilis voluptatis effectum. Tiberius longa post convivia, Suetonio teste, Siriam provinciam Pompeio Flacco tam temere permisit quam Lucio Pisoni Romanam profecturam.

Et enim iocundiores quidem homines commesatio facit, quin etiam insanos interdum. Neronem accepimus post saturitatem laudatum a Grays, irrisum, illusum, dum eorum semet ipse tam vanis quam falsis laudibus plectro voceque iactaret citaredus imperator, usque adeo hebetata mente ut proferret unice Grecos nosse et scire, solosque et se et suis dignos studiis fore. Qui eque stultum imperatorem ridere quam miserrimos iudicare qui tali subesse paterentur imperatori valuerunt. Etsi Romanarum tum gloria rerum totum per orbem haberetur illustrior, poterat dignius diffamari predicarique miseria, qui tres succes-

LETTER: You so completely silence my objections that even though there remains something which I could (and would like to) bring up, I have decided to keep quiet. Otherwise I'll hold you up with useless work and you'll send me off burdened with a longer text! See, I'm hurrying to take off. But—what am I to say?

GIOVANNI: I hope, with God as your leader, that you may go more successfully than I, Letter. As soon as you arrive there safely, be sure you do not approach him inconveniently when he is attending to sacred or other important matters. Choose a time when his mind is free of external affairs, since a message delivered when people are busy is ineffectual and cannot take root in a heart where persistent business worries are sprouting.

I advise you not to stay for a meal, even though it is said that men are usually more approachable at table. This is true concerning the kind of men who glut themselves with food and wine, to the point of being overcome and reduced to torpidity, so that even the light of reason is extinguished. Such men, although very often found to be generous and kind, are also exceedingly cruel and generally very troublesome. Clitus suffered for the drunkenness of Alexander of Macedon when he attempted to commend his father's virtues to him. A harlot, because she had never seen a man beheaded and was eager to do so, obtained from Flaminius at a banquet the fulfillment of her wicked and detestable desire. Tiberius after a lengthy feast, according to Suetonius, turned over the province of Syria to Pompeius Flaccus as irresponsibly as he gave the Roman prefecture to Lucius Piso.[117]

Feasting makes men more cheerful, to be sure, but also sometimes insane. We have learned that after Nero was sated with food and drink, he was praised by the Greeks; but they also mocked and ridiculed him when, because of their empty and false praise, he boasted about his playing and singing, a musician-emperor.[118] His mind was so dulled that he announced that Greeks alone were learned and knowledgeable and were the only ones worthy of him and his efforts. They were able not only to laugh at the stupid emperor, but also to judge as most wretched all who suffered subjection to such a ruler. Although at that time the glory of the Roman state was considered illustrious throughout all the world, it would have been more appropri-

sive tales dominos, imo carnifices suos, Gaium, Claudium, Neronem, toleraverunt. Sed ignavius populo nichil, denique nichil imprudentius, qui publico numquam malo, nisi extrema perurgente necessitate, succurrit.

Atque cerno te iamdudum hiantem ac dicere incipientem quod fuerit plerisque succedens ab epulis dexterque postulationis effectus. Neemias restruendi sancte menia civitatis ab Artaxerxe occasionem accepit a mensa. Nec non post cenam Darii nobilis questio versata, veritas approbata, gratia, et gloria data Zorobabel. Herodes Agrippa Gaium imperatorem, licet omnibus sevissimum, in prandio tamen facilem habuit ut de statua sua in Dei templo viventis collocanda irritari pateretur edictum. Quid Ester? Nonne Assuerum a convivio non solum mitem Iudeis sed faventem quoque habuit? Fateor, Litera, quamquam evenerint ista nutu Dei, qui novit interdum de lupis agnos facere, hilariores esse refectos, contra ieiunos tristes ac querulos, ut ait Seneca. Nam Stacianus ille Neptunus "letus ventabat° Occeano ab hospite mensis." Quippe nutrimentum ipsum cibationis ingeste conservatio caloris fomentumque est, qui pro sui copia vel inopia reddit audaces, iocundos, item pusillanimes turbidosque.

Habes quoque in Esdra, habes ab Ecclesiastico, nec psalmidicus liber tacet letificari animos potu, quod Flacci quoque carmine didicisti. Quid Ypocrates medicine doctissimus artifex, qui vini usum corpori humano quam accommodissimum amphorismo ccclxviii docet. Sed de moderate sumpto locutos intelligas, quoniam uti certo cum temperamento admodum iuvat, sic diffusius hausto mens hebet, ratio caligat, enervatur absumiturve corpus. Accelerat enim senectam catervatimque morbos vehit ebrietas. Quanta quoque animo vitia imprimat ne dici quidem opus est, quoniam id apostolus, id Proverbia, id Gregorius, Ieronymus, id litere omnes, id exempla tam multa quam vera docent. Profecto in regno Liberi Patris nec virtus habitare nec integra ratio potest.

ate to publicize and noise abroad the misery of those who endured
successively three such overlords, or rather executioners: Gaius,
Claudius, Nero. But nothing is slower to rouse or more short-sighted
than the populace, who never act to remedy a public evil unless extreme necessity compels them.

I perceive that you have now for a long time been eager to speak
and are about to say that many have had good and profitable results
from requests made during banquets. Nehemiah received from Artaxerxes, while at table, permission to restore the walls of the Holy
City. Also, after dinner, the noble Darius held an investigation, approved the truth, and gave favor and glory to Zorobabel. Herod Agrippa found the emperor Gaius, usually cruel to everyone, so compliant
while dining that he permitted the cancellation of the edict concerning the placement of his statue in the temple of the living God. What
about Esther? Did she not find Assuerus during a banquet not only
lenient to the Jews but even indulgent to them? I admit, Letter, that
although such things came about by the will of God (who knows how
sometimes to make lambs out of wolves), well-fed men are happier
and, on the other hand, hungry men are ill-humored and querulous,
as Seneca says. For in Statius' poem, Neptune "came away from Ocea-
nus, his host, gladdened by the banquet."[119] To be sure, the nourishment from food that is eaten is the fuel and conservator of the heat
which, in proportion to its abundance or deficiency, makes men spirited
and jovial or timorous and gloomy.

In Esdras, Ecclesiasticus, and the Psalmist you read that minds are
made genial by drink. This you know too from the poem of Horace,
and from Hippocrates, the most skilled practitioner of medicine, who
teaches in his three hundred sixty-eighth aphorism that wine is the most
useful thing possible for the human body. But you must understand that
they referred to moderate consumption; although a limited amount is
helpful, wine drunk in too copious quantities dulls the mind, clouds the
reason, and enervates and destroys the body. Drunkenness hastens old
age and is a carrier of a vast number of diseases. I need not even mention
how many vices it imprints upon the mind, since the Apostle, Proverbs,
Gregory, Jerome,[120] all of literature, and object lessons as true as they
are many, give illustration of this. Certainly neither virtue nor unsul-
lied reason can inhabit the kingdom of Father Bacchus!

Hos igitur homines qui palato ventrique morigeri sunt nonnumquam adiri a mensis laudo, ut tum effusiores et hoc iuris alieni futuros
magis quo temulentia plus a se ipsis devios trahit. Hinc evenit sepe
ut ab huiusmodi hominibus° vel turpiter donata fleantur vel turpis-
sime repetantur.

Homines autem sobrios et ita ab omni lenocinio carnis exhaustos
ut non parendum corpori verum tamquam improbum contumaxque
iumentum fuste ac inedia domandum censeant, incenes aut refectos
petas minimum refert. His ratio sic fundata quadrataque est ut non
perverti modo nullis queant illecebris sensuum sed ne concuti quidem
Apud hos utique non preces, non munera, non temporis differentia,
sed honesta, sed equa, sed iusta moderataque peticio valet. Eiuscemo-
di noster hic extat. Eadem illi constantia semper, maturitas eadem,
una dictorum factorumque maiestas, et par tranquillitas hilaritasve ie-
iuno atque refecto.

Itaque observare moneo tantummodo ne qua moles extranearum°
occupationum sevocet mentem sacram. Tum confestim profer tete et
sacros osculata pedes vertice succiduo persevera, nec si non bis terque
iusserit erigitor. Talem nempe cultum simili paternitati debes. Mox
demisso vultu, lepida ac remissa sed nec extenuata nimium voce, geminis
offerens volumen palmis, reverendis illud manibus trade.

LITERA: Si rogaverit, "Quidnam offers?" quo pacto satisfaciam ne mendax redarguar edoce. Haud enim cum pueris agitur causa coram sed
mortalium cordatissimo. "Heccine epistola," deposcet, "historiane, an
liber? Ede nomine quicquid exhibes." Quid ergo reddam?° Frons prima librum simulat, sed liber non est. Nam ubi elegantia festivitasque
verborum? Sententiarum pondus et maiestas abest, diluciditas ordinem, conpositionem nervi deficiunt, caret gravitate et dignitate materia.
Forte mentiar si epistolam voco, quoniam vultus, sonus, habitus refel-

Therefore I recommend that men who indulge their palate and belly are sometimes to be approached when they are at table, as they are then generous; and the more their minds are led astray by drunkenness, the more they fall under some one else's control. Consequently they often are shameless enough to regret gifts they have made, or even most shamefully demand them back!

But as for men who are serious minded and so detached from every enticement of the flesh that they think the body should not be catered to but should be subdued like a stubborn and unruly mule, with club and starvation, it makes no difference at all whether you visit them before or after they have eaten. In them, reason has been so well-constructed and solidly based that it is impossible not only to corrupt them by the attractions of the senses but even to interest them. Among such as these, certainly, neither entreaties, gifts, nor selection of the right time has any influence – but only an honorable, equitable, just, and modest request. This man of ours is of this sort. He always preserves the same steadfastness and maturity, together with a majesty of words and deeds, and the same calmness and cheerfulness, whether he has eaten or not.

Therefore I advise you to make sure only that no weighty outside business is distracting his saintly mind. Then immediately introduce yourself and, kissing his saintly feet, remain with bowed head. Do not stand up until he has requested it two or three times. Of course you owe such courtesy to one like the Paternity. Then with lowered eyes and a pleasant, gentle, yet not too weak voice, offer the volume on both your palms and give it into his reverend hands.

LETTER: If he asks, "What are you offering me?" tell me how I can answer without being condemned as a liar! For this case is not being presented before children but before the most intelligent of mortals. He will inquire, "Is this a letter, a history, or a book? Tell me the name of what you are presenting." What then am I to reply? The outside cover looks like a book, yet it is not a *book*. For where is the refinement and liveliness of its words? Its ideas lack weight and grandeur, there is no clarity of arrangement or vitality of composition, the subject matter has no seriousness or dignity.

As it is, I shall be untruthful in calling it a *letter*, since its appear-

lunt; transilit enim epistolarem metam et numeros. At si appellaver‹
historiam, in ipso limine orationis videbor falsidica. Quippe non re
rum proprietates, non gestorum fortunas seu varietates exprimit. Nis
ideo forte libeat historiam appellare, quod pauca de sancto presul
atque ea quidem incidenter ac cesim intexuisti. Verum idcirco nor
est historia vocanda sed descriptio potius vel commendatio vite que
dam. Quod igitur vocabulum tribuo? Premone!

JOHANNES: Non refert tua, neque ut ipsa tibi nomen usurpes decet
Ideoque pedibus genuflexa verendis taciturna maneto, prestolatura ti
tulum ipse designet. Et quodcumque taxaverit nomen, sempiternun
habeto, ea denique nominatione e divino quasi oraculo manant‹
gavisura, seu historiam, librum, vel epistolam maluerit dicere.

Postquam vero ius acceperis fandi, humili ac ferventi me primun
recommendatione memorabis, orationibus supplex ne me creaturan
suam relinquat exortem beatitudinis sue. Quod si alius ad manum serm‹
non currit, dic saltem ut Egionem ganeo Terentianus oravit: "In t‹
spes omnis, Thoma, nobis sita est, te solum habemus, tu es patronus
tu pater. Conversinus tibi moriens commendavit senex; si deseris tu
nos perimus." Quin etiam expones valere utcumque domum hanc
honestam magis quam felicem, lugubrem nunc tabescentem, attonitam
que lacrimis et dolore, imo velut in funere patris familias dissolutam

Estis conscii, Deus et tu, Litera, qui cor meum, ubi sum, quisqui
sum cernitis, me sepius ex ubertate tum gaudii, tum meroris illacrima
tum. Hinc sublimatio tanta celesti quadam alacritate mentem dilatat
inde fortune mee tenax et sinister flatus animum perstringit, meditan
tem sane quam procul a benefactore meo, a spe, a fiducia mea contin
gat abesse. Recolo item proficiscentem me Venetias humanissimus pate
quanta clarissimi vultus sui iocunditate visebat, receptabat, honorabat
Videbar ipse michi e terris celum petisse maiestati quotiens illius in
tereram. Numquam adii sanctum virum quin monitus sacros, exempl‹
virilia, sententias divinas inde reportarem, quin melior inde saniorqu‹

nce, sound, and style belie that. Indeed, it exceeds the limit and meas-
urements of a letter. Yet if I call it a *history*, at the very beginning
I shall be seen to describe it falsely, because it does not express the
qualities of things nor the fortunes or varieties of deeds. Possibly you
may choose to call it a history because you have inserted a few facts
about the holy prelate, but these are merely incidental and brief. It
should not be called a history on this account, but is rather a description or praise of a life. What name therefore shall I give it? Please
tell me!

GIOVANNI: It is no concern of yours, and neither is it proper for you
to claim a name for yourself! So just remain silent, kneeling at his
reverend feet, waiting until he himself designates the title. And whatever
name he assigns, keep it forever, rejoicing in this appellation as if coming
from a divine oracle, whether he prefers to say *history, book,* or *letter.*

Then after you have received permission to speak, you will mention me first with a humble and heart-felt commendation, entreating
him with prayers not to leave me, his creation, without a share in
his blessedness. And if another topic of conversation does not easily
occur to you, at least say, as Terence's parasite begged Hegio: "All
my hope rest in you, Tommaso, I have only you, you are my patron,
my father. On his deathbed the elderly Conversino entrusted me to
you. If you desert me, I perish."[121] Moreover you are to explain that
this household is getting along as best it can, more respectable than
prosperous, now sadly wasting away, stricken by tears and grief, in
fact, heartbroken as if the head of the family had died.

God and you, Letter, who know my heart, where I am, who I
am, are aware that I have wept as often from overflowing happiness
as from sadness. At one moment my mind swells with the exaltation
of heavenly joy; at another, the persistently baleful winds of my fortune abrade my spirit when I realize how far away I am from my
benefactor, my hope, and my source of help. I recall also, when I
went to Venice, with what great pleasure on his distinguished face
my most kindly father used to look at me, welcome, and honor me.
I felt that I had reached Heaven from earth whenever I was in the
presence of his majesty. Never did I go to that holy man without bringing back from him saintly advice, manly examples, and divine precepts,

remearem. Enunciare poteram ut fidelis ille piscator, domino Iesu rogan-
ti num ipse quoque abire vellet cum plerique alii recessissent discipu-
li: "Nolo," ait, "abs te dividi; verba vite eterne habes."

Prorsus dum vigebat rerum suarum in mea mente vestigium, non
labor me quotidianus, non onera domestica gravabant, non illecebre
mundi, non blanda sed falsa potius quam utilis aura popularis inflabat,
nec reddebat anxium desideriis peritura felicitas. Sic me confirmabat
conformabatque vita eius et exhortatio doctrine. Probe veteranus illo
me comitatus, dum enim redeuntem quererent quam bene sibi in patriarchali tecto fuisset, respondit, "Opipare! Consedebat," inquit, "deus
ille in mensa medius, debitas eidem escas circumsidentibus imper-
tiens,° spectandus moribus, spectandus seriis, dictorum factorumve
prestantia spectandus."

At nunc, o Litera, pergam ipse Venetias. Quo divertam cum absit
qui paterno me colligebat affectu? Quis posthac rudimenta salutis dabit?
Ubinam erunt illa tam fida quam sana consilia? Non accipiam responsa Thome que contemptum seculi, amicitie fidem, celestium desiderium edocebant. Nuspiam michi spectabitur Paternitas illa, vere
humilitatis et prudentie exemplar, non erit quoque qui abeuntem me
benedictionis munimine dimittat.

Coniecta igitur quo valeam modo iacturam tantam sine querimo-
nia, sine tristicia preterire. Namque eo degente cominus poteram cum
propheta clamare: "Pater meus et mater mea dereliquerunt me. Dominus autem assumpsit me." At vero nunc qui me assumpserat dominus
assumptus est, elevatus est, exaltatus est. Elevandum ad superos et
meliorem in sedem reponendum Heliseus Heliam comitatus trans Ior-
danem cum fletu, clamore, mesticia transferri vidit. Sed duplicis
prophetie, sed palii munus accepit. Ergo sine lacrimis ego, sine dolore,
sine eiulatu superesse valeo, cum nec propheta relinquor, nec sacris
ut ille reliquiis fungor, vel saltem ut oportuit benedictione novissima?

Piguit° hactenus adolescentie mee fervoribus et pie severitatis

or without coming away better and more sensible. I was able to proclaim like the faithful fisherman, when his Lord Jesus asked him whether he too wished to leave since most of the other disciples had gone: "I do not wish to be parted from thee," he said. "Thou hast the words of eternal life."[122]

At that time, when the evidence of his activities was fresh in my mind, neither daily labor nor domestic duties were a burden to me, nor did the enticements of the world and the agreeable (though deceptive and useless) breeze of popularity puff me up; nor did that sort of happiness which is destined to perish distress me with its desires. In this way his life and the encouragement of his teaching strengthened and shaped me. A veteran who had accompanied me there, when asked on his return how well he had been treated under the patriarch's roof, accurately answered: "Lavishly! He sat like a god at the middle of the table, passing to those around him the food meant for himself. He was remarkable for his character, seriousness, and excellence in words and deeds."

And now, Letter, I myself shall proceed to Venice. Where am I to turn, since he is gone who cherished me with a father's love? Who will hereafter give me the lessons of salvation? Where will there be counsel both reliable and sound? I shall not be receiving Tommaso's answers, which taught me contempt for this age, trust in friendship, and a longing for the celestial. Nowhere shall I see that Paternity, the exemplar of true humility and wisdom, and there will not be anyone to send me off with the protection of his blessing when I leave.

Do you imagine, therefore, that I could pass over so great a loss without complaints and sadness? For when he was living nearby, I could exclaim with the Prophet: "My father and my mother have left me; but the Lord hath taken me up."[123] But indeed now the lord who took me up has been taken up, elevated, and exalted. When Elisha accompanied Elijah across the Jordan, with tears, laments, and sadness he saw him taken away to be raised on high and placed into a better home.[124] At least he received the gift of a two-fold prophecy and a mantle. So how can I survive without tears, grief, or lamentation when I neither am left as a prophet nor enjoy, like Elisha, sacred relics, not even, at the least (as would have been fitting), a last blessing?

Tommaso was previously displeased because of the ardors of my

fronte me receptabat. Tum mallem si habendus procul semper erat
sublimatum, mitius passus, utpote manus et ferramenta medicorum
morbosi quidam horrescunt. Porro impresentiarum quo vulnus meum
esset cruentum magis, cum tenerrime, dulciter, ac blande me com-
plecteretur. Atque non in mense modo et seriorum sobriorumque
solaciorum participium adhiberet, verum ambulando, colloquendo,
in ipsis quoque penetralibus stando, non ut servulum humilem, sed
ut filium aut comitem pium admitteret—ipsum perdo. Quo fit ut iugi
merore tabescam. Scis ipsa quotiens lacrimas increpuisti meas, quotiens querulum tristemve cohortati sunt amici.

LITERA: Assentior hec et testor crudum valde vulnus tuum, et spei tibi
in hac precipue regione degenti ac virium excidisse plurimum, cum
solus, nunc unicus, expes, orphanus patronum talem lugeas ademp-
tum. Sed quid illo abeunte restitisti? "Quid iuvat insano indulgere
dolori," ut Maro ait? Ceteris sequentibus cur usque adhuc perstas?

JOHANNES: Interogas cum noris ipsa quibus istic affixus clavis, quo vis-
co, quibus demum nodis continear? Non me coniugis cura velut ar-
gumentari plerique nituntur, auctore Deo, sic instructe° moderateque
nullum ut sobrium michi impetum rumpat. Cui abunde iam illud per-
suasum est, habendos esse viros ut custodes fragilis sexus et vite huius
laboriose comites, minime autem pro commercio concubitus, nimirum in supplementum nostre misere propagationis, non autem in bes-
tialem quandam voluptatem permissi.

Sed nec liberorum iocunditas tenuit, quos qua voluptate habeam,
quis audiens me quotidie spectansve nescit? Enimvero iamdudum ad-
verti, arentibus ubique virtutibus et fruticante vitio, rara provenire bene
institutis animis de prole solatia. Coalam domi qui forsan olim luxuria diffluat, qui afficiat contumacia parentes, qui potando, scortando,

youth, and he used to receive me with a frown of pious sternness. I would have preferred his promotion at that time — if it was his destiny to be gone permanently — since I then could have borne his departure more easily: I was like sick persons who dread the hands and instruments of the doctors. But as things are now, my wound is all the more bloody because he has embraced me with tenderness, love, and affection. He not only invited me to share in his table and his serious and sober words of comfort, but he also admitted me to his walks, his conversation, even to his innermost thoughts, not as a humble servant but as a son and loyal companion. This is the man I am losing. And this is why I am continually pining away with grief. You yourself know how often you have reproved my tears, how often my friends have tried to cheer me up when I am fretful and unhappy.

LETTER: Yes, it is true. I can witness to your very bloody wound and to the fact that the greatest part of hope and purpose has been lost to you, especially since you live in this region; because now you are grieving alone, solitary, hopeless, and bereft, for the loss of such a patron. But why did you stay behind when he left? "Of what avail is it to yield thus to frantic grief?" as Vergil says?[125] Since others are following him, why do you still stay here?

GIOVANNI: Do you ask this question when you well know the nails by which I am pinned down to this place, the glue, the knots which bind me? I am not tied down by worry about my wife, as many try to prove; for as God is my authority, she has been so taught and trained that she interferes with no serious purpose of mine. She has now been fully convinced that men are to be regarded as protectors of the frail sex and companions in this life of troubles; of least importance, however, is their part in sexual intercourse. This naturally is permitted for the purpose of our miserable reproduction but not for brutish gratification.

Neither has enjoyment of my children held me back, although everyone who hears and sees me daily knows the happiness I have in them. For indeed I have long since observed that, because of the withering of virtue everywhere and the proliferation of vice, there is little solace in children for those who are well-informed. Perhaps I am rearing at home the kind of son who in the future will run wild in extrava-

lusitando, scurrando mille fraudibus ac sudoribus partum et insonni-
bus curis turpique avaricia servatum patrimonium profundat. Cui ut
impune liceat in hereditate iactare sese suamque explere libidinem ac-
celeratum parentis obitum non prestolatur modo sed expetit, vivaci
maturat ipse plerumque.

 Si vero religiosa ceteri ac munda caritate diligeremus, non mehercule plus exule filio vitioso vel etiam pereunte quam extrario tor-
queremur. Maxime cum sanctus Ecclesiastici liber clamet: "Utile est
mori sine filiis, quam relinquere filios impios." Qui quidem "testes ipsi
sunt impietatis adversus parentes," ut Sapientie volumine dicitur. Atqui persepe laudasti cum non solum Euripedem cum Severino
laudarem, verum ipse de meo quoque diffinirem prolem cupiscenti-
bus infortunium minus nullum occurrere quam liberos non habere.

 Sed armantur plurimi Augustini sententia docentis xviiii De Civitate Dei libro: "Pertinere ad virtutis officium vivere patrie et propter
patriam filios procreare." Propter patriam, aiunt; propter opem senecte
et propagandi nominis studium gignendos esse filios, neu quoque divitie
in quibus desudavimus et parci viximus extraneis direptionibus distra-
hantur. Quasi mentientem Ecclesiastem faciant, qui proferat: "Laboravi
studiosissime habiturus post me heredem quem ignoro utrum stultus
an sapiens futurus sit, et dominetur in laboribus meis, quibus desuda-
vi et anxius fui. Et est," intulit, "quicquam tam vanum?" Ceca ista quidem et insipida cogitatio, gignere hominem patrie nec ullis quibus°
regitur patria servaturque artibus adornare, sed inscitia plenum, libidine plenum, ambitione plenum, incastigatum et incompositum, veluti
ferum et indomitum animal linquere. Unde fit ut cum civem despon-
derimus, tradamus sevam et sediciossimam beluam. Nec aliunde
crediderim, si ulle nunc dicende sunt, tam deformes et expilatas ia-
cere respublicas. Tum sane ut Satirus ait:

gant living, obstinately disobey his parents, and, with drinking, wenching, sporting, and foolery, waste the estate which was acquired by a thousand stratagems and exertions and preserved by unsleeping care and base avarice. In order to glory in his inheritance and sate his lusts with impunity, such a son not only awaits his father's swift death but longs for it, and often hurries it up himself if his father is long-lived.

But if we loved our children with a pure religious affection, we would not, by Hercules, agonize more over the exile or even the death of a corrupt son than over that of a stranger. The holy book of Ecclesiasticus proclaims: "It is better to die without children than to leave ungodly children," who indeed themselves "are witnesses of wickedness against their parents," as is said in the book of Wisdom. And you very often approved not only when I praised Euripides along with Severinus,[126] but also when I asserted on my own part that for those who long for offspring, nothing is more fortunate than not to have children.

However, many arm themselves with the opinion of Augustine, who teaches in the nineteenth book of the *City of God:* "It is part of virtue's duty to live for one's fatherland and on behalf of the fatherland to beget sons."[127] On behalf of the fatherland, they say, and also for assistance in our old age and from the desire to perpetuate our name, ought we to beget sons; and in order that the riches for which we have toiled and lived frugally not be destroyed by the depredations of strangers. They would make Ecclesiastes a liar, since he says: "I had earnestly labored, being like to have an heir after me, whom I know not whether he will be a wise man or a fool, and he shall have rule over all my labors with which I have labored and been solicitous! And is there," he adds, "anything so vain?"[128] Truly it is a blind and senseless idea, to beget a man for one's country and then, instead of endowing him with any skills by which a country is directed and preserved, to leave him full of ignorance, lust, and ambition, undisciplined and uncontrolled, like an untamed wild animal. Consequently, although we have promised a citizen, we hand over a savage and recalcitrant beast. I think it is for this very reason that republics (if any are to be so named) lie prostrate, plucked, and ugly. Then, as the Satirist says:

Gratum est quod patrie civem populoque dedisti,
si facis ut patrie sit ydoneus, utilis agris,
utilis et bellorum et pacis rebus agendis.

Age, quot non modo non fuere decrepitis adiumento patribus sed
impie deseruerunt, quodque scelestius est, pulsatos fugarunt, interdum
etiam necaverunt. Cum interim ipse ciconie deplumatos etate parentes
ac senio fovere et alere dum replumescant ipsi tradantur. Alia quoque avis nomine merops non solum veterascentes sed omni demum
coalere fertur etate. Volvamus annales et utriusque legis codices: plures
patres numerabis infelices. Evilmorodac, genitoris cadaver ne revivisceret
metuens, trecentis frustatim vulturibus, ut memorant historie, tradidit,
tam filius novo sceleris invento quam pater inaudito notandus° busto.
Taceo iniquitatem Absalon et Ninum Samiramis filium qui licet sceleribus inquinatam matrem tamen extinxit. Cassandri regis filius Antipater
nonne Thesalonicem parentem etiam per materna quidem ubera
deprecantem vitam peremit? Non impudicam quemadmodum Ninus
verum quod alius filii Alexandri partibus favorabilior videbatur. Sed
valuit magis regnandi libido quam sacra necessitudo nature. Eadem
in Suetonio Neronem cauteriat infamia. Artaxerxi cxv fuere sed tres
legitimo tantum matrimonio suscepti. Quorum Darius, a patre vivente
rex constitutus et omni favoris indulgentia promotus, parricida ipse
quinquaginta e fratribus in parricidii factionem involvit. Herodes Ascalonita filiorum suorum Aristoboli et Alexandri venena et gladios
vix evasit, quem attendebant omnes per angulos domestice semper
insidie; ut merito diffinitum sit, felix° unus° qui in externis fuisset° in
domesticis infelicissimus fuerit. Metridatem quoque Pharnaces filius
non solum haurire venenum verum etiam hosti sponte iugulum offerre
coegit.

It is good that you have presented your country and your people with a citizen, if you make him serviceable to his country, useful for the land, useful for the things both of peace and war.[129]

Consider this, how many men have not only failed to help their decrepit fathers but have even unfilially deserted them, or, what is more wicked, have driven them away with beatings, sometimes even killed them! Yet at the same time the very storks are said to take care of their parents when defeathered by time and old age, and to feed them until the feathers regrow. Also another bird, called the bee-eater, is reported to look after its parents not only when they are old but at every age. If one studies the histories and the books of the Old and New Testaments, one finds most fathers unhappy. Evilmerodach, in fear lest his father's dead body come back to life, gave it piece by piece to three hundred vultures, so the histories relate, the son as famous for his innovation in crime as the father for his previously unheard-of funeral rites. I need not mention the wickedness of Absalom, or of Ninus, the son of Semiramis, who killed his mother. No matter how besmirched she was by crimes, she was still his mother. Did not Antipater, son of King Cassander, murder his mother Thessalonice even as she begged for her life by her maternal breasts? Unlike Ninus's mother, she was not a shameless woman, but was killed because she seemed more favorable to the side of her son Alexander. The passion for ruling was stronger than the sacred bond of nature. The same infamy brands Nero, according to Suetonius. Artaxerxes had one hundred fifteen sons, but only three conceived in lawful wedlock. Of the three, Darius, made king by his father when he was still alive and advanced by the bestowal of every kind of favor, himself a parricide enrolled fifty of his brothers into a party for parricide. Herodes Ascalonita barely escaped the poison and swords of his sons Aristobolus and Alexander.[130] Domestic ambushes were always awaiting him in every corner, so that it has been asserted with good reason that, although fortunate in his external affairs, he was most unfortunate in his personal affairs. Mithridates was compelled by his son Pharnaces not only to drink poison but even to offer his throat voluntarily to his enemy.[131]

Sed quid vetusta cum sint in oculis recentia atque domestica?
Blanorem Seravallensem nec reverentia paterna nec amor nec etas se-
nis repressit; quin Zanucium parentem in ipso quidem quo natus, ali-
tus, excretusque fuerat lare veneno extrudit, qui diis tandem paterne
maiestatis ultoribus penas dedit. Non opus est deterere tempus tum
prisci tum nostri temporis in explicandis parentum iniuriis cum omnis fere angulus inveniat parricidas.

Quos ab annis si mollibus incurvarent, ut Proverbiorum doctrina
sonat, atque ostentarent avariciam fugere, frugalitatem perferre,
amicitias colere, fidem venerari, mendacium vereri, preque omnibus
amare Deum, timere Deum, tunc sane rempublicam exornari et ipsis
parentibus qui tales sustulissent filios consuli sponte concederem. Siquidem eruditos disciplinis° huiusmodi debere patrie donari doctorem
acutissimum arbitror persensisse. Talem Tobias, tales Mathathias patrie
sustulit. Huiusmodi dotibus preditos liquerunt patres illi primevi
Abraam et Thare pater eiusdem. Quanta Adeodatus° virtute cresce-
bat nimirum intelligit quisquis Confessionum librum nonum presignati doctoris legat. Iisdem itidem ego insignibus decusatos optem fore
si quos dedit vel daturus est Deus omnipotens, quos non tam patrie
terrene cives aut mee "baculum senectutis" quam Civitatis Eterne colo-
nos et Christi servos fieri studeo.

Cumque hanc michi spem fugiendo facienda vel fugienda faciendo
amputabunt, nedum caripendam sed ne meos quidem patiar appellari. Malo enim sustantiam comparatam quivis integer habeat alienus
quam ex ossibus meis quis editus perditissimis moribus dissipet. Dum
sanis filii documentis obtemperant, semitam virtutis non spernunt, animi
non carnis imperia sectantur, fovendi, colendi, multipendendique sunt.
Veluti cetera ex nobis sponte nascentia, cesariem, barbe prolixitudi-
nem, ungues, reputamus dum ornamento existunt. Que posteaquam°

But why cite ancient examples when we have before our eyes recent instances at home? Blanor of Seravalle was restrained by neither reverence nor love for his father nor by the old man's age; indeed he poisoned Zanucio, his father, in the very home where he himself had been born and reared and had grown to adulthood.[132] He finally paid the penalty when the gods avenged his father's dignity. There is no need to spend more time relating injustices to parents either of former times or of our own, when almost every corner reveals parricides!

If parents controlled their children from a tender age, as the book of Proverbs teaches,[133] and showed them how to avoid greed, practice frugality, cultivate friendships, respect loyalty, shun falsehood, and above all things to love God and fear Him, then indeed I would gladly agree that the republic is honored and looked after by the parents who have brought up such sons. For I believe that most keen-witted teacher observed that sons educated in lessons like this ought to be given one's country.[134] Tobias brought up such a one, and Mattathias also such sons, for their country. Those ancient fathers, Abraham and his father Thare, left children equipped with similar gifts. Whoever reads the ninth book of the *Confessions*, by the previously mentioned teacher, certainly knows the great virtue in which Adeodatus grew up.[135] I would wish my sons to be marked with the same signs of honor, if omnipotent God has given or is going to give sons to me, whom I fervently desire to become not only citizens of our earthly fatherland and "the staff of my old age,"[136] but inhabitants of the Eternal City and servants of Christ.

And if they cut off this hope from me by avoiding what ought to be done or doing what ought to be avoided, much less than holding them dear I shall not even allow them to be called mine. For I prefer that some good man, although an outsider, should have the substance I have acquired rather than that one born of my bones should waste it by his depraved habits. When sons are obedient to sound precepts, they do not spurn the path of virtue but follow the commands of the mind and not of the flesh, and are to be cherished, loved, and deemed of great worth. Like other things produced spontaneously from our bodies, such as hair, beard, and fingernails, which we value when they are becoming to us and which we later cut off and throw away

in magnitudinem indecorem ac noxiam excreverint amputamus
abicimusque, ita, me dii ament, perversantem filium, quoniam ex me
sit, haud aliter curem ac decisos ungues, abrasam barbam, obtonsos
capillos, ceteraque alia humani corporis excrementa que velut inutilia
ac dannosa spernunt calcantque homines. Quid sane sit pluris natus
cum libidine et immundicia carnali quam prenominata hec sponte ex-
orientia lege nature? Utrumque meum est, utrumque ex me et in mea
nascitur carne, forte ex humorum utrumque redundantia meorum,
si ut° medici perhibent huiusmodi propago ex tertie digestionis resi-
duo seminetur. Sicuti quoque ex humorum fumis enasci pilos Galie-
no teste proditur.

Verum sicut Aristoteles ait: "Animantibus ita cuntis permanendi
natura infixit amorem ut enitantur universa sui simile gignere." Hinc
nostre in filiis spem virtutis amplectimur, et velut quibusdam in surculis non permansuram diu speciem nostram in his vivere diffundique
gaudemus. Qui quidem si perniciosi supervicturi sunt, non decorant
indolem domesticam sed funestant; sed certe notionis nostre celebritatem melius sanctiusque clarorum splendor operum diuturnaret.

Omnino autem insano quidam amore, ne dicam furore, cunta liberorum acta dictave amant, probant, admirantur, quamvis mendosa, quamvis scelerata, quamvis impia, dira. Dolum sodali fraudemve fecerint,
rident, laudant, sapere et sibi providulum instrepunt. Si iniuriosum
altercacemve cernant, applaudunt, fortem iurant, gratantur domi quod
vindicem alunt, sed tortorem forte patris futurum. Si libidinosum ac
prodigum, profusum, edacem, magnificum ac liberalem asseverant. Instituti disciplinis° huiuscemodi quidni piam, sobriam, plenam, sanctam parentibus rependunt vicem!

Quare non est ut presumas hac me opinione preditum quo minus
inter mei pontificis vernas memet ipse dicarem filiorum indulgentia
retractum. Prorsus siquidem michi corporis ut animi libertas fuisset,

after they have grown to an unattractive and troublesome length: so, may the gods love me, I would treat a profligate son (since he too is from me) – just like cut fingernails, shorn beard, trimmed hair, and other outgrowths of the human body which men detach and reject as useless and detrimental. Why indeed is a son who is born of lust and carnal impurity worth more than these aforementioned items which grow spontaneously by the law of nature? Each is mine and each is born from me and in my flesh, perhaps from an overabundance of my humors, if, as the doctors claim, products of this sort are begotten from the residue of the third digestion. It is also claimed, according to Galen, that the hair originates from the fumes of the humor.[137]

But as Aristotle says: "Nature has fixed in every living thing such a love of survival that all strive to reproduce a likeness of themselves."[138] Hence we seize eagerly upon the hope of our own virtue in our children, and we rejoice that our image, itself of short duration, lives and continues in them, like off-shoots from a tree. If they are destined to survive as evil men, they do not honor the family character but defile it; but certainly glory from their distinguished accomplishments would better and more virtuously prolong the praises of our own fame.

However, some people through a demented love, not to say madness, fully enjoy, approve, and admire all the words and deeds of their children, no matter how wrong, wicked, impious, or dreadful. Suppose they have committed a treacherous or deceitful act against a companion: the parents laugh, praise them, and proclaim it is clever to look out for oneself. If parents observe that their son is insolent and pugnacious, they applaud him, swear he is brave, and congratulate themselves on rearing a champion at home (but perhaps one who will be his father's tormentor!). If he is wanton and extravagant, wasteful and gluttonous, they claim he is lordly and generous. Educated by such lessons as these, children naturally do not repay their parents with filial devotion, sobriety, generosity, and virtuous conduct.

Therefore you have no reason to presume that I have been kept back by my devotion to my children and consequently believe it impossible to present myself among the servants of my pontifex. Furthermore, if I had had freedom of body as well as of mind, certainly

nulle profecto compedes, nulli unci, nulle moles obstruxissent iter meum, et peroptatum hactenus et acceptissimum nunc. Obligatus namque promissis, vinctus pactionibus, imo et stipendiis venditus, peregrinandi liber non fui. Rursum accepisti me Venetias ad patrem ipsum novissime profectum quam egre tulerit, quam ingratas in me ferreasque sententias invidia fabricaverit, quodque bellum cum malignitate gestavimus. Nam cavillas in nos fingere et morsibus laciniare tentavit, quod unum speravit posse, sed frustra quidem, saltem opinionis bone decorem nobis denigrare congressa.

Que stilo mandarem adhortata es plurimum et quotidie stimulos acuis. Verumtamen prima nostri otii vigilatione petito tibi labore satisfiet, quatenus huiusmodi certamen in posteros hibernis noctibus fabula sit.

Preterea liberum solutumque finge; hostiles circum turme errabant. Nesciebam quoque egregii patris et domini de mea conditione sententiam, atque unus hic me clavus potissimum fixit viderique fecit hebetem. Deum celi testor quod intaminata fide, ignito amore, zelo filiali illum colui et veneratus sum, semperque nomen eius preciosum et quoddam veluti numen habebo. Ita ut Maroneo carmine:

In freta dum fluvii current, dum montibus umbre,
. . . convexa polus dum sidera pascet,
semper honos nomenque suum laudesque manebunt.

Utinam sicut frons ipsa cetereque portiuncule corporis, ita protinus animi cura palpari visuque deprendi valeret. Mortua siquidem esset humane confederationis venenum suspicio. Plurimi quoque, virium quos imbecillitas negligentie seu frigiditatis calunniatur, ferventissimos affectuosissimosque amoris vivax fomes ostenderet. Quid plane gravius toto pectore amanti quam nullis sese notis designare posse? Atque unam hanc vel maximam semper iniuriam benegrata mens patitur, reconditum benevolentie thesaurum explodere non posse. Sentit quantum integritatis suo ipse sinu baiulet, sed nisi per fallacissimam rem atque incerti iudicii verba nequit exerere. Quid ista iactura maius?

no fetters, no fastenings, no responsibilities would have prevented a journey long desired and now most welcome. For, obligated by promises, bound by agreements, in fact, in bondage for my salary, I have not been free to travel. Also you know, when I last went to Venice to see my father, how vexed he was, what thankless and unfeeling sentiments envy fabricated against me, and what a war I waged with men of malice. They tried to fashion sophistries against me and rend me with criticisms, because they hoped (vainly) to accomplish one thing—to join battle with me and at least to blacken the beauty of my good reputation.

You have very often urged me to write of these matters, and daily you prod me on. Nevertheless, as soon as leisure gives me an opportunity to do so, my pen will satisfy you with the performances you have requested, so that this combat of mine may be a tale for posterity on winter nights.

Now, picture a man free and unfettered, surrounded by hostile throngs. I did not know the opinion of my distinguished father and lord about my situation, and one nail in particular pinned me here and made me seem lacking in energy. I call as witness God in Heaven that I have cherished and venerated Tommaso with unblemished loyalty, ardent love, and filial zeal, and will always regard his name as precious and even god-like. As is said in Vergil's poem:

While rivers run into the sea, while on the mountains shadows pass over the slopes, while heaven feeds the stars, ever shall his honor, his name, and his praises endure.[139]

If only the love in the heart could be touched and seen as easily as the face and other parts of the body! Then indeed suspicion, which poisons human concord, would have perished. Also, many people who are falsely accused of negligence and coldness, because of their bodily weakness, would be shown by the lively fire of their love to be most ardent and affectionate. What is clearly more grievous for one who loves whole-heartedly than to be unable to reveal himself by any signs? The one and always greatest injury suffered by a grateful mind is the inability to open up its hidden treasury of good-will. The possessor is aware of how much integrity he bears in his bosom, but he cannot express it except through very misleading situations and words of misunderstood import. What is a greater deprivation than this?

Domestici canes herile diligunt secunturque vestigium. Quosdam
nedum canes verum etiam equos accepimus dominorum in funere con-
sumptos inedia. Ministris aves complodunt notis. Forem nimirum feris
immanior si beneficiorum immemor benefactorem ipse° non recog-
noscerem ego meum, et ad tam alta vocatum visere magna absque
necessitate differrem. Sed non ita ferreus ego, nec, ita ut Persius ait,
"est michi cornea fibra." Nec usque adeo generis humani pudor fugit
ut bene meritis gratia nulla sit, et occasio, tempus, pudor, conscientia
pectus interdum non pungat quatenus benevolentie vicissitudo
retribuatur.

Et in re dico, vel saltem ipsa professione benegrati animi, sinon
patefacta, at tacita certe delitentique gratificatione, atque leta debendi
memoria plenave obsequendi voluntate. Profecto esset impar nimium atque deterior hominum sors inopum, si consciencia bona non
equivaleret datum bonum. Namque amare, familiari° cupere, quod
debeas letari, reddere quidem est. Nescio an id ipso ingenti desiderio
converti in beneficium incipiat.

Nempe cum illo tum pro multitudine meritorum atque gratiarum
in me, tum pro amplitudinis excellentia nil apud me dignum in-
venirem.° Quod unum potui pro rebus verba surrogavi, laudando,
diffamando, extollendo, de amplitudine quoque virtutis, de profunditate scientie, de sapientie claritate, de morum ornatu, deque moderatione vivendi; calamo certatim° et ore historiam intexui, haud habens
ipse rem decentiorem neque honestiorem ipsa gratitudinis amorisve
confessione. Hoc quidem animi pignore quo bonus patefieret affectus
meus usus fui. Et si quis facundie superest honos, utar in futurum,
dictorum eius factorumve summam, si longior michi et quietior vita
prestetur, venustiori perfectiorique meta clausurus. Quatenus qui hominem ipsum fama virtutis audient, velut presentem in oculis, mea

Family dogs love and follow their masters' footsteps. Some animals, not only dogs but even horses, we hear, have died of starvation because of the death of their masters. Birds flutter their wings at the sight of familiar attendants. Indeed, I would be more brutish than wild animals if I myself, forgetful of kindnesses, did not acknowledge my benefactor and if I postponed visiting him, now that he is called to such heights, except under pressure of great necessity. But I am not so unfeeling, nor as Persius says, "have I a heart made of horn."[140] The self-respect of the human race has not yet so completely disappeared that there is no gratitude to those deserving it, and that opportunity, time, sense of honor, and conscience sometimes do not prick the heart to repay a kindness.

I speak of this matter with, at any rate, the avowal of a grateful mind. I have, if not a manifested, at least a silent and hidden gratitude, a happy memory of obligations, and an overflowing will to serve. Surely the situation of men without resources would be exceedingly unfair and hard, if a good conscience were not the equivalent of a good gift. For to love, to wish a close friend well, to rejoice in being under obligation to him, is indeed to make him a repayment. I am inclined to think that it is the very strength of the desire which begins the transformation into a gift.

Of course, concerning Tommaso, not only in proportion to the multitude of his merits and his favors toward me, but also in proportion to his outstanding eminence, I could find nothing worthy in myself. But one thing I have been able to do: I have substituted words for deeds, praising, heralding, extolling him for the greatness of his virtue, the depth of his knowledge, the clarity of his wisdom, the luster of his character, and the temperance of his life. With both my pen and my voice I have set forth his history, since I do not possess anything more suitable or honorable than this profession of my gratitude and love. I have used this pledge of my mind to reveal my true devotion. And if any respect for eloquence still survives, I shall use it in the future to round off my summation of his words and deeds with a more graceful and polished conclusion, provided a longer and quieter life is granted me. My purpose is that those who hear of him through the fame of his virtue may, by reading about him thanks to my labor (for what it is worth), grow to know him as if he were before their

qualicumque industria perlegendo cognoscant; ut quisquis vel exemplar honestatis vel requisierit virtutis imaginem Thome vitam discere
discendoque imitari possit. Quamquam opulenti et fortunati complures
ampliori largitione donaverint donentque quotidie, ex maximis illi certe
copiis quod largirentur decerpserunt° retentaveruntque plura sibi. Ego
quod habui unum et maius exhibui, otium meum et siquid est ingenii
atque hoc in diuturnitatem nominis eius, quod vix aliusmodi munere
fieri queat.

Superest nisi quod Socrati dedit Eschines, ipsum videlicet individu-
um. "Nihil," inquit, "quod te dignum habeam invenio. Do itaque me
ipsum, hoc usui ut libet habe." Quodsi donationem huiusmodi ap-
probat laudatque Seneca, quid est cur ego simili munere donare patrem
et dominum vereor meum? Quasi eiusmodi sit largitionis impatiens
quam philosophus tantus admisit iocunde et habuit humaniter! Atqui
vera si discutimus ne huiusmodi quidem promissum largiri valeo. Nam
me ipsum antehac donatum a genitore meo longa iam diuturnaque
possessione prescripsit et suum in ius vertit. Quid igitur vult ista sibi
professio? Consignat certe refiteturque dominium.

Invitus igitur, Litera, steti. Magnaque et invisa necessitas ab optato
me expectatoque semper eventu suspendit. Ipse enim recognosco, uti
pars sine toto suo abiecte ac deformiter iacet, sic fede culpabiliterque
illo abeunte moram traho. Et equum id, fas, honestum, caritas, debi-
tum, pudor inclamant. Atque amici potissimum canunt verecundum
michi, probrum, ac improbum esse celestem huiusmodi vocationem
minime consequi. Verumtamen persuadentes ipsi quod tam michi
necesse est velle quam iocundum, quodque omnium ante° sugges-
tiones ingenti desiderio precurri, nesciunt "quanta Caribdi laborem,"
ut ille ait, quibusve intricationibus solvendi pedes sint. Non ignoro
"quid distent era lupinis," ut Flaccus ait.

Nemo rursus tardum ita me natura hebetemque fingat ut que mortalibus innata est cuntis, sciendi multa et visendi nova me quoque non
vexet accendatque cupido. Quodsi nec amor tanti patris nec reveren-

very eyes; and that everyone who seeks an exemplar of honor or a model of virtue may be able to learn of Tommaso's life and, by learning, imitate it. Although many wealthy and fortunate men have made, and make daily, more lavish donations to him, they have drawn what they give from very great resources and have retained even more for themselves. I have presented the only thing which I have, and it is a greater gift: my time and my talent, such as it is, and this for the preservation of his name. Almost no other service can accomplish this.

There remains only what Aeschines gave to Socrates, namely, his own person. "I find nothing," he said, "which I have that is worthy of you. Therefore I give myself. Take this and use it as you please."[141] If Seneca approves and praises an offering of this sort, why do I scruple to present my father and lord with a similar gift? As if he could be intolerant of the kind of tribute which the great philosopher received with pleasure and regarded with kindness! And yet, to tell the truth, I cannot make even such a pledge as this, for I myself was previously bestowed on him by my own father, and Tommaso recorded me long ago as a permanent possession, transferring me to his own authority. What then does such a declaration mean? It solidly establishes and reaffirms his ownership.

Against my will, therefore, Letter, have I stayed back. Also, great and hateful need makes me dependent on a longed-for, always hoped-for successful outcome. For I realize that, as a part without its whole is prostrate, spiritless, and unsightly, so, with him gone, I prolong my continued stay with shame and guilt. And that this is just is proclaimed by morality, honor, love, obligation, and self-respect. My friends especially reiterate that it is shameful, a reproach to me, and disloyal not to attend him in his celestial vocation. However, in their urging a course which is as needful for me to desire as it is pleasing, and which prior to anyone's suggestions I already longed to follow, they do not know "in what a fatal whirlpool am I caught," as Horace says, nor the snares from which I must disentangle my feet. I am aware of "how coins and counters differ," again to use the words of Horace.[142]

Further, let no one imagine me so spiritless and dull that I too am not tantalized and excited by what is natural to all mortals, that is, the desire to learn many things and visit new places. Even if neither

tia nec familiaritas blanda, at sacrarum ac ignotarum michi rerum dignitas atque amplitudo, tum res quoque Romanas et maximis cantata
carminibus loca visendi cognoscendive studium potuisset allicere. Expressim igitur affirmabis maturaturum me venerabilem sacramque
presentiam adire; et quod non potuit exiguo longo queretur itinere.

Ab Ethiopie finibus illustrem reginam sapientia Salomonis excivit,
Platonem Archite doctrina, sic Pithagoram Memphitici vates, sic quosdam ex Hispaniarum finibus testante° Ieronimo Titi Livii facundia
vocavit. Par caritas Paulum Damasco Syriaque lustratis Ierosolimam
traxit. Ylarionem a Palestina orbe toto queritavit Ysichius, tandem
Siculis delitentem finibus letus invenit. Quidni beati viri quos ultro
citroque conglutinat spiritus sanctus indefesso labore, vicaria caritate,
se petant, cum legamus ipsos quoque latrones in Laternina statione
degentis Affricani presentiam, veluti quoddam virtutis° numen admirari, profectos?

Non ergo me pigeat quod hosti collibuit nec premissa illustrium
exempla imitari piger omittam. Benivolos illi vel quorum scientie virtutisve fulgor invitabat percontabantur. Ista merito cunta meo instant,
pater, patronus, preceptor, dominus, benefactor, quovis utimur nomine nichil fallimur. Quam primum igitur adeundi sese facultas libertasque dabit, quod ut sit enitemur, evestigio limen transiliemus, forte
"cum Zephiris et hirundine prima," sicut ait Oratius.

LITERA: Domum pariter ages, an seorsum tacita sede diis penatibus credis? Meministi apud Ieronimum Theofrasti: peregrinari cum uxore
difficile, relinquere vero tam culpandum quam dannosum plerumque.
Quamquam ista tu quidem suspicione metuque tum pudicitia tum fide
coniugis, Deo largiente, ire securus vales. Ceterum in laudatione huiusmodi rei presertim sue taciturnitas pulcrior est.

my love and respect for so great a father nor our fond and close relationship could draw me, I could have been enticed by the dignity and
majesty of sacred rituals unfamiliar to me, as well as by my eagerness
to visit and become acquainted with Rome and places celebrated in
the greatest poetry. Therefore you will explicitly affirm that I shall
hasten to approach his venerable and sacred presence, when what is
not possible in a short visit will be sought in a long one.

Solomon's wisdom drew the illustrious queen from the land of Ethio-
pia, the learning of Archytas attracted Plato, Pythagoras was drawn
by the seers of Memphis, and, according to Jerome, certain men from
the lands of the Spanish provinces were lured by the eloquence of
Titus Livius.[143] A similar esteem led Paul to Jerusalem after he had
traversed Damascus and Syria. Hesychius searched for Hilarion from
Palestine through the whole world and finally rejoiced to find him
in retirement in Sicily.[144] Why should not blessed men whom the
Holy Spirit bonds together seek out each other with tireless efforts,
in mutual love, when we read that even robbers set forth to the presence
of Africanus, living in Liternum, as if to marvel at the divine nature
of his virtue?[145]

I therefore could not be averse to what pleased even an enemy,
nor could I be so lazy as to fail to imitate the aforementioned examples of illustrious men. They sought out kindly persons or those whose
brilliance of knowledge or virtue attracted them. All these things press
insistently upon me, as I deserve: he is father, patron, teacher, lord,
benefactor—whatever name I use, I do not go wrong. As soon, then,
as the opportunity and freedom to go presents itself (and I shall strive
for this to come about), I shall immediately cross my threshhold,
perhaps "with the Zephyrs and the first swallow," to quote Horace.[146]

LETTER: Will you take your family with you, or do you entrust them
to your household gods while you are away from your quiet home?
You remember Jerome's words about Theophrastus: to travel with
his wife was difficult, but to leave her behind was as rash as it was
disastrous.[147] However, you certainly can go free of this kind of suspicion and fear because of the chastity and fidelity of your wife, thanks
to God's bounty. But in commending this state of affairs, especially
when it is one's own, reticence is preferable.

JOHANNES: Non agam. Imo instructa rebus et circumspecta° quarum rerum familiaris eget inopia, decerno remaneat, ne quis prestolantibus querimonie iuste locus dimittatur, proficiscenti vero conscientia animum nulla detorqueat. Domi pergravis est feminarum sarcina, quisquis percenseat cultum, sumptus, vestes, ancillas, variam supellectilem, ceteraque que matronarum quotidie usus voluptasque exigit. Preterea querulum semper ac impos affectuum animal femina est, quam sola necessitas erudit. Adde adversam earum et repugnacem voluntatem, que iuxta Terentianum illud: "Ubi nolis volunt, nolunt ubi velis." Preterhec honesta causa vocante gemunt, trepidant, queruntur, nauseant, imbecillitatem pretendunt. Ubi vero impudica ratio sexum urget, impetuose sunt, audent, furunt, valent, instrepunt. Iuxta Satiri carmen, "fortem animum prestant rebus quas turpiter audent."

Multo amplioris igitur molis tam inertem laboriosamque sarcinam quam femina est per itinera trahere, precipue mille completa discriminum, latronum, predonum, et in alienam iniuriam atque exicium hiantium hominum. Quid in hospitum imo hostium diversoriis colligi, in quibus insidie, doli, mendacia, fraudes? Cunta suspecta sunt. Fidei parum, perfidie multum inest. Tot offert hostes tibi caupona quot servos. Quin uti licentius fallant blandam nescio quam caritatem fronte gestant, introrsus omni musipulatione constipati, nisi infitiemur Ecclesiasticum monentem: "Non iustificabitur caupo a mendaciis labiorum suorum."

Memorare possem viros quosdam minime revocatos filiorum seu coniugis solicitudine a peregrinationis affectu. Alexius pia fraude novam et egregiam sponsam, ipsos quin etiam parentes, illusit. Moysem ad divina iussa pergentem comitante familia minax angelus terruit, quasi vero impedimento foret domesticum onus quo minus divina iussio perfici valeret. Quod cum ad socerum Ietro redire compulisset, divi-

GIOVANNI: I shall not take her. In fact, since she is trained in household matters and is careful about the needs of our poverty-stricken family, I have decided that she is to stay behind, so that no cause for justified complaint may be afforded those awaiting me, and indeed so that conscience may not distract my mind when I leave. At home women have a lot of possessions, if one reckons up personal adornments, foodstuffs, clothing, maids, various household furnishings, and all else which matrons daily demand for their use and pleasure. Besides, a woman is always a complaining creature of uncontrolled emotions, teachable only by necessity. Add to this their contrary and obstinate will, as Terence describes it: "When you are unwilling, they will it; they are unwilling when you will it." Furthermore, when an honorable business summons them, they groan, tremble, complain, become ill, feign weakness. But when a shameful reason motivates the sex, they are impetuous, bold, impassioned, strong, and vociferous. According to the poem of the satirist, "if she be doing a bold, bad thing, her courage fails not."[148]

Therefore it is a very great trouble to drag along on trips as useless and bothersome an encumbrance as a woman, especially when the journey is filled with a thousand perils, with highwaymen, brigands, men keen to inflict suffering and death on others. Think about the inns, run not by hosts but by hostile men, where there are ambushes, cunning, lies, swindles. Everything there is suspect, there is too little honesty and much treachery. A lodging house holds for you as many enemies as it has servants. In fact, in order to deceive more readily, they wear on their faces agreeable expressions of friendliness; but within they are crammed full of all sorts of entrapments, if we are to believe Ecclesiasticus when he warns: "An innkeeper shall not be justified from the sins of his lips."[149]

I could mention certain men who were not dissuaded from their intent to travel by worry over their children or wives. Alexis tricked his distinguished new bride, as well as his parents, by a righteous deception.[150] Moses was deterred by a menacing angel from pursuing the divine commands in the company of his family, on the grounds that domestic encumbrances would prevent the accomplishment of the divine instructions. When he had compelled his family to return to his father-in-law Jethro, he completed his divine journey with greater

num liberius iter implevit. Non pudet unius femine exemplum viris
annectere, eo quidem efficacius quo muliebris expugnabilior animus
suapte natura quam virorum est. Quamquam ipsa mollicie non inter
homines multi sed infra conditionem feminarum tantum computandi
sunt quantum sensui preesse ratio debet. Paulam nobilissimam matronarum, dum Roma Ierosolimam peteret, non amicorum blande preces,
non propinquorum obsecrationes, non denique pie filiarum lacrime,
non postremo suarum et magnarum quidem rerum mordax cura revo-
care potuerunt.

Erone femina mollior ego? Quas ob res huiuscemodi ipse quoque
onera seponens solus vel maiore contentus nato comite, omnibus domi
relictis curarum sarcinis, callem arripiam, ni fors emergens laudabile
michi votum hoc decretumque detorqueat. Cum vite mortalium tam
sit rerum incerta conditio quam bene certissimus labor est.

LITERA: Qua mente? Quenam illo te voluntas agit? Mansurusne fortasse an illicet unicum adversarum tibi rerum solatium, librorum otium, repetes?

JOHANNES: Primum uti celebrem illam patris ac semper amandam michi
maiestatem venerer, ipsius fruar presentia, contemplatione delecter.
Cuius nutu reditus meus festinus aut serus erit. Demum quatenus urbem almam dudum orbis matrem imperiosamque totius, que sanctorum meritis indulgentiarum extat velut commune quoddam erarium,
visitando cognoscam. Et hoc quidem corpus priusquam deponendum
sit, iuvenilibus infectum sordibus, tum quotidianis quoque mendis,
a tergo instante senecta, visitatione sanctorum liminum expiem. Cunti me dies in bustum, perpendo, detrudunt, insonante auribus apostolica
michi sententia: "Omnes oportere duci ante tribunal Christi." Igitur
omni quidem luce memor novissimorum ac metuens maculas peccato-
rum, quibus mortalium nullus me magis abundat, aqua satifactionis
paro diluere.

Interim vero apud dominum Thomam nostro munere, Litera, fun-
gere, et fideli ac sobria narratione creditorum tibi verborum deposi-

freedom.[151] I am not ashamed to add one example of a woman to those of men; actually, it is more effective, because a woman's mind by its nature is more easily overcome than a man's. (Although many men on account of their weakness ought to be reckoned not among men but as much below the status of women as reason is superior to feeling!) When Paula, noblest of matrons, left Rome for Jerusalem, neither the persuasive pleading of her friends, the entreaties of her relatives, the filial tears of her daughters, nor even, finally, her keen anxiety over her own great possessions could hold her back.[152]

Shall I be softer than a woman? Therefore, I too, putting obstacles aside, shall leave at home all my burden of worries and take the road alone, or content with the companionship of my elder son, unless fate turns up and deflects me from this praiseworthy hope and decision. After all, the condition of mortal life is as unsure as its hardships are assured!

LETTER: What is your intent, what purpose leads you there? Do you perhaps mean to stay, or will you come back quickly to your one consolation in adversity, namely, leisure for your books?

GIOVANNI: First, my purpose is to do reverence to that distinguished majesty of my father's which I shall always love, to enjoy his presence, and to delight in looking upon him. My return will be either soon or late, as he desires. Finally, I intend to visit and become familiar with the city which has long been the kindly mother and ruler of the whole world and which is, so to speak, the common treasury of indulgences through the merits of the saints. And before this body of mine has to be laid aside, stained by the debaucheries of my youth and afterwards too by every-day faults, now that old age is creeping up on me from behind, I wish to purify myself by visiting the holy threshholds. Every day, by my reckoning, is thrusting me toward my tomb, as the Apostle's words sound in my ears: "All must be led before the judgment seat of Christ."[153] Therefore each morning, being mindful of my most recent sins and fearing their stains—sins which no mortal has in greater abundance than I—I prepare to wash them away with the water of atonement.

But, meanwhile, carry out my mission to lord Tommaso, Letter, and, using an accurate and sober narrative, deliver the deposit of words

tum ede. Quodsi cunta favorabili suscipientur auditu, sacro protinus patri subice: "Iohannes ille vester, inclite domine, quem pio sinu puerum sustulistis et labore tanto ac indulgentia ad scientie culmen virtutisque perducere nitebamini, sordida et inutili occupatione deteritur nec altius evolare nisi alas contuleritis potest. Quare per amicitie deos,° per fidei sacrum, per Conversini parentis memoriam, perque tua in eundem, sancte domine, studia, per Dei quoque omnipotentis, quod premitti decuit, reverentiam, et humane pietatis cultum supplicamus quatenus nunc dum potes liberiorem ei vacationem tua clementia provideat. Largitus illi gratuito munere tot nuper libros, equum est quoque vacuum tempus prepares ut celebritatem nominis tui gloriamve gestorum sua venturi industria perlegant. Quid iuvat accepisse ingenium a natura si illud discendo, legendo, scribendo, dictando excolere non valet?

"Novisti, pater benignissime, florem eloquentie sine fortunatorum hominum umbra vel favore exolescere numquam posse; quia 'non facile emergunt quorum virtutibus obstat res angusta domi,' ut Iuvenalis ait. Tot illustrium virorum facta dictave quibus instruitur vel excitatur humanus vigor, tot sanctorum historie, tot rerum mundi vices documentaque obscure ac sepulte iacerent, magne nisi amplitudinis homines privatis otia ingeniis suppeditassent. Non est enim frugefera res nec lucrosa facundia, sed ut laboris sic venerationis admirationisque plena, atque per hoc aliene semper felicitatis ut ornatrix laudatrixve, ita quoque pedisequa. Divus Augustus Maronis fovit ingenium, Ennium superior Africanus non emolumentis et otio tantum sed auctoravit honoribus. Magnus quoque Pompeius Theopanem Mitilenensem rerum suarum descriptorem honore et gloria prosecutus est. Sic Flaccum Mecenas, sic Dantem Guido Ravennas, sic me puero heros ille magnanimus Bernardinus de Polenta, quam amicissimus tibi pater, Iohannem de Certaldo rebus otioque donavit. Sic amplis nuper honoribus Petrarcham princeps Euganeus.

which has been entrusted to you. And if everything receives a favorable hearing, say at once to the holy father: "That Giovanni of yours, distinguished lord, whom in his childhood you took into your loving arms and with great effort and devotion strove to lead to the peak of knowledge and virtue, is being worn down by a mean and useless occupation and can fly no higher unless you give him wings. Therefore, by the gods of friendship, by the sanctity of good faith, by the memory of his father Conversino and your regard for him, holy lord, by reverence for almighty God (which should properly have been mentioned first), and by respect for human piety, we beg that now, since you have the power, your clemency may provide for him a greater period of freedom. Because you have recently bestowed upon him, as a free gift, so many books, it is right for you to provide also free time so that, thanks to his industry, posterity may read about the fame of your name and the glory of your deeds. What good is it for him to have received talent from nature if he cannot develop it by learning, reading, writing, and composing?

"You know, most kindly father, that the flower of eloquence can never blossom without the protection and favor of successful men. 'It is no easy matter anywhere for a man to rise when poverty stands in the way of his merits,' as Juvenal says.[154] So many words and deeds of illustrious men, by which human energy is guided and motivated, so many stories of the saints, so many vicissitudes and instructive examples in the history of the world, would be lying buried in obscurity if eminent men had not provided leisure for the talents of private citizens. For eloquence is not a lucrative or profitable commodity; but although attended by hardship, it commands respect and admiration. Therefore it is always the companion of another's good fortune, as enhancer and extoller. The divine Augustus fostered the genius of Vergil, the elder Africanus rewarded Ennius not only with financial aid and leisure but with honors. Pompey the Great conferred honor and glory upon Theophanes of Mitylene, the historian of his accomplishments.[155] Horace was rewarded by Maecenas, Dante by Guido of Ravenna, and in my boyhood Giovanni [Boccaccio] da Certaldo was presented with property and leisure by that noble hero, Bernardino da Polenta, who was a most loving father to you. And recently the Paduan prince bestowed impressive honors upon Petrarch.[156]

"Ego nempe cui adherescam te preter non habeo, presertim diser-
titudinis obsoleta iam dignitate. Tu igitur spes, refugium, portus,vec-
tor, auctor huius mee quantulacumque vel fingi potest vel esse virtutis,
quam obsecro supplex ne sopitam vel mortuam potius dimitti patiaris.
Sed equum est magis 'ut auctoritas vestra industrie mee adiutrix fautrix-
que sit,' ut Comicus ait.

"Ita demum sine vacationis et otii commodo libros pridem accepisse
iuvat, ut conferunt arma pacem habenti, que exedet ipsa rubigo, quantum ligna profutura sunt algenti si non, quo ardeant, ignis addatur,
quantum sana fantasia diffluente et evanescente memoria, et sine exercitatione disciplina. Quantum vero sine opere fides aut sine satisfac-
tione confessio, quantum sine caritate operatio mortalium, vel quantum
amicitia potest sine beneficentia firmitatis habere. Quasi vero non ideo
liberales artes appellate sint, quod illas adiscerent liberi, cum Enodius
quoque testetur: 'Ornamenta dicendi non sunt negotii sed quietis.' "

LITERA: Mendacem vereor ipsa deprendi, que defuisse tibi ferias enun-
ciem, tanta cum nugarum serie onusta profectura sim! Vix factivum
ut ab occupato tanta verborum emanaverit moles.

JOHANNES: Imo et quotidiane mentem nobis iniurie, ingrata vero fe-
dave servitus sibi vendicat corpus, ut vix quicquam vacui remaneat,
si non aliquid quotidie temporis voluptatibus ipse naturalibus ut
comesationi, deambulationi, somno, theatrorumve conversationi sub-
duxero, et amicorum illud quidem literis responsa suppeditat. Atque
utinam indicare ipsa sufficeres quanto rerum turbine, quam sevis fortune insultibus impetiti, quantis quoque curis ac solicitudinibus morsi
exaravimus orationem huiusmodi. Imo contra invidiam, iniquum, et
odium stantes in acie dictavimus, ut aliis forte videtur plura sed pro
animi quidem ubertate obligationisque nodo paucissima.

Verumtamen nil habemus preter huius qualecunque vocis obse-

"I, of course, have no one to rely on except you, especially since eloquence is no longer esteemed. You therefore are the hope, refuge, haven, conveyor, and initiator of this talent of mine, however small it may be supposed, or may be; and I beg humbly that you not allow it to be dismissed as torpid or even dead. And it is still more fitting that 'your authority support, help, and assist' my diligence, as Terence says.[157]

"Finally, as to the books which I received some time ago, since I lack the advantage of leisure and respite from work, they are no more useful than weapons to a man in peacetime, which will be eaten up by rust; or than firewood to a shivering man if no fire is put to it so it will burn; or than a sound imagination when memory is faded and gone, or training without exercise! Indeed, they are of no more value than faith without works, confession without atonement, human activity without love, or friendship without benefit of constancy. After all, the liberal arts were so named because free men, i.e., men with liberty, learn them. Ennodius also testifies to this: 'The ornaments of speaking are not the products of business activity but of leisure.' "[158]

LETTER: I am afraid I'll be caught giving a false impression if I announce that you have no holidays, when I shall be setting out loaded down with so great an array of trivia! It is scarcely believable that such a quantity of words has emanated from a busy person.

GIOVANNI: On the contrary, daily insults punish my mind, and my body is held in a base and thankless servitude, so that hardly any freedom remains to me, unless I steal some time each day for natural pleasures like eating, walking, sleeping, or attending the theater. And this also gives me an opportunity to answer letters from my friends. Now if only you could manage to point out the great disturbances of my life, the cruel blows of fortune which have assailed me, the cares and worries which have vexed me while working on this treatise! In fact, it is while marshaling myself to do battle with envy, injustice, and hatred that I have written, composing a great deal, perhaps, in the opinion of others, but in proportion to the fertility of my mind and to my obligations, only very little.

Nevertheless, I have nothing to offer except this service of my voice,

quium. Hoc ita dicendi ordine locutus sum, in oculis quasi clementissimi antistitis mei, sortem, eventum, conditionem mearum omnem ipse, ut solebam hactenus, rerum deplorarem. Quis enim amplius restat cui omnes pectoris impetus velut patri fidissimo credam? Cui medico saucii cordis vulnera° detegam? Ad quem consultum ancipiti laborantem sententia animum traham? Abiit instructor meus, consultus meus, sospitator meus, cui quo gravaris tam longa processit oratio.

Nec id sine iniuria causaris, cum in sancto Iob legas esse difficile "concepta verba tenere." Ardebat enim diu mens, cum ire nequiret, in decus celebritatemque tanti nominis dictamen ordiri et ebullire quicquid in pectore coxeram diu. Erat quidem presto materia sed otium deerat. Ceterum natali Domini Iesu cum vacarem ipse pauculis a labore diebus inerti nolui vacatione transire, nec rursus indignis studioso homine voluptatibus languescere. Sed quicquid otii opere discipulorum subduxi libenter id domino meo dispensatum est. Dumque alios epulatio haberet, iocis alii laxarentur, his vicatim otiose vagantibus, preciosa res prudenti tempus elaberetur, quosdam libido transversos perdite vexaret, illi patrimonia tesseris ponerent—cellula memet indulgentem calamo habebat, intra bibliothece parietes corpore, tota sed intentione cum beatissimo patre Thoma cohabitantem. Hoc quidem uno benemerita de hominibus natura, quod gladios, tela, ignes, mare, montes penetrantem elargita est animum. Qui si angustari ut membra cohercerive queat, quid infimius homine reperire queas? Itaque dum volverem ipse mecum laudes domini Thome et virtutis amplitudinem admirarer, ita quidem plerumque afficiebar ut esse una michi videretur, ex quo nulla potuit voluptas antiquior offerri.

In qua re gratias omnipotenti Deo, qui sic me hactenus castigatum sua misericordia circumfulsit, quod deprendenti michi orbis huius men-

such as it may be. And so I have used this method of speaking, as
if I were deploring the fate, the outcome, the whole condition of my
affairs before the very eyes of my most clement priest, as I used to
do formerly. For who else is there to whom as a most loyal father
I can entrust all the emotions of my breast, to whom as a doctor I
can reveal the injuries of my wounded heart, or to whom as an adviser I can bring my mind laboring under indecisive thought? My
teacher has gone away, my adviser, my preserver, for whom I have
created the lengthy treatise with which you are burdened.

And you do wrong to complain of it, since you read in holy Job
that it is difficult "to withhold the words he hath conceived."[159] For
my mind had long been eager, since I could not go, to embark on
a literary composition to promote the glory and fame of that great
name, and to bring to a boil what I had been stirring in my heart
for a long time. The material was ready at hand, but time was lacking. But at the birthday of the Lord Jesus, when I was free from work
for a few days, I was unwilling to spend my vacation in idleness; and
on the other hand I did not wish to fritter away the time on pleasures
unworthy of a scholar. Whatever time I have stolen from work with
my pupils has gladly been given over to my lord. So while partying
occupied some, and others amused themselves with merrymaking or
wandered idly through the streets, letting time (a precious commodity to the wise man) slip away; while wanton passions drove some
upon a reckless and depraved course, and others were betting their
inheritances on the dice—my little room was holding me, dedicated
to my pen, physically within the walls of my library, but in my entire mental concentration dwelling with my most blessed father Tommaso. For this one gift nature deserves thanks from mankind, that
she has bestowed upon us a mind which can overcome swords, spears,
fire, seas, and mountains. If the mind could be restricted and confined
like the body, what could you discover more worthless than a human being? Therefore, whenever I reflected upon the renown of lord
Tommaso and admired his great virtue, I was usually so strongly affect-
ed that he seemed to be in my presence. No finer pleasure could be
given me than this.

I thank almighty God, who, after previously chastising me, merci-
fully shed His light upon me; so that, as I recognize the crafty wiles

dacis atque fugacis versutias terrena blandimenta sordescunt, asper-
norque que mundanis illecebris devios agunt. Eos° autem qui vulgo
felicissimi predicantur infelices cum Seneca iudico. Quo fit ut ridens
ipse procul e tutissimo velut scopulo vite presentis letiferos Syrenarum cantus, otio et solitudine contentus degam, meliora de michi pol-
licens. "Nunc," inquam, "valere, bone vir, nunc rectum quid sit incipis
sapere, quam periculosa vulgi frequentia, quam frugi et sancta solitu-
do. Advertis," inquam, "ubique gentium quam scelerate, quam infide
res mundi, et omnia super, infidelissimus ac ultro infestissimus homini homo, quo nullum natura animal edidit miserius neque superbius.
Saltem proprie fragilitatis oblitum Ecclesiasticum admoneret elogium:
'Quid superbis, terra et cinis?' " Ideoque tutam hanc atque optimam
partem capesso et literis et studio meme dedens, sic optime ratus hominum temporumque molestias declinare posse. Sic vulgi calco favorem,
tam mehercule fedum quam volatilem. Sat lucubratiunculis meis sit,
conscientia optimus quidem testis.

Interdum illud michi Virgilianum despondeo: "Macte virtute, puer,
sic itur ad astra." Ita plane affectus huiusmodi extimatione plerumque
ut instantis vite, imo peregrinationis seu exilii potius calamitatibus fessus,
tum amplissima spe immortalitatis erectus, crebro illud apostoli cla-
mem: "Infelix homo, quis me liberabit de corpore mortis huius?" Quotiens vero septimum Plinii volumen Naturalis Historie verso, Democriti
vicem nunc Eraclii comprobo, quorum Seneca teste alter flebat, risabat
alter cum procedebat in publicum. Democrito cunta ineptie, Eraclio
miserie censebantur, quasi vero conditio mortalium vana sit omnino
vel misera iudicanda. Hactenus cuntis ego quas mediocris certe fortuna conferre valet blandiciis usus, quid impresentiarum sentio? Quid
teneo? Quid omni ex humana superest voluptate nisi peccatum? O
felix hominum genus, si anteiret annos nostros et non sequeretur sapientia, que pene sero semper mortalibus advenit. Quodsi animadvertere-

of this deceptive and transitory world, earthly enticements grow sordid to me, and I scorn the things which lead men astray by their worldly charms. Moreover, those who are commonly called most happy, I along with Seneca judge as unhappy.[160] As a result I laugh from afar off, as if from a very safe rock, at the death-bearing Siren songs of this present life and live content in peace and solitude, promising myself better things from myself. "Now," I say, "my good man, you are beginning to be strong and to know the right, the perils of associating with the crowd, and the value and sanctity of solitude. You notice everywhere," I continue, "how wicked and undependable is the business of the world, and above all how exceedingly treacherous and deliberately inimical man is to man, of all animals which nature has produced the most wretched and the most proud. At least this verse of Ecclesiasticus admonished one who was heedless of his own frailty: 'Why be proud, earth and ashes?' "[161] And so I take this good and secure position, devoting myself to literature and study, thinking that in this way I can best avoid the problems of men and of the times and ignore the favor of the crowd, which is as base, by Hercules, as it is fickle! My conscience is the best witness that there is good reason for me to burn the midnight oil.

Sometimes I despair of achieving what that verse of Vergil's expresses: "Well done, my child, so man scales the stars."[162] I am frequently so deeply moved by this sort of judgment that, after being wearied by the misfortunes of a demanding life, and, even more, of my wanderings (or rather exile), then restored by the great hope of immortality, I often cry out these words of the Apostle: "Unhappy man that I am, who shall deliver me from the body of this death?" Indeed each time I read the seventh book of Pliny's *Natural History*, I approve first the position of Democritus, then that of Heraclitus, of whom Seneca claimed that the latter would weep and the former would laugh whenever he went out in public.[163] To Democritus all seemed folly, to Heraclitus, misery, as if the human condition is to be adjudged either entirely foolish or entirely wretched. Formerly I relished all the pleasant things which a modest fortune can procure. What do I now enjoy, what do I possess, what is left from all human pleasure except sin? Oh happy race of men, if only wisdom, which always comes to mortals nearly too late, could precede our years in-

mus ista, quam fugax et fragilis conditio nostra est, quam feda origo, quam culpabilis laboriosaque vita, denique meticulosus miserque exitus, nichil prius meliusve foret quam seculi contemptus et amor Dei. Vel forte Eraclii fletibus adderentur eiulatus et planctus.

Hec peccator ego miser contuens sed necdum complectens, nam id divini quidem muneris est. Si quis michi deus eius quod optem hic ego prestet optionem, sobriam et sibi suppetentem° supellectilem atque a rebus solitudinem ultro ac libens deligam, bonis amicam mentibus, honestissimis quoque studiis complectendam nostra etate presertim. Quandoquidem hominum conversatio periculosior numquam, nec exemplar honesti minus hesurum mentibus, nec erudicio profutura minus in populis. Ad scelera docile, ad virtutem insolens genus nostrum est, orbe gravido bellis, fraudibus, rapinis, avaricia debellatrice virtutum atque federis humani pernicie. Ideoque conducit a corruptorum atque corrumpentium turba procul in recessu degere, et legendo, meditando, sibi ac generi humano consulere.

Olim forte scripturis honor erit, quamvis ut fit scriptorum parentibus auctoritas veneratioque nulla prebeatur. Quin imo bene si exprobratio improbatioque desit. Si quando autem errori publico repugnare quis posse videatur, cum Ieronimo, cum Cicerone, tum ipse fatebor subduci minime debere studiosum, quin ultro gerendis rebus capessendam esse materiam. Ubi vero actio sterilis appareat, boni quamquam viri opera numquam salutaris esse nequeat, tum deliteat, secedat. Sic Benedictus veneficos fratres, sic Paulus Damascum, sic Romanum Ieronimus clerum fugit. Cicero quoque, armis Cesaris libertate reque publica succumbente, excedens urbe rure se continebat. Metellus Numidicus exulare maluit quam Saturnini, quos irritare non valebat, interesse° conatibus. Itaque vir sapiens cedet interdum, non subtrahendo tamen operam suam sed conservando in tempore profuturam.

Interim negotium suum aget, "sibi canet et musis," ut Antigenidas

stead of following them! Yet if we should concentrate on how fleeting and frail our condition is, how base our origin, how reprehensible and wearisome our life, and finally how fearful and wretched our death, there would be nothing more important or desirable than contempt for the world and love for God. Perhaps our weeping and wailing would be added to Heraclitus' tears.

I, a wretched sinner, contemplate these things but do not yet embrace them, for this is a divine gift. If some divinity should offer me a choice of what I would like here, I would gladly and freely choose a sober, adequate means of support and, far from business matters, solitude, which is a friend to good minds and which also ought to be embraced for honorable studies, especially in our age. For indeed never will association with men be more full of peril, or an example of honor less likely to cling to their minds, or learning less valuable among the people. Our race is receptive to crime and insolent to virtue, in a world pregnant with wars, impostures, rapine, and with avarice which is the vanquisher of virtue and the destroyer of human concord. Therefore it is expedient to live in a retreat far from the throng of the corrupted and the corrupters, and by reading and meditating to take thought for one's own welfare and that of the human race.

Perhaps in time to come there will be respect for written works, although as it is now no esteem or honor is bestowed upon the creators of such compositions. In fact, one is lucky if there is no reproach or censure. If ever it seems possible to take a stand against public error, then I myself, along with Jerome and Cicero, will confess that a scholar ought not simply to retire but instead ought to find his subject matter in the world of affairs. But when activity appears fruitless (although a good man's effort can never fail to be salutary), then let him go into retreat, let him withdraw. In this way Benedict escaped the murderous monks, Paul fled Damascus, and Jerome escaped the Roman clergy. Cicero too, when freedom and the republic were succumbing to the armed might of Caesar, left the city and lived in the country. Metellus Numidicus preferred exile rather than involvement in the designs of Saturninus which he could not counteract.[164] And so a wise man will sometimes retreat, without however giving up his efforts but saving them to be of use at a proper time.

Meanwhile he will attend to his own business, "sing for himself

ait. Vacabit bone menti, edet monimenta quibus proficiant vel delectentur posteri. Vacabit pre omnibus creatori suo, contemplando, orando, et relique studiose vacationis munera implendo. Que liber sanctus Ecclestiastici meminit: "Sapientiam antiquorum exquiret, in prophetis vacabit. Narrationem virorum nominatorum conservabit et in versutias parabolarum introibit. Occulta proverbiorum exquiret . . . Deinde cor suum tradet ad vigilandum diluculo ad Dominum° qui fecit illum, et in conspectu altissimi deprecabitur. Aperiet os suum in oratione, et pro delictis suis deprecabitur." Ista inquam est beate solitudinis excubatio, ista quidem milicia. His intentum non inflat ambitio, non urit cupiditas, libido non vexat.

O bonum supernum, o numquam infestum, o non intellectum superbis! Quid Flaccus clamat:

> Quam beatus ille qui procul negotiis,
>> ut prisca gens mortalium,
> paterna bobus exercet rura suis,
>> solutus omni fenore.

"O rus," inquit,

>> quando te aspiciam quandoque licebit
> nunc veterum libris, nunc somno et inertibus horis
> ducere solicite iocunda oblivia° vite?

Cui non vehementer beate solitudinis amorem desideriumque gignat Ypolitus apud Anneum, cum fructum vite delitentis et gaudium tangit? "Non alia," inquit,

> magis est libera et vitio carens,
> ritusque melius vita que priscos colat,
> quam que relictis menibus silvas amat.
> Non illum avare mentis inflammat furor
> qui se dicavit montium insontem iugis,
> non aura populi et vulgus infidum bonis,
> non pestilens invidia, non fragilis favor;
> non ille regno servit ac regno iminet,
> vanosque honores sequitur aut fluxas opes,
> spei metusque liber; aud illum niger

and the Muses," as Antigenidas says.[165] He will have time for his
good mind, he will produce literature in which posterity will find profit
and enjoyment. He will have time above all for his Creator, as he
meditates, prays, and performs the other duties of his scholarly seclusion. The holy book of Ecclesiasticus reminds us: "He will seek out
the wisdom of the ancients, he will be occupied in the prophets. He
will keep the sayings of renowned men, and will enter into the sub-
tleties of parables. He will seek out the hidden depths of proverbs. . . .
Then he will give his heart to resort early to the Lord that made him,
and he will pray in the sight of the most High. He will open his mouth
in prayer, and will make supplication for his sins."[166] This, I say, is
the guard duty of blessed solitude; this is its army service. Ambition
does not puff up the man intent upon these things, greed does not
inflame him, passion does not harry him.

Oh heavenly boon, never harmful, unknown to the proud! Why
does Horace proclaim:

Happy the man who far away from business cares, like the
pristine race of mortals, works his ancestral acres with his steers,
from all moneylending free?

"Oh rural home," he says,

when shall I behold you! and when shall I be able, now with
books of the ancients, now with sleep and idle hours, to quaff
sweet forgetfulness of life's cares?[167]

Who does not find created in himself a passionate love and desire
for solitude by the words of Hippolytus, in Seneca, when he touches
upon the rewards and joy of the secluded life?

There is no life so free and innocent, none which better cherishes the ancient ways, than that which, forsaking cities, loves
the woods. His heart is inflamed by no mad greed of gain who
has devoted himself to harmless ranging on the mountain-tops;
here is no shouting populace, no mob, faithless to good men,
no poisonous hate, no brittle favor. No slave is he of kings, nor
in quest of kingship does he chase empty honors or elusive wealth,
free alike from hope and fear; his venomous spite assails not with

edaxque livor dente degeneri petit;
nec scelera populos atque inter urbes sita
novit, nec omnes conscius strepitus pavet.

Hec et cetera que colligit, quis bonus non admiretur, amet, optetque?
Sic vocat fortunatos agricolas Maro, sic Ylario sexaginta et tres annos
natus almam solutudinem suspirabat, sic tranquillum Gregorius cenobii
recessum.

Sic denique, ut domestica quoque prebeamus exempla, Petrarcha
in solitudine floruit et finivit. Quam vero nedum literis accommoda
sit, verum propior quoque saluti procul a mundi turba secessio, divinitus
beatus ille Arsenius audivit. Cui quidem oranti quonam pacto salvari
posset, divina vox insonuit: "Arseni, fuge homines et salvaberis." Fac-
tus tali deinde oraculo monachus iterum audit: "Arseni, fuge, tace,
quiesce." Supervacuum addere beate solitudinis gaudia quive in eadem sanctitatis profectus vel literarum exorti sunt, cum Bernardus
precipue testetur literas se inter silvas et fagos didicisse. Nempe si in
lucis didicisse ut Bernardus, si quas habeo, fateri non possum, utinam
saltem augere contingat.

Atque hoc unum te deprecatum iri nunc, Litera, iubeo, non autem
opes, gloriam, potentatum:° si libris otium donatis prestetur, accipi-
mus satis magna. Sed quid hoc facilius tanto domino et cardinali quam
uni homini dare otium, et suo et suam ad gloriam vigilanti?

Verumtamen tempus est amodo limen exeas, Litera. Dictatoris tui
memento. Ne quid titubes cave, quo minus omnia recolas, neve lin-
gua trepidante verba confringas. En vestibus decoram et vario te, Litera,
ornatu dimittimus, veluti mangones quos exponunt equos consuevere
faleris, freno, et variata auro atque ebore sella concinnare. Sicuti quoque virguncule que, ut procos irritent inescentque, nisi purpurismo
cerusave ac reliquis muliercularum fucis vultum depictas non offe-

the bite of base-born tooth; those crimes that spawn midst the
city's teeming throngs he does not know, nor in guilty consciousness does he quake at every sound.

What good man would not admire, love, and desire these and other
things which he possesses? Hence Vergil calls farmers happy, Hilarion at the age of sixty-three sighed for kindly solitude, and Gregory
for the tranquil seclusion of the monastery.[168]

Finally, to use as well some instances from home: Petrarch flourished
and ended his life in solitude,[169] and blessed Arsenius learned through
divine inspiration that retirement far from the world's tumults is not
only congenial to learning but also closer to salvation.[170] For when
he was asking in prayer how he could be saved, a divine voice came
to him: "Arsenius, flee the company of men and you will be saved."
After he had then become a monk because of the oracular utterance,
he again heard: "Arsenius, flee, be silent, be at peace." It is superfluous to add the joys of blessed solitude and the benefits to sanctity
and erudition which have arisen from it, since Bernard in particular
declares that he learned literature in the midst of forests and beech
trees.[171] To be sure, if I cannot confess like Bernard that I acquired
my learning (such as I have) in woodland groves, I hope that it may
at least succeed in increasing.

And there is one thing which I now order you to plead for, Letter—
not, however, wealth, honor, or a position of power: if only time
could be furnished me for the books which I have received, then this
is a sufficiently great gift. But what is easier for so eminent a lord
and cardinal than to give leisure to one man, who is his own and
is ever watchful for his glory?

However, now it is time for you to leave our threshhold, Letter.
Remember your author. Be careful not to slip up and forget anything,
nor mangle your words with stammering tongue. See, I am sending
you off beautifully dressed, Letter, with many-colored ornaments—
just as merchants are accustomed to deck out horses which they put
up for sale, with metal trappings, a bridle, and a saddle of contrasting
gold and ivory; and just as young maidens, in order to excite and entice
suitors, offer themselves to public view only after their faces have been
painted with rouge and powder and other cosmetics of silly women.

runt sese spectaculo.° Quodsi te orante successum fero, amplioribus decoramentis nedum honestabere sed miro te quotannis honore celebrabit hec domus.

LITERA: En pergo. Tu prosperum interim michi iter, faustum deinde successum ac reditum superos ora. Vale.

Anno imperii domini nostri Iesu Christi millesimotrecentesimoseptuagesimonono. Indicione secunda Nonis Ianuariis.

Vertice purpureo sacro qui in cardine mundi
Fulge, Thoma, tui pueri dignare volumen.
Quamquam te resonet totum tua fama per orbem,
Hoc quoque venturis nostro discere labore.

Then if I achieve success as a result of your request, not only will you be ornamented with more elegant decorations, but also this household will sing your praises with wondrous honor every year.

LETTER: Well, then, I'm off. Meanwhile, pray to the gods for a good trip for me, then a successful outcome and return. Farewell!

In the year of the reign of our Lord Jesus Christ 1379, second indiction, January 5.

Tommaso, cardinal-hatted, you shine on the world like
a beacon.
Consider this volume I send you and find it worthy, I pray
you.
Although your fame has resounded throughout the civilized nations,
This volume will add to your glory even for men of the
future.

oditum superos ora. Vale.
Anno imperij dni nri Jesu
xpi Millesimotrecentesimosep
tuagesimonono Indicaoe secda
Nonis Januarijs;

Vertice ppureo sic q in caidine mudi
fulges Thoma tui pueri digne uolum.
Quaq te resonet totu tua fama poebez
boocq ueturis nro discere labore;

libe Coluccij pxxri de Stigno

APPENDIX
NOTES
BIBLIOGRAPHY
INDEX

Appendix

Document One

[see introduction, n. 21 and historical notes, n. 60]

Archivio di Stato di Venezia, Maggior Consiglio, reg. 19 (Novella), fol. 140v.

From margin: Dominus, consiliarii et capita.

1374, 23 April. Capta.

Cum Reverendus pater dominus Patriarcha Gradensis dispositus in omnibus ad honorem nostri dominii comparuerit coram nobis asserens quod quando placeret nobis facere reformari pacta clericorum, ut cessarent rixe et scandala inter clericos et laycos. Ipse esset paratus facere plenam iusticiam contra clericos suos delinquentes, taliter quod pro certo dominium haberet merito contentari. Et similiter dicit vicarius castellanus. Et pro honore nostro faciat in hoc salubriter providere, taliter quod maleficia non transeant impunita. Vadit pars quod eligantur quinque sapientes, scilicet una manus, per dominum, consiliares et capita, et due alie per duas manus electionum in maiori consilio, qui debeant esse cum dicto domino Patriarcha et conferre etiam cum vicario castellano super predictis. Et diligenter examinare et providere super modo tenendo pro correctione et reformatione excessuum occurrentium inter clericos et laycos, et super dependentibus ab eis, dando nobis suum consilium in scriptis, cum quo erimus hic et fiet sicut videbitur. Et quilibet possit ponere partem et habeant terminum unius mensis.

Et possint accipi de omni loco et officio, etiam si haberent plures sensus, non accipiendo ultra unum pro officio.

Document Two

[see introduction, n. 22 and historical notes, n. 60]

Archivio di Stato di Venezia, Maggior Consiglio, reg. 19 (Novella), fols. 145v–147r.

1374, 19 November, 13th indiction. Capta omnes.

Sapientes: Ser Marcus Contareno, Ser Franciscus dale Bochole, Ser Andreas Basilio.

Infrascripte sunt provisiones ordinate per dictos sapientes cum beneplacito et consensu domini Patriarche Gradensis et vicarii domini Episcopi Castellani super correctione excessuum committendorum sive perpetrandorum inter clericos et laycos. Que quidem provisiones nove simul cum provisionibus veteribus contentis in libro spiritus ad cartam cxliij [i.e., reg. 18, fol. 143r], firmate sunt usque annos quinque, ut in ista subsequenti parte eciam declaratur.

Quia provisiones et correctiones facte per tempora preterita super clericis et laycis, cum omni diligentia examinate sunt per sapientes presentes. Et habent ipsi sapientes quod huiusmodi provisiones preterite nullam correctionem recipiant quoniam sapientes illi, qui illas consuluerunt, mature et prudenter, ipsas ordinaverunt, sapientes presentes nullam correctionem, vel mutationem, super illis faciunt. Sed quia leges non possunt precise providere omnibus casibus occurentibus. Et per tempore elapsa occurrerint maleficia et casus, quibus provisum non est. Ad corrigendos ipsos casus de novo provisum est per sapientes prout in subsequentibus septem capitulis continetur. Que quidem capitula sunt visa, audita, et sub magna deliberatione pensata, et per consequens libere approbata per dominum Patriarcham Gradensem, et per dominum Nicolaum Hermolaum Zierra vicarium Episcopi Castellani, asserentes scilicet ipsum dominum Patriarcham et vicarium antedictum hec capitula in se omnem honestatem, equitatem et iustitiam continere. Que quidem capitula sunt ipsa in sequentibus, scripta, cap-

ta et confirmata per annos quinque simul, cum aliis provisionibus
veteribus.

In nomine Dei. Capta.

[1] Super iustitia in criminalibus ministranda declaretur et intelligatur
talem esse et fieri debere iusticiam, quod si clericus perpetraverit
homicidium in persona layci vel tale maleficium, delictum vel exces-
sum propter que laycus, qui talia commisisset, deberet mori secundum ordinamenta dominationis laicalis, ipse talis clericus iudicatus per
dominationem clericalem debeat finire vitam suam, seu supplitium mortis sue in carcere nominato Grandonia deputato clericis talia committentibus ad requisitionem et beneplacitum domini Patriarche Gradensis
et domini Episcopi Castellani, seu vicariorum suorum. Et si mors dic-
ti clerici statueretur publica [sic] per dominationem clericalem, in hoc
casu officiales dominationis secularis, causa favoris exequende iustitie,
debeat esse simul cum officialibus dominationis clericalis, donec exe-
quuta et consumata fuerit iustitia publica talis clerici delinquentis.

De parte 259

De non 76

Non sinceri 36

|fol. 146r| [2] Capta.

Si vero aliquis clericus inculparetur de morte alicuius et dictum
homicidium non fovet probatum legittime, sed contra talem clericum
essent presumptiones vel indicia, tunc dominatio clericalis procedat
contra dictum clericum ad questionem et torturam, eo modo quo sibi
videbitur. Et in casu quo talis clericus fuerit confessus delictum, tunc
fiat et procedatur, ut continetur in capitulo proximo precedenti, quod
incipit: "super iustitia in criminalibus ministranda." Sed si purgatis
presumptionibus vel iudiciis habitis contra clericum per torturam vel
questionem sibi exhibitam, confessus non fuerit, tunc dominatio clericalis, habito Deo preoculis, faciat in hoc, ut iusticia et equitas suadebunt.

De parte 258

De non 72

Non sinceri 47

[3] Capta.

Verum si aliquis clericus commiserit furtum, robariam, vel aliud delictum propter quod secundum constitutiones et ordinamenta nostra laycus deberet perdere membrum vel membra, tunc talis clericus

condemnetur arbitrarie in carcere antedicto Grandonia nominato et deputato, ad requisitionem et beneplacitum domini Patriarche Gradensis et Episcopi Castellani, seu eorum vicariorum, talibus clericis talia committentibus. Et finito tempore pene carceris sibi date, per dominationem clericalem debeat ipse clericus relaxari cum conditione quod sit perpetuo bannitus de Veneciis et districtu et privatus beneficio et titulo que haberent in Veneciis et districtu et privatur beneficio et titulo que haberet in Veneciis vel districtu. Et si ullo tempore contingerit reperiri quod iterum capiatur et stet in carcere antedicto Grandonia nominato per tempus limitatum per dominationem clericalem, quo finito, iterum relaxetur, ita quod hoc totiens servetur quociens fuerit per dictum clericum contrafactum, in banno semper ipso clerico remanente.

De parte 271

De non 70

Non sinceri 37

[4] Capta.

Insuper, eciam si aliquis clericus commiserit delictum propter quod laycus deberet bullari et frustari, quod talis clericus tantummodo banniatur perpetuo de Veneciis dicto modo contento in capitulo proximo precedente, ipso clerico ut predictum est in banno perpetuo remanente.

De parte 260

De non 98

Non sinceri 46

|fol. 146v| [5] Capta.

Et quocienscumque aliquis clericus detentus fuerit per officiales ad quos spectabit quod isti officiales licite possint pro aliquo delictorum predictorum detineri facere in carcere Grandonia antedicta clericos talia comittentes. Et illa die vel sequente denuntiare dominationi clericali detentionem talium clericorum ut de ipsis fiat debita punitio et condigna. Et teneantur domini de nocte et alii officiales ad quos spectat facere inquisitiones et processus criminales mittere copiam huiusmodi processuum et inquisitionum dominationi clericali super omnibus que habebunt contra clericum inculpatum pro informatione dicte dominationis clericalis, ut ipsa dominatio procedere valeat secundum Deum et iustitiam.

De parte 276
De non 54
Non sinceri 39
[6] Capta.

Preterea ut servetur intentio utriusque dominationis statuatur quod quocienscumque facta fuerit aliqua condemnatio contra clericum in casibus specificatis, quod ipsa dominatio clericalis mittat ipsas condemnationes dominis de nocte, qui, ut hoc servetur, faciant ipsas registrari in quaternis sui officii.

De parte 285
De non 53
Non sinceri 37
[7] Capta.

Quia sepe contingit quod clerici dimissi commissari per seculares non bene nec legaliter administrant bona sui commissi. Et seculares eciam dimissi commissarii per clericos idem faciunt quod quidem vertitur in maximum contrarium mentium testatorum, ut talia reformentur sub debita regula. Statuatur et sic de cetero debeat observari quod quicumque clericus dimissus fuerit commissarius per aliquem secularem teneatur et debeat ipse clericus sub pena privationis notarie, si erit notarius, et sub pena eciam privationis commissarie, atque etiam standi in dicto carcere, per menses tres Grandonia nominato, facere si scribi ad officium dominorum de nocte. Et facere se notari commissarium testatoris per quem dimissus fuerit. Et pro dicta commissaria iuste et legaliter ministranda, si illam voluerit acceptare, teneatur dare dominis de nocte idoneam et sufficientem plezariam, ut in casu quo non ministrasset seu non ministraret recte, et secundum intentionem testatoris aut in alio casu quo ipse talis clericus haberet de bonis testatoris. Et |fol. 147r| illa bona per aliquem casum non posset administrare, ipse clericus aut fideiussio data per ipsum clericum teneatur ad restitutionem bonorum omnium que haberet et restarent ipsi clerico. Et consimiliter et versa vice in omnibus et per omnia sic intelligatur et observetur de quolibet seculari dimissio commissario per quemcumque clericum.

De parte 296
De non 52
Non sinceri 30

Nota, ut supra scriptum est, quod iste provisiones nove comprehense in supradictis septem capitulis simul cum provisionibus omnibus veteribus notatis in libro Spiritus ad cartam cxliii [reg. 18, fol. 143]. Capte et confirmate fuerunt et ordinate debere observari per annos quinque futuros, in capite quorum veniatur ad maius consilium. Et si videbitur predicta omnia iterum confirmari debeant per illud tempus quod videbitur.

Document Three

[see historical notes, n. 132]

Giovanni Conversini da Ravenna, *Memorandarum rerum liber.* cap. 18. De perfidia, parag. 1. Blanor Serravallensis, in Venice, Biblioteca Querini-Stampalia, MS 1006, fol. 54r/b–v/a. Capitula de perfidia.

Educatur nolens licet impium scelus in lucem, ne penam latendo aut infamiam evitet. Invalescit enim latebris nequicia torpet conspectu, et sicut predicacione virtus inclarescit, ita dum vulgantur vicia langue— |fol. 54v| scunt. Egredere igitur infelix filius, sed infelicior anima, patrie dedecus exitium parenti, Blanor Seravalensis, qui Zanucium patrem, quia, veluti pro senii morbo contractioris spei, ita parcioris in suos licencie, haud omnifariam liberum nato rerum usum, ceu diuturno partam labore substanciam et mox profligaturo impartiretur, veneno substulit. Is felix diu scelere, cum luxuria, luxu, abusu, omni postremo vanitate intemperanciaque hereditatem profligaret, tandem impii facinoris penas dedit. Enimvero increbuerat vulgo, nam diu eciam scelera obmutescentibus linguis oculi tota inclamante natura queunt. Increbuerat, inquam, sed incerto quidem auctore Blanorem patricidam usque adeo, ut ducalis aures dominii rei atrocitas perculisset. Ceterum forte profecturus presidis Seravali de rei publice commodis ad summum litteras magistratum accepit; quibus iuxta imperium traditis, ad amicos notosve, quorum rerum afluencia largicionesque profuse plurimos ceu blandos, sic labantes peperere, divertit et festive opipareque suscipitur. E quibus non defuere qui reum patrocidii vul-

go haberi dicerent. Atque id quidem e censorum numero nec asseve-
rabant vanum modo rumorem, sed ducali archano ratione constare.
Consulunt, hortantur cedat ultro dum rumor ipse languescat. Contra
ille, sic precipitem agebat impietas, et ante Deum paterna iniuria clami-
tans monitus ridebat, contempnebat, assertans ceu nullius conscium
ullo timore ullove rumore perstringi non posse. Tandem re profectu-
rus, si quid allatis respondere mandaret litteris, ducem adit. Qui admonitus nomine censente principe magistratu litteras ad Seravali
prefectum, quibus de sceleris questione mandabatur, accipere iubet.
At ipse quid ferret ignarus Seravalum festus remeat. Iocunde preses
atque amice recipit ceterique applausu socio concives, ubi vero lateri
presidis colocatus assedit. "En," ait, "ducales litteras offero," elatus sane
elatione quasi tacitum quid sueque dumtaxat fidei credendum pertulis-
set. Quibus tamdem resignatis atque perlectis, preses haud libens inquit, "Age, doleo, hac animadversione in te, Blanor, quam in alium
utendum esse verum imperia superioris, iusticia, tuum denique peccatum te deposcunt. Coripite hunc Blanorem satelites, vincite, in car-
cerem trudite." Idque raptim et conctorum stupore complectum. Inde
mox dignum de confesso convictoque sumptum patricidio supplicium.

Document Three (English Translation)

Although reluctantly, an impious crime should be brought forth into
the light, lest it avoid punishment or infamy by being hidden. For
wickedness grows strong in the darkness, weakens when seen, and
just as virtue grows bright with publicity, so crimes languish when
noised abroad. Therefore, depart, unhappy son, unhappier soul, disgrace to his fatherland and death to his parent: Blanor of Serravalle,
who poisoned his father Zanuzio because, through old age's disease
of lessened expectations and being more sparing in privileges to his
family, the father did not give entirely free use of things to his son
as if he would waste the estate acquired by long labor. The son did
waste his inheritance with riotous living, extravagance, misuse, in short,
with complete lack of judgment and intemperance, yet he finally paid
the penalty for his wicked crime. Indeed, his crime was well known,

for though the tongue may be silenced for a long time about crimes, eyes are able to perceive with all nature protesting. It was noised about, I say, but anonymously, that Blanor was a parricide, so that the atrocious deed came to the ears of the ducal government. It happened that Blanor was about to set out on some public business for the podestà of Serravalle and took a letter to the supreme magistrate. When he had delivered it, as per order, he went to see some friends and acquaintances, whose wealth and great generosity made many people compliant, also easily swayed. He was received genially and lavishly. Some of these said that he was commonly considered to be guilty of parricide. And this indeed by a number of judges, and they claimed it was not just an idle rumor, but had been discussed in the Doge's private chambers. They advised and urged him to go away until the rumor died down. But on the contrary, so rashly did his impiety drive him, decrying before God the injustices done him by his father, he laughed at their warnings, scorned them, claiming that being guilty of nothing he could not be constrained by any fear or rumor. Finally, as he was about to depart, he approached the Doge to see if he wanted to send any reply to the letter he had brought. Being advised of his identity, the Doge, following the opinion of the chief magistrate, ordered him to take to the podestà of Serravalle a letter in which he gave orders for punishing Blanor for his crime. And Blanor, ignorant of what he was carrying, returned happily to Serravalle. The podestà received him cheerfully in a friendly manner, as did his fellow citizens with friendly greetings, and he seated himself being placed at the side of the podestà.

"See here," he said, "I bring you a letter from the Doge." He was puffed up with pride as though he had brought some secret which was to be entrusted to his confidence alone. When the letter had been unsealed and read, the podestà reluctantly said, "I am sorry that the same punishment must be inflicted upon you, Blanor, as on anyone else. Indeed the commands of my superior, justice, demand that you are punished for your sin. Seize this Blanor, attendants, put him in chains and throw him in prison." This was done immediately and to the amazement of all. Soon thereafter the ultimate penalty was exacted from the confessed and convicted parricide.

Textual Notes

22 necessitudinis] nectitudinis Z   proprii] proprius Z   vero] non Z
   ut] unde V   Anneus] amicus Z   lapseque] lapse quem Z   num-
   quam] umquam O
24 avidius] dulcius V, Vi   tantus] tantos V
26 num] non V   parenti] matri V, Vi   quidem] quid V
28 vix] vis V
30 ut ipsius fruaris] ut matum ipsum revisos ipsius fruaris V, Vi
32 numquam] umquam *codd.*   quam penitentia] quam locos penitentie V
   frustra] nequiquam V, Vi   doceberis] docebis O
34 ceteri] ceteris O   aerem] aserem V
36 computum] compotum O
38 Possidius] Possidonius O, Vi
40 quoniam] quando V, Vi
42 quam] quantum V, Vi
44 Hirtio] urio O   prolixique] profluxique V, Vi
46 venerabilis] pater V, Vi   seu] sui V, Vi   ut] unde V
48 non] nemo V
50 obliquavit] afflavit V, Vi   ut] unde V   illinc] hinc V
52 retulit] respondit V, Vi
54 precipue] precipue non V
56 quod] quam V, quem Vi   non] ut V   eventa] cuncta V
64 ac] dum V, Vi   viri] verum V, Vi   duellatum acriter] duellum acre
   susceptum V, Vi
66 convitia] cum vitia V
68 sustulisse] substillisse V
72 sudandoque] studendoque V, Vi
74 erigunt] exigunt V

78 hunc] hoc V
80 diviserunt] disserunt V, Vi
84 obsequar] parebo V, Vi
88 deprendit] dependit V, Vi
90 attingendi] attingi O   iam iam] in animam V, Vi   inperterritusque]
   impreteritus V
92 quanam] quam nam V
94 delirantium contentionem] delirantium atque errantium conten-
   tiones V, Vi
96 nisi] ubi V
98 cum sorte] consorte V, Vi   profectura] profutura V, Vi   statu] cul-
   mo V, eulimo Vi
100 exerceatur] exercitetur V, Vi   quatenus] ut V, Vi   comitem] so-
    ciam V, Vi   miserabiliter] mirabiliter V
102 tedas] cendas eo V, cedas ac Vi   fore] fori *codd.*
104 regnantium] regum V, Vi   a facto] affacto V, affectu Vi   inde]
    ut V, Vi   nichil] nisi V
108 iri] ire *codd.*   extimaverim] existimaverim V, Vi   nunc] non V
    verecunda] verenda V
110 provectos] productos V   minime] non V, Vi   unicum] unum O
114 ventabat] venit ab V
116 hominibus] *addidi*   extranearum] extraiarum O, V   reddam] red-
    damus V
120 impertiens] impertinens V   piguit] riguit V, Vi
122 instructe] instruente V
124 quibus] qui V
126 notandus] natandus V, Vi   felix] falax V   unus] unum
    codd.   fuisset] fuisse *codd.*
128 disciplinis] discipulis V, Vi   Adeodatus] Deodatus *codd.*   postea-
    quam] preterea quam V
130 si ut] sive V, Vi   disciplinis] discipulis *codd.*
134 ipse] ipsum V   familiari] re familiari *codd.*   invenirem] invenien-
    tem V   certatim] certantem V
136 decerpserunt] descripserunt V   ante] an V
138 testante] testant V   virtutis] virtus O
140 circumspecta] circumferta *codd.*
144 deos] pignora V, Vi
148 vulnera] ulnera O
150 eos] eo V
152 suppetentem] suppetem V   interesse] interesse sevis V, Vi
154 Dominum] Deum O, Vi   oblivia] oblivio V, Vi
156 potentatum] potentum V
158 spectaculo] spectandas V, Vi

Historical Notes

N.B. All quotations from the Bible are taken from the Douai translation of the Vulgate, and all from classical Latin authors from the Loeb series translations, with only minor changes as necessary because of Conversini's slight paraphrasing of the texts.

1. Cicero, *De officiis* 3.13.56.
2. Pseudo-Cicero, *Invectiva in Sallustium* 1.1.
3. Juvenal, 1.3.143–44.
4. Cf. Ovid, *Metamorphoses* 2.1–400; 8.184–235.
5. Cicero, *De amicitia* 9.32; Seneca, *Epistulae* 9.9.
6. Cf. Seneca, *Agamemnon* 934.
7. We have not been able to identify the source of this saying attributed to Socrates.
8. Valerius Maximus 4.3.6; 8.11.1; 5.1.ext.1.
9. Cicero, *De amicitia* 7.23.
10. Valerius Maximus 4.7.1.
11. Strophilus is apparently a corruption of Strophius, king of Phocis, brother-in-law of Agamemnon and tutor to Orestes, who lived at his court as the best friend of his own son, Pylades. See Hyginus, *Fabula* 117 and Ovid, *Epistula ex Ponto* 2.6.26; Lycurgus, the Spartan lawgiver, is praised for his protection of the state in W. Burley, *De vita et moribus philosophorum antiquorum*, ed. H. Knust (Tübingen, 1886) cap. 15, p. 64, and Cicero, *Tusculanae disputationes* 2.14.33.
12. 2 Kings 9; 19.31–40.
13. Ovid, *Tristia* 1.9.33.
14. Cicero, *De amicitia* 7.23.
15. A reference to Giovanni's marriage in Belluno in 1375 to the well-to-

do widow Benasuda, and, hence, his present ineligibility, as a married man, to receive a benefice in Rome from his Uncle Tommaso or Pope Urban VI. See R. Sabbadini, *Giovanni da Ravenna, insigne figura d'umanista (1343–1408)* (Como, 1924) 44, 156.

16. Jacobus de Voragine, *Legenda aurea*, 3d ed. (1890) cap. 15, p. 95; cap. 49.15, p. 212.

17. Vergil, *Aeneid* 1.748.

18. Cicero, *De amicitia* 4.15; Saint Jerome's friendship with and advice to Paula was proverbial by this period, see, for example, Petrarch, *De vita solitaria*, bk 2, in *Opere latine*, ed. A. Bufano et al., 2 vol. (Turin, 1975) 1:418, 420. Sulpicius Severus, *De vita Beati Martini* 1 (PL 20.159–60).

19. Persius 5.41–44.

20. Giovanni's mother died while he was still an infant, and his father Conversino, physician at the court of King Louis of Hungary, sent him back to Italy accompanied by one Michele of Zagreb to be placed under the guardianship of Uncle Tommaso da Frignano.

21. Psalms 118.136.

22. Psalms 24.7.

23. Psalms 72.18.

24. Tommaso da Frignano was elected Minister of the Franciscan Order in the Province of Bologna in 1352, a post which he held for the next fifteen years until elected Minister General of the Order at Assisi in 1367.

25. A reference to Tommaso's election as Minister General of the Franciscan Order at Assisi on 6 June 1367 by the General Council. See Luke Wadding, ed., *Annales Minorum*, 2d ed. (Rome, 1731ff.) 8:200.

26. A reference to Tommaso's election by his friend Pope Gregory XI on 19 July 1372 as Patriarch of Grado, resident in Venice. See C. Eubel, *Bullarium franciscanum*, vol. 6 (Rome, 1902) 6:484, no. 1211.

27. A reference to Giovanni's visit with his uncle Tommaso in Venice in the late summer and fall of 1373, before they quarreled and he took up a position as schoolmaster at Belluno. See Sabbadini, pp. 39–41. Ricciardo Cancellieri the Elder, a soldier and noble of Pistoia, was at the Este court in Ferrara from at least 16 April 1362, when he served as procurator for Niccolò II d'Este concluding a defensive league with Cardinal Albornoz, the Carrara, and the Scaligeri, against the Visconti of Milan. See J. Glenisson and G. Mollat, *Gil Albornoz et Androin de la Roche (1353–1367)* (Paris, 1964) 252–53. He continued in the service of the Este family until his death at Ferrara in 1378.

28. Cf. Sallust, *Bellum Jugurthinum* 102.

29. Cf. Sallust, *Coniuratio Catilinae* 54.1; Seneca, *Epistulae morales* 79.13.2.

30. To give sanction to his attempt at a biography of his Uncle Tommaso da Frignano, Giovanni lists the most famous biographers of the great Latin fathers: Possidius for St. Augustine, Paulinus of Nola for St. Ambrose, Pope

Gregory the Great for the founder of western monasticism, Benedict of Nursia, and the historian Paul the Deacon for Pope Gregory the Great himself.

31. We have not been able to identify the source of this quotation attributed to Livy, which is not, however, in the *Ab urbe condita*.

32. St. Anthony, the Desert Father, as showing a path to virtue by his example, was a commonplace by this time, as in Petrarch's *De vita solitaria*, bk. 2, in *Opere latine* 1:390, 392.

33. A description of Tommaso's rugged native country in the Apennines above Modena on the Panaro River.

34. Justinus 2.2.10.

35. Cf. Justinus 1.4–5; the youth of Cato is mentioned in Valerius Maximus 3.1.2; Poppaedius Latinus is discussed in Valerius Maximus 3.1.2.

36. Tommaso entered the Order as a novice in 1318 and after studying grammar at Bologna and perhaps Venice took his vows in the Franciscan Order, probably in the late 1320s.

37. Socrates' hatred of marriage and his difficulties with his wife Xanthippe were proverbial by the later Middle Ages. For mention of this, see, for example, Burley, 118, 136; and Petrarca, *Rerum memorandarum libri* 3.71.6–7, 22–27, ed. G. Billanovich (Florence, 1945) 156–57, 159.

38. Juvenal 6.268; cf. St. Jerome, *Adversus Jovinianum* 1.47 (PL 23.289).

39. The proverb on not being able to serve wife and philosophy is mentioned in Burley, cap. 95, p. 318, and in St. Jerome, *Adversus Jovinianum* 1.48 (PL 23.290).

40. The incident of the fashionable friars at Bologna took place at some point between 1352 and 1367, where Tommaso was Provincial General of the Franciscan Order in that city.

41. Galatians 1.10.

42. Gregory the Great, *Regula pastoralis* 3.4 (PL 77.54).

43. Apparently a reference to Tommaso's study of theology in Venice and receiving the laurea there, something that is not recorded in any other sources known to us.

44. Evidently Tommaso was ill when elected Minister-General of the Franciscan Order at Assisi in June 1367, but attempted to reconcile opposing parties within the Order in the early months of his office.

45. Cf. Gregory the Great, *Epistola* 11.45 (PL 77.1157).

46. A reference to the accusations of heresy brought against Tommaso in 1368 after his granting of a monastery to Paoluccio de' Trinci in Umbria in 1368. See Wadding, 8:210–11 and the introduction above.

47. Cf. Esther 37.

48. Seneca, *De providentia* 2.9.8

49. The anecdote of Father Pellegrino from Trieste visiting Tommaso in Rome is not known to us from any other source.

50. Echo of Luke 1.74.

51. Cf. Luke 23.34.

52. Cf. Seneca, *De constantia* 2.3; the exiles of Metellus Numidicus and Rutilius Rufus are mentioned in Valerius Maximus, 3.8.4 and 6.4.44, respectively, as well as the dialogue on exile in Petrarch's *De remediis utriusque fortune* 2.117, in *Opera omnia* (Basel, 1554) 1:233.

53. Cf. Cicero, *De officiis* 1.26.90.

54. Cf. Jeremiah 11.19 ff.; cf. 2 Corinthians 11.20-28; St. John Chrysostom from Voragine, *Legenda aurea*, cap. 138, p. 617.

55. 2 Timothy 3.13.

56. A reference to the official rehabilitation of Tommaso da Frignano from the charges of heresy made at the meeting of the General Chapter of the Franciscan Order at Naples on 2 June 1370. See Wadding, 8:231.

57. Valerius Maximus 3.8.ext.2.

58. Reference to Pope Gregory XI's appointment of Tommaso as Patriarch of Grado on 19 July 1372 after his strenuous service as ambassador and peacemaker on behalf of the papacy for several years before. See Wadding, 8:249-56.

59. Gregory the Great, *Regula pastoralis* 1.1 (PL 77.14); Hosea 8.4.

60. An accurate report and summary of Tommaso's activities of reform and reconciliation at Venice while Patriarch of Grado there after July 1373. See Documents 1-2 of the Appendix below.

61. A reference to the fierce Chioggia War just begun in 1378 between Venice on the one hand, and Genoa, the Carrara of Padua, and the forces of the King of Hungary, on the other; we have not been able to find the exact quotation in Aristotle, but he argues this point in *Politics* 7.4 (1326a1-b15).

62. Reference to Tommaso's investigation of abuses and reform of the churches and monasteries at Venice ordered by Pope Gregory XI in a letter of 29 January 1374, and again of the reform of the Benedictine monastery of San Zaccaria on September 25 of the same year. See Wadding, 8:296-97, and G. Cappelletti, *Le Chiese d'Italia* (Venice, 1854) 9:84-85.

63. Gregory the Great, *Epistola 8.33, Ad Dominicum* (PL 77.855).

64. Habacuc 2.19.

65. Croesus and Solon from Burley, cap. 2, p. 14.

66. Cf. Seneca, *De constantia* 18.5.

67. The story of the visit of Silvestro, a citizen of Conegliano, to Giovanni and the Patriarch in Venice in the autumn of 1373 is not known to us from any other source.

68. Seneca, *Epistulae morales* 65.22.

69. The boyhood visit of Tommaso da Frignano to Giovanni at Ravenna probably happened in 1354-1356 when Giovanni was a pupil at the school of Donato Albanzani in that city.

70. Socrates' death by drinking of the hemlock and the labors of Her-

cules were proverbial by the fourteenth century. Giovanni could have known the tales from both a classical source, such as Cicero, *Tusculanae disputationes* 1.41.97–100; 4.22.50, and a contemporary source, such as Petrarch, *De remediis utriusque fortune* 2.116; 2.56, in *Opera omnia* 1:232, 175, respectively. Cato Uticensis' death in Africa was known from several sources available to Giovanni, including Cicero, *Tusculanae disputationes* 1.30.74, as was the voluntary return of M. Attilius Regulus to a certain death by torture in Carthage; see for example, Aulus Gellius, *Noctes Atticae* 7.4.4, and Cicero, *De officiis* 3.26 ff. – On Fabricius see Valerius Maximus 4.4.3. – Valerius Maximus 5.3.ext.3, reports that Aristides was driven into exile by the Athenians.

71. On Joseph, cf. Genesis 39 ff.; cf. 1 Maccabees; cf. Tobias 2 ff.; cf. Job 7; probably the Eustachius of Tuscany, whose trials are recorded in the life of Saint Donatus in Voragine, *Legenda aurea*, cap. 115, p. 485; on Paul, cf. Acts of the Apostles 9.15.

72. Cf. Ecclesiasticus 34.9; Seneca, *De providentia* 3.3.4; cf. Seneca, *De providentia* 4.1.4; the famous man is Boethius, *De consolatione philosophiae* 2.8.

73. Wisdom 3.5; Apocalypse of St. John 3.19; Seneca, *De providentia* 1.6.7; Luke 16.25.

74. Gregory the Great, *Homilia in Evangelia* 2.40.6 (PL 67.1307); 2 Corinthians 4.17.

75. A reference to the creation of many new cardinals in September 1378 by the recently elected Pope Urban VI.

76. A reference to the two major wars raging in Italy in the late 1370s: the Chioggia War pitting Venice against Hungary, Genoa, and the Carrara rulers of Padua in 1378–81, and the War of the Eight Saints of Florence against the papacy in 1375–78.

77. Isaiah 59.2.

78. Vergil, *Eclogae* 1.25; Pseudo-Cicero, *Rhetorica ad Herennium* 4.32.47; Justinus 31.5, on Hannibal's judgment that Italy could not be conquered without Italian troops.

79. This boast is found in Ovid, *Epistulae (Heroides)* 16.177; cf. Pliny, *Naturalis historia* 3.40.

80. Cf. Ovid, *Metamorphoses* 13.433–34.

81. Typical of Giovanni's naïveté is this roseate prediction that an Italian pope and Italian College of Cardinals resident in Rome will end factional strife and warfare in Italy and restore peace to the peninsula.

82. Joel 1.17.

83. Pseudo-Cicero, *Rhetorica ad Herennium* 4.18.25.

84. Apocalypse 2.23.

85. Cf. St. Jerome, *Translatio homiliarum Origenis in Lucam* 1 (PL 26.234).

86. A reference to Tommaso's diplomatic missions for Popes Urban V and Gregory XI to Florence, Hungary, the dukes of Austria, and to mediate the end of the border war between Venice and Padua in the summer of 1373.

See Wadding, 8:249–56, 274–76, and Eubel, 6:470, no. 1174; 6:475, no. 1188; 6:476–77, no. 1195; 6:482, no. 1204; 6:483, no. 1206; 6:493, no. 1234.

87. Apparently a reference to Tommaso's role as mediator in the war between Florence and Pisa fought in the 1360s.

88. Macrobius, *Commentarium in Somnium Scipionis* 4.2.

89. Valerius Maximus, 4.1.13.

90. The poet is Ovid, *Metamorphoses* 1.264; the names of the winds are perhaps a reminiscence of the storm described in Vergil, *Aeneid* 1.81 ff.; Vergil, *Aeneid* 1.91.

91. Cf. 2 Corinthians 11.25.

92. Luke 21.18.

93. Cf. Cicero, *Tusculanae disputationes* 1.43.102; 1.43.104; and Burley, cap. 50, p. 212.

94. Cf. Seneca, *Epistulae morales* 97.15.

95. Vergil, *Aeneid* 6.664; Philippians 1.21; for Andreas see Voragine, *Legenda aurea*, cap. 2.8, p. 18.

96. Gregory the Great, *Epistula 13.23. Ad Rusticianam patriciam* (PL 77.1276).

97. Pliny, *Naturalis historia* 7.190.

98. Terence, *Adelphi* 43–44; Giovanni's first marriage as a teenager to Margherita Furlan of Ravenna was filled with quarrelling and ended tragically in the early death of his young wife at Conegliano in 1370 from disease and malnutrition.

99. Cf. Job 2.9; Tobias 2.13; 2 Kings 6.16, 24.

100. Cf. 4 Kings 8.1 ff.; see 3 Kings 11.1 ff.; Matt. 6.14–22.

101. On the death of Aruns, cf. Valerius Maximus 9.11.1; the murder of Candaules, King of Lydia, by his wife is from Justinus 1.7; for Deianira killing Hercules see Boccaccio, *De mulieribus claris*, ed. V. Zaccaria (Milan, 1967) cap. 24, p. 106; for the death of Agamemnon see ibid., cap. 36, p. 144; for Samson see Judges 15–16; for the betrayal of Amphiaraus, see Boccaccio, *De mulieribus claris*, cap. 29, p. 124; ultimately from Statius, *Thebaidos* 1.394 ff. Caesonia killing Caligula, Agrippina killing Claudius, and Eurydice killing King Arideus are from Suetonius, *Gaius Caligula* 50.2; Boccaccio, *De mulieribus claris*, cap. 92, p. 368; and ibid., cap. 61, p. 248, respectively. The murders are also mentioned in Boccaccio, *De casibus virorum illustrium*, ed. V. Zaccaria and P. G. Ricci (Milan, 1983) 598, 602, 336, respectively.

102. Cassiodorus, *Variae* 11.40.7, ed. A. J. Fridh, Corpus Christianorum, Series Latina 96 (Turnholt, 1973): 459 (PL 69.852); Ovid, *Epistulae ex Ponto* 2.7.9; Cicero, *Tusculanae disputationes* 1.111; 1 Corinthians 7.27.

103. Cf. Genesis 27 ff.; we have not found the source of the anecdote of the Roman women condemned for poisoning.

104. The source of the proverb has not been found.

105. Seneca, *Oedipus* 982; ibid., 983–84, 981–82, 988.

106. Cf. Proverbs 10.6.

107. A reference to Giovanni's visit to Uncle Tommaso at Venice in the summer of 1373 hoping for employment as a tutor in the household of a Venetian family, thwarted by intrigues at the curia of the Patriarch. See Sabbadini, pp. 39–41, and B. G. Kohl and J. Day, "Giovanni Conversini's *Consolatio ad Donatum* on the Death of Petrarch," *Studies in the Renaissance* 21 (1974): 13, 29.

108. A reference to an earlier work of Giovanni's on marriage, perhaps the fragmentary, *De miseria humane vite*. See B. G. Kohl, "The Works of Giovanni di Conversino da Ravenna: A Catalogue of Manuscripts and Editions," *Traditio* 31 (1975): 349–67.

109. Romans 8.8.

110. Horace, *Sermones* 1.9.49.

111. Seneca, *Hercules furens* 251.

112. Terence, *Andria* 68; Lucan, *De bello civili* 8.493; Juvenal 3.105; Terence, *Eunuchus* 251–53.

113. Another instance of Giovanni's fulsome praise of the recently elected Pope Urban VI, deriving in part no doubt from the author's hope for a position at the papal court.

114. Baruch 5.2–4.

115. An expression of hope for employment and patronage from Francesco il Vecchio da Carrara, already famous as friend and patron of Petrarch in his later years.

116. Cicero, *De officiis* 1.48.

117. Valerius Maximus 9.3.ext.1; for the story of the harlot see ibid., 2.9.2; Suetonius, *Divus Tiberius* 42.1.

118. Suetonius, *Nero* 22.3–23.3.

119. Nehemiah 2; 1 Esdras 5.2–3; the anecdote of Herod Agrippa and Caligula derives ultimately from Josephus, *Antiquitates Judaicae* 18.8.7–8; Esther 10 ff.; cf. Seneca, *De ira* 4.19.5; Statius, *Achilleis* 1.52.

120. No such phrase appears in Esdras, but in Judges 9.13; Ecclesiasticus 31.37; and Psalms 103.15.—Cf. Horace, *Carmina* 1.18; 3.21.—Cf. Hippocrates, *Aphorisms*, ed. E. Marks (New York, 1817) 47: "Fames vini potio solvit."—Galatians 5.21; Proverbs 6.27 and 23.20; Gregory the Great, *Homilia in Ezechielem* 10.7 (PL 76.888–89); and St. Jerome, *Epistola 21, Ad Damascum* (PL 22.385).

121. Cf. Terence, *Phormio* 470.

122. John 6.69.

123. Psalms 26.10.

124. 4 Kings 2.6 ff.

125. Vergil, *Aeneid* 2.776.

126. Ecclesiasticus 16.4; Wisdom 4.6; Boethius, *De consolatione philosophiae* 3.Prosa 7.

127. Augustine, *De civitate Dei* 19.1–2 (PL 41.622).

128. Ecclesiastes 2.18–19.

129. Juvenal 14.70–72.

130. Evilmerodach is the son of Nebuchadnezzar mentioned in 4 Kings, chap. 25.—Absalom in 4 Kings 15.16.—Ninus is mentioned in Justinus 1.9 and Boccaccio, *De mulieribus claris*, cap. 2, p. 38.—For Antipater see Justinus 16.1.1.—On Thessalonice's shamelessness, cf. Justinus 1.1.6.—Cf. Suetonius, *Nero* 28.—On Artaxerxes' 115 offspring see Justinus 10.1.2, and Petrarch, *De remediis utriusque fortune* 2.12, in *Opera omnia* 1:139.—On Darius' parricide, see Justinus 10.1.1.—The anecdote of Herodes Ascalonita derives ultimately from Josephus, *Antiquitates Judaicae* 16.10.3–5.

131. Justinus 38.6.2.

132. The murder of Zanucio by his son Blanore in Serravalle (the present Vittorio Veneto) near Conegliano was apparently an infamous event in the Trecento. Giovanni set down the particulars at length at the end of his life in his unfinished *Memorandarum rerum liber*, cap. 18, which is published below as Appendix, Document 3, from Venice, Biblioteca Querini-Stampalia, MS 1006.

133. Proverbs 22.6.

134. Cf. St. Augustine, *Confessiones* 9.6.

135. Tobias 5 ff.; 1 Maccabees 2; cf. Genesis 11 ff.; cf. St. Augustine, *Confessiones* 9.6.

136. Cf. Tobias 5.23.

137. The residue of the third digestion comes from Avicenna, *A Treatise on the Canon of Medicine*, Sect. 111, ed. and trans. O. Cameron Gruner (London, 1930) 90–91, and hair from the fumes of the humors from Galen, *Comm. I in Hippocr. de humor.* cap. 8, in *Claudii Galeni Opera omnia*, ed. C. G. Kuehn (Leipzig, 1822; repr. Hildesheim, 1964) 16:89.

138. Aristotle, *De generatione animalium* 2.1 (733b1), trans. G. de Moerbeke, *Aristoteles latinus* 27.2, ed. H. J. Drossaart Lulofs (Bruges-Paris, 1966) 46.

139. Vergil, *Aeneid* 1.607–9.

140. Persius 1.47.

141. Seneca, *De beneficiis* 1.8.1–2.

142. Horace, *Carmina* 1.27.19; Horace, *Epistolae* 1.7.23.

143. Giovanni took his account of the wisdom of Solomon and Archytas' learning from the famous letter to Paulinus of Nola by St. Jerome, *Epistula* 53.1–2 (PL 22.540–41).—The story of the man journeying to Rome from Spain just to lay eyes on Livy is found in Pliny, *Epistolae* 2.3.8.

144. For Paul's journey see Acts of the Apostles 25; on Isychius' search for Hilarion see St. Jerome, *Vita Hilarionis* 38 (PL 23.55–56).

145. Valerius Maximus, 2.10.2.

146. Horace, *Epistulae* 1.7.13.

147. St. Jerome, *Adversus Jovinianum* 1.47 (PL 23.289–90).

148. Terence, *Eunuchus* 813; Juvenal 6.97.

149. Ecclesiasticus 26.28.

150. See Voragine, *Legenda aurea*, cap. 94, p. 404.

151. Cf. Exodus 4 ff.

152. St. Jerome, *Epistolae 108.6, Ad Eustochium* (PL 22.881–82).

153. 2 Corinthians 5.10.

154. Juvenal 3.165.

155. Augustus' patronage of Vergil was proverbial by the fourteenth century; see, for example, F. Petrarch, *Rerum Senilium XIV. Ad magnificum Franciscum de Carraria, Epistola I. Qualis esse debeat qui rem publicam regit*, ed. V. Ussani (Padua, 1922) 43; English trans. in B. G. Kohl and R. G. Witt, eds. *The Earthly Republic* (Philadelphia, 1978) 76.—On Ennius' rewards see Valerius Maximus 8.14.1; for the honors of Theophanes see Valerius Maximus 8.14.3.

156. Giovanni provides the same list of ancient and contemporary patrons of arts and letters in his *Dragmalogia*, p. 114, paralleling Petrarch's list in *Seniles* 14.1 (cited in n. 155) and drawing on his own personal experience of Boccaccio at Ravenna and Petrarch at Padua.

157. Terence, *Hecyra* 48.

158. Ennodius, *Libellus adversus eos qui contra synodum scribere praesumpserunt*, Praef. (PL 63.183).

159. Job 4.2.

160. Cf. Seneca, *De brevitate vitae* 6.3–4.

161. Ecclesiasticus 10.9.

162. Vergil, *Aeneid* 9.641.

163. Romans 7.24; Pliny, *Naturalis historia* 7.55.189; Pliny, *Naturalis historia* 7.19.80; cf. Seneca, *De tranquillitate animi* 15.2.

164. For the escapes of Benedict, Paul, and Jerome, see Voragine, *Legenda aurea*, cap. 49.3, p. 205; cap. 90, p. 380; cap. 146, p. 654, respectively.—Cicero's exile from Rome in the country was proverbial by the Trecento in humanist writings; see, for example, Petrarch, *De vita solitaria*, bk 2, in *Opere latine* 1:510.—On Metellus' exile see Valerius Maximus 3.8.4.

165. Valerius Maximus 3.7.ext.2.

166. Ecclesiasticus 39.1–3, 6–7.

167. Horace, *Epodes* 2.1–4; *Sermones* 2.6.60–62.

168. Seneca, *Phaedra* 483–95; Vergil, *Georgica* 2.458; St. Jerome, *Vita Hilarionis* 29 (PL 23.44); Voragine, *Legenda aurea*, cap. 46, p. 198.

169. A reference to Petrarch's last years spent in retirement in Arquà south of Padua where Giovanni visited him at the Christmas season of 1373. See Sabbadini, 43, and Kohl and Day, "Conversini's *Consolatio ad Donatum*," 13, 19.

170. Voragine, *Legenda aurea*, cap. 178, p. 807.

171. Voragine, *Legenda aurea*, cap. 120, p. 531.

Bibliography

Primary Sources

Boccaccio, Giovanni. *De casibus virorum illustrium*. Edited by V. Zaccaria and P. G. Ricci. Vol. 9 of *Tutte le Opere*. Milan, 1983.

Boccaccio, Giovanni. *De mulieribus claris*. Edited by V. Zaccaria. Vol. 10 of *Tutte le opere*. Milan, 1967.

Burley, Walter. *De vita et moribus philosophorum antiquorum*. Edited by H. Knust. Tübingen, 1886.

Conversino, Giovanni di, da Ravenna. *Dragmalogia de eligibili vite genere*. Edited and translated by H. L. Eaker with introduction and notes by B. G. Kohl. Renaissance Society of America Text Series, vol. 7. Lewisburg, Pa., and London, 1980.

Conversini, Giovanni, da Ravenna. *Rationarium Vite*. Edited by V. Nason. Florence, 1986.

Conversini, Giovanni, da Ravenna. *Two Court Treatises*. Edited and translated by B. G. Kohl and J. Day. Munich, 1987.

Eubel, Conrad, ed. *Bullarium Franciscanum*. Vol. 6. Rome, 1902.

Gatari, B. and G. *Cronaca Carrarese*. Edited by A. Medin and G. Tolomei. Rerum italicarum scriptores, vol. 17, pt. 1, N. ed. Bologna, 1909–32.

Petrarca, Francesco. *Opera omnia*. 3 vols. Basel, 1554. Reprint. Ridgewood, N.J., 1965.

Petrarca, Francesco. *Opere latine*. 2 vols. Edited by A. Bufano et al. Turin, 1975.

Petrarca, Francesco. *Prose*. Edited by G. Martellotti et al. Milan, 1955.

Piana, C., ed. *Nuovi documenti sull'Università di Bologna e sul Collegio di Spagna*. Studia Albornotiana 26. Bologna, 1978.

Voragine, Jacobus de. *Legenda aurea*. Edited by T. Graesse. 3rd ed. 1890. Reprint. Osnabrück, 1969.

Wadding, Luke, ed. *Annales Minorum*. Vols. 8–9. Rome, 1733.

Studies on Tommaso da Frignano and Religious History

Brongio. L. *L'Osservanza francescana in Italia nel secolo XIV*. Rome, 1963.

Bughetti, B. "Documenta quaedam spectantia ad sacram inquisitionem et ad schisma Ordinis in provincia praesertim Tusciae circa finem saeculi XIV." *AFH* 9 (1916): 347–83.

Callebaut, A. "Thomas de Frignano, Ministre générale, et ses defenseurs: Pétrarque, Philippe de Cabassol et Philippe de Maizières, vers 1369–70." *AFH* 10 (1917): 239–49.

Cappelletti, G. *Le Chiese d'Italia*. Vol. 9. Venice, 1854.

Cappelletti, G. *Storia della Chiesa di Venezia*. Vol. 6. Venice, 1850.

Cenci, C. "I Gonzaga e i Frati Minori dal 1365 al 1430." *AFH* 58 (1965): 3–47, 201–79.

Eubel, C. *Hierarchia Catholica Medii Aevi*. Münster, 1913.

Faloci Pulignani, D. M. "Il beato Paoluccio Trinci da Foligno." *Miscellanea francescana di storia, di lettere, di arti* 6 (1896): 96–128.

Lippen, H. "Une nouvelle recension du 'Catalogus Generalium Ministrorum' O.F.M." *AFH* 15 (1922): 333–48.

Mollat, G. "Thomas de Frignano, O.F.M. et la diplomatie pontificale." *AFH* 55 (1962): 521–23.

Moorman, J. *A History of the Franciscan Order from Its Origins to the Year 1517*. Oxford, 1968.

Nimmo, D. "Poverty and Politics: The Motivation of Fourteenth Century Franciscan Reform in Italy." *Religious Motivation: Biographical and Sociological Problems for the Church Historian*. Edited by D. Baker. Studies in Church History, vol. 15. Oxford, 1978. 161–78.

Péano, P. "Jacques de' Tolomei, éléments de biographie." *AFH* 68 (1975): 273–97.

Pergamo, B. "I Francescani alla facoltà teologica di Bologna (1364–1500)." *AFH* 27 (1934): 3–61.

Piana, C. *Chartularium studii Bononiensis S. Francisci (saec. XIII–XVI)*. Analecta Franciscana, vol. 11. Quaracchi, 1970.

Pistoni, G. "Un modenese amico del Petrarca, il Cardinale Tommaso Frignani, con lettera inedita di Coluccio Salutati." *Atti e Memorie dell'Accademia di scienze, lettere ed arti di Modena*, 5th ser., 12 (1954): 82–96.

Tiraboschi, G. *Biblioteca modenese*. Vol 2. Modena, 1782. 366–68.

Tondini, G. B. *Delle memorie istoriche concernenti la vita del cardinale Tommaso da Frignano*. Macerata, 1782.

Ullmann, W. *Origins of the Great Schism*. 2nd ed. Hamden, Conn., 1969.

Studies on Giovanni Conversini da Ravenna and Humanism

Biasuz, G. "Giovanni Conversini da Ravenna, maestro di grammatica a Belluno." *Archivio storico di Belluno, Feltre e Cadore*, 25 (1954): 37–39.

Billanovich, Giuseppe. *Petrarca letterato, 1. Lo scrittoio del Petrarca*. Rome, 1947.

Foresti, A. "Pietro da Muglio a Padova e la sua amicizia col Petrarca e col Boccaccio." *L'Archiginnasio* 15 (1920): 163–73.

Gargan, L. "Giovanni Conversini e la cultura letteraria a Treviso nella seconda metà del Trecento." *Italia medioevale e umanistica* 8 (1965): 87–159.

Gargan, L. "Per la biblioteca di Giovanni Conversini." *Vestigia: Studi in onore di Giuseppe Billanovich*. Edited by R. Avesani et al. Rome, 1984. 1:365–85.

Gargan, L. "Il preumanesimo a Venezia, Treviso e Venezia." *Storia di cultura veneta*. Vol. 2, *Il Trecento*. Vicenza, 1976. 159–67.

Kohl, B. G. "Conversini, Giovanni, da Ravenna." *Dizionario biografico degli Italiani* 28 (1983): 574–78.

Kohl, B. G. "Readers and Owners of an Early Work of Giovanni Conversini da Ravenna: New College, Oxford, MS D.155." *Scriptorium* 40 (1986): 95–100, and plates 6–7.

Kohl, B. G. "The Works of Giovanni di Conversino da Ravenna: A Catalogue of Manuscripts and Editions." *Traditio* 31 (1975): 349–67.

Kohl, B. G. and J. Day. "Giovanni Conversini's *Consolatio ad Donatum* on the Death of Petrarch." *Studies in the Renaissance* 21 (1974): 9–30.

Lazzarini, L. *Paolo de Bernardo e i primordi dell'umanesimo a Venezia.* Geneva, 1930.

Martellotti, G. "Albanzani, Donato." *Dizionario biografico degli Italiani* 1 (1960): 611–12.

Sabbadini, R. *Giovanni da Ravenna, insigne figura d'umanista (1343–1408).* Como, 1924.

Schullian, D. "Valerius Maximus." *Catalogus translationum et commentariorum.* Vol. 5. Ed. F. E. Cranz. Washington, D.C., 1984, pp. 287–403, esp. pp. 340–42.

Szur, R. C. A. "Giovanni of Ravenna and his *History of Ragusa.*" M. Phil. thesis. University of London, Warburg Institute, 1972.

Trinkaus, C. *The Scope of Renaissance Humanism.* Ann Arbor, 1983.

Ullman, B. L. *The Humanism of Coluccio Salutati.* Padua, 1963.

Ullman, B. L. *Studies in the Italian Renaissance.* 2nd ed. Rome, 1973.

Wilkins, E. H. *Petrarch's Later Years.* Cambridge, Mass., 1959.

Witt, R. G. *Hercules at the Crossroad: The Life, Works, and Thought of Coluccio Salutati.* Durham, N. C., 1983.

Zaccaria, V. "Il *Memorandarum rerum liber* di Giovanni di Conversino da Ravenna." *Atti dell'Istituto Veneto, classe di scienze morali et lettere,* 106. Pt. 2 (1947–48): 221–50.

Index

The **Dialogue** takes place between Giovanni Conversini da Ravenna (1343–1408) and a letter sent to his uncle, the Franciscan prelate, on the occasion of his elevation to cardinal in 1378. Inspired by Petrarch's writing on the status of the religious, Giovanni treats the same theme but in a more intimate way. As one of the earliest humanist writings on the religious calling, it provides a vivid portrait of a church leader at the time of the Great Schism, elucidating his emotional and professional concerns.

This first critical edition of the Latin text has a facing-page translation acclaimed by readers as an accurate and graceful rendition. The introduction provides historical, literary, and biographical background, and the volume is completed by a comprehensive bibliography and an index.

Helen Lanneau Eaker is a Lecturer in Classics at Rice University. **Benjamin G. Kohl** is Professor of History and Coordinator of the Program in Medieval and Renaissance Studies at Vassar College. The two authors also collaborated on *Giovanni Conversini: Draqmalogia de eligibili vite genere* (Bucknell, 1980).

mRts

medieval & renaissance texts & studies
is the publishing program of the
Center for Medieval and Early Renaissance Studies
at the State University of New York at Binghamton.

mRts emphasizes books that are needed —
texts, translations, and major research tools.

mRts aims to publish the highest quality scholarship
in attractive and durable format at modest cost.